The Cosmopolitan Ideal

The Cosmopolitan Ideal

Challenges and Opportunities

Edited by
Sybille De La Rosa
and Darren O'Byrne

**ROWMAN &
LITTLEFIELD**
INTERNATIONAL

London • New York

Published by Rowman & Littlefield International, Ltd.
Unit A, Whitacre Mews, 26-34 Stannary Street, London SE11 4AB
www.rowmaninternational.com

Rowman & Littlefield International, Ltd. is an affiliate of Rowman & Littlefield
4501 Forbes Boulevard, Suite 200, Lanham, Maryland 20706, USA
With additional offices in Boulder, New York, Toronto (Canada), and London (UK)
www.rowman.com

British Library Cataloguing in Publication Information Available
A catalogue record for this book is available from the British Library

ISBN: HB 978-1-7834-8229-0
ISBN: PB 978-1-7834-8230-6

Library of Congress Cataloging-in-Publication Data

The cosmopolitan ideal : challenges and opportunities / edited by Sybille De La Rosa and Darren
O'Byrne.
pages cm
Includes bibliographical references and index.
ISBN 978-1-78348-229-0 (cloth : alk. paper) — ISBN 978-1-78348-230-6 (pbk. : alk. paper)—
ISBN 978-1-78348-231-3 (electronic)
1. Cosmopolitanism. I. De La Rosa, Sybille
JZ1308.C6665 2015
306—dc23
                                2015000495

∞™ The paper used in this publication meets the minimum requirements of American
National Standard for Information Sciences Permanence of Paper for Printed Library
Materials, ANSI/NISO Z39.48-1992.

Printed in the United States of America

Contents

Introduction

Sybille De La Rosa and Darren O'Byrne

This volume is the product of a successful conference held at the University of Roehampton, London, UK, from 10–12 July 2013. This was the annual conference of the Global Studies Association, and the theme was 'The Cosmopolitan Ideal: Challenges and Opportunities'. The underlying rationale for the conference was to present a sympathetic but intellectually engaged critique of the concept of *cosmopolitanism* and to make the case for a *critical cosmopolitanism*, and this is reflected in the papers reproduced herein.

What, precisely, we mean by cosmopolitanism and why it was deemed necessary to dedicate a conference to presenting such a critique of it are themes that will be taken up in this introduction. Suffice it to say now that the term is—perhaps surprisingly—very much in vogue in the social sciences at present (Appiah 2006; Archibugi 2003, 2009; Archibugi and Held 1995; Beck 2000, 2006; Beck and Beck-Gernsheim 2002; Beck and Grande 2007; Beck and Sznaider 2006; Brown and Held 2010; Delanty 2009, 2012a; Delanty and Inglis 2010; Held 1995, 2003, 2010; Rumford 2006, 2008). There are all sorts of reasons why this may be surprising: The term is too vague and too easily contested, it is too normative, it is too deeply entrenched in Western ways of thought. Even its most ardent champions would concede that there is some truth in such concerns. Even now, among those dedicated advocates of cosmopolitanism, there are tensions between those who use the term in a purely normative sense, and those whose approach is more analytical or empirical. Such tensions are taken up in this volume in the chapter by Nascimento, so there is little point in repeating them here.

Cosmopolitan ideas, embracing calls for human rights and citizenship of the world (and in some cases world government), can be traced back to the ancient Greeks, were developed through the classical Roman philosophers and further extended by the Christian moral universalists, and found their most famous political statement in the Enlightenment philosophy of Immanuel Kant (Heater 1996; Nussbaum 1997; O'Byrne 2003; however, see Inglis 2012, for a slightly more complex reading of this history). Historically, they have existed within the framework of political ideology, and have been easily dismissed as utopian. They have, of course, been significant insofar as they have provided the conceptual base which underpins the activities of many global social movements, and it is with such movements and in the generic category of *global civil society* that they have been most commonly associated (Hensby and O'Byrne 2012; O'Byrne 2005).

The revival of cosmopolitan thinking at the end of the twentieth century is, in no small part, a response to the numerous dangers facing the world at this critical point in history, and to the opportunities facilitated by the emergence of transnational institutions (Held 1995, 2003). *Globalization* (which is, of course, itself a hugely contested term) ushers in a new world of possibilities, and the cosmopolitan response is rooted in respect for diversity as well as for transnational institutions (Appiah 2006).

For such cosmopolitan theorists, globalizing processes enable the institutionalization of transnational forms of governance, legal and political structures operating above the level of the nation-state, which, by denying the nation-state its historical excesses, can help to build a more peaceful and sustainable world, and deal with the numerous ecological, economic, and political risks it faces (Beck 2006; Beck and Sznaider 2006). For this to happen, though, these structures need to possess a legitimacy that empowers them and overrides the self-interest of individual nation-states; there has to be a cosmopolitan will driving the direction of these cosmopolitan structures (Bauman 2002; Beck and Sznaider 2006). Cosmopolitanism cannot, its advocates insist, begin and end with transnational governance: It has to be entirely democratic, embracing the active participation of global citizens (Archibugi 2003, 2009; Archibugi and Held 1995).

But cosmopolitanism is—its defenders insist—more than just a perspective within the emerging field of global studies (that interdisciplinary field of inquiry concerned with interpreting the different manifestations of contemporary global change). As Gerard Delanty (2012b) stresses as part of his efforts to define the scope of cosmopolitanism studies as distinct from global studies, the latter is a relatively recent development while the former goes back to ancient Greece. Also, the latter is by definition the study of globalization, which is not a normative concept, while the former is unavoidably normative. In short, insists Delanty, 'the attraction that cosmopolitanism has today is not unconnected with the implicit tension between cosmopolitanism and globalization, with cosmopolitanism suggesting a critique of globalization. The world may be becoming more and more globally linked by powerful global forces, but this does not make the world more cosmopolitan. If the normative underpinnings of cosmopolitanism are taken seriously, it must be apparent that it is not reducible to the condition of globalization' (ibid: 2).

Underpinning cosmopolitanism as a social and political theory, then, is a particular kind of progressive, left-leaning ideology. However, insofar as it is underpinned by this normativity, it is a hugely contested and polarizing term. For as long as there have been those who have advocated a 'cosmopolitan' outlook (whether or not they used the language), whether through advocacy of international laws, transnational political structures, or simple recognition of human rights, there have been those quick to dismiss it as utopian and naïve, for misrepresenting either the realities of the political system or the basic human condition. Conservatives and communitarians since Burke have sought to embed values and ways of life more firmly in local customs which are articulated in the form of the nation. Realists since Macchiavelli and Hobbes have sought to prioritize the importance of security as a political project, reflecting as it does the fundamentally *human* project of protecting and promoting self-interest. Among contemporary writers, cosmopolitan ideas have been met with somewhat vitriolic criticism from neorealists such as Danilo Zolo (1997, 2002). Liberals since Locke have presented a distinctly non-cosmopolitan worldview grounded in bourgeois individualism and the primacy of economic relations, which has in the twentieth century become more aggressively articulated as an ideology of the inherently globalizing tendencies of the market. Marxists and socialists since Marx have remained largely trapped within the particularist assumptions of historical materialism despite the obviously cosmopolitan possibilities of socialist internationalism.

Struggling against such dominant philosophies and ideologies on both right and left, cosmopolitanism has existed as a somewhat esoteric, even quirky, alternative. Indeed, against the apparent pragmatism of the realists, the materialism of the Marxists, the romanticism of the conservatives, and the pro-capitalist individualism of the liberals, it had apparently little to offer and had little or no influence on the emerging social sciences of the nineteenth century (one exception, of course, being in the field of international relations, where cosmopolitan ideas underpinned the tradition of 'idealism', or liberal institutionalism).

Yet a critically informed cosmopolitanism can offer us social scientific as well as philosophical insight into the contemporary global condition. To do so, however, it must be liberated from its limitations, which are themselves, sociologically speaking, bound up in unequal social relations—class, ethnicity, gender. That cosmopolitanism as an outlook on the world—rather like globalism—can be read as a form of cultural capital, bound up within and reproduced through a Western middle-class value system is evident (O'Byrne 1997, 2003, 2013). Critical cosmopolitanism, as advocated to varying degrees within this volume, would treat the project of cosmopolitanism as one capable of breaking down hegemonic discourses and practices as a natural extension of the project of critical theory, to look beyond the apparently 'closed' dynamics of dominant forms of rationality and seek out alternatives (Delanty 2009, 2012c; Mignolo 2000, 2001; Rumford 2008). Let us now consider the contributions made to this volume in the context of this emergent *critical cosmopolitanism*.

OVERVIEW OF THE BOOK

The book is organized in three sections. The first section—'The Debate on Cosmopolitanism and Connected Discourses'—contains contributions which give an overview about the debates on cosmopolitanism and the debate on global distributive justice. The second section, 'The Challenges of Intercultural Communication', is comprised of contributions which show the challenges of intercultural communication and its power aspects for cosmopolitan concepts in as different fields as historiography, public use of speech, text interpretation, and cosmopolitan ideology or narration. The third section, 'The Challenges of Pluralism and Difference', contains contributions that highlight the challenge of pluralism and difference as a starting point for a more dialogical understanding of democratic processes on a global scale.

Amos Nascimento's contribution gives an overview of the cosmopolitan debate of recent years and points out some of the central aspects. The author goes through the variety of cosmopolitanisms such as cosmopolitan studies as proposed by Gerard Delanty, the social theoretical approach of Ulrich Beck, liberal cosmopolitanism, and feminist cosmopolitanism, and reinforces or questions their contributions to the cosmopolitan debate. He then proposes an answer to the question of what critical cosmopolitism should involve by drawing on the tradition of critical theory and the decolonial theories of Latin American writers in order to emphasize that 'the conditions for a critical cosmopolitanism are daunting but relatively simple: a critical cosmopolitanism needs to be cosmopolitan enough. A critical cosmopolitanism shall be a truly cosmopolitan cosmopolitanism', which is only possible if we are able to make the claims of the excluded visible and audible 'so that change may eventually happen', and by expressing solidarity with minorities. This sets the scene for the following chapters, which mainly identify aspects of the debate that have not, or have rarely, been discussed so far.

Angie Pepper contributes to the debates on global distributive justice, and therefore to the basic question of why we owe justice to those who suffer injustice on Earth. She highlights and analyses the differences between relational and non-relational approaches and argues that feminists should be non-relational cosmopolitans because justice should not be contingent on certain relationships. Going through the approaches of Okin, MacKinnon, Nussbaum, and finally Kittay, she argues that relational approaches like Kittay's should not be seen as incompatible with non-relational approaches because 'the important thing is not that a person stands in particular relationships with others but that they have the capacity to do so'.

Intercultural communication has been addressed as an academic topic in different fields such as philosophy (Gadamer 2004; Kögler 2007; Taylor 1985) and in postcolonial and decolonial theories (Bhabha 1994; Mignolo 2003; Spivak 2004). The postcolonial and decolonial thinkers have focused primarily on the communication between colonizers and colonized or subaltern speakers and former colonizers, and therefore have paid much more attention to violent forms of interaction. In turn, they have given little attention to the possibilities of dialogical communication.[1] The philosophical debate, in contrast, has been mainly focused on the possibility of dialogical communication, and it has produced a variety of concepts that we cannot discuss here. But both theoretical approaches share the constructivist assumption that human actors construct their reality through their utterances, which gain their materialistic force when they form discourses or narrations that become guiding.

But it is also important to mention that these concepts show that there are two main modes of intercultural communication: an instrumental one which appropriates the Other by negating his claims and wish for self-determination and leads towards a powerlessness of the Other through exclusion and misrecognition, and another mode of communication which dialogically includes the Other into narrations by listening to his claims and self-description, which leads towards inclusion and empowerment (De La Rosa 2012). The contribution of the chapter shows how communicative power aspects challenge cosmopolitan thinking and political practices.

Martin Hewson's contribution, for example, points out that a new cosmopolitan world order needs a new world history. Therefore, he critically analyses the polycentric approach of history which aims to overcome Eurocentric historicity by denying that Europe was exceptional in generating capitalism, economic development, and the modern nation-state, and also, the assumption that where capitalism goes modernity follows. Hewson criticizes that to de-exceptionalize the West to this extent only loses sight that the West was in some points exceptional. Therefore, he asks for a post-polycentric model of historicity.

The contribution from Sae-Hee Lee elaborates on the question of how to reach a shared ideological basis for cosmopolitanism. In this context, such a question is articulated in respect of how basic philosophical concepts can be translated from one language and culture into another without being subordinated into a dominant discourse. Lee proposes a concept of practical universalism in order to answer this question. She argues for a methodology to attain and foster a cosmopolitan community. This, says Lee, could be based on a comparative analysis of political thought in order to find and compare the 'core indicators of political thoughts embedded in each culture' with the goal being to understand different speech cultures so as to open up a global dialogue. She develops and exemplifies her methodology with an analysis of Kant's concept of 'practical reason' and Wang Yangming's concept of 'pure knowing'.

Sneja Gunew develops the argument that cosmopolitanism needs a critical interpretive methodology for cultural texts that brings in minority ethics and different knowledges in order to distinguish a critical cosmopolitism from an elitist or banal cosmopolitism. Here again, power aspects become visible insofar as cosmopolitan concepts have to position themselves and to point out to what kind of cosmopolis they contribute. Whereas Lee intends to establish a universal basis to ground cosmopolitism, Gunew points to the necessity to acknowledge the traces of difference and, similar to Spivak, asks for a cosmopolitan pedagogy. This pedagogy would have the task to demonstrate that all cosmopolitanisms are vernacular. So it is a kind of deconstructivist method that critically reminds us that cosmopolitan concepts, just as other concepts, remain contingent but in this way also open for changes and the inclusion of former excluded knowledges.

Anne Surma's contribution describes a case of instrumental communication which strongly strives for the exclusion of refugees in Australia, and that claims the need to understand writing as 'a critical, careful and self-reflexive practice in a global context'. Based on Australia's 'No Advantage' brochure aimed at stopping asylum seekers trying to reach the country by boat, Surma argues that writing 'constitutes a form of human subjectivity, however disguised that may be, since it necessarily addresses the other, even when indirectly, unwittingly or even unwillingly'. Although the examples used in this chapter are taken from the Australian context, their impact and significance have global relevance. The paper thus addresses a fundamental challenge to the cosmopolitan ideal within academic research: How does one write in a cosmopolitan way from the national perspective?

It is fairly commonplace to acknowledge that pluralism challenges the conventions of everyday life. However, developing a concept that describes how to deal with it adequately has led to very different strategies and concepts, including those of Robert Dahl (1971) and Hannah Arendt (1998). But what these diverse answers to the question of how to deal with pluralism (in a democratic way) share are its nation-state context. Taking cosmopolitanism seriously calls for a revision of this question in light of the cosmopolitan challenge. The contributions of the third section in this volume take up again the problematization of power aspects by asking how concepts that have been connected to the nation-state, such as representation, sovereignty, citizenship, democracy, and civilization can be reinterpreted as democratic practices that contribute to the cosmopolitan challenge.

Geneviève Souillac's contribution highlights the necessity for a global democratic consciousness that is oriented by an understanding of the civilizing process as a 'reflexive cultural process designed to identify, and to restrain, certain forms of violence seen as contrary to civilization itself'. To sustain the civilizing process, she identifies the necessity of new skills such as respect for diversity, dialog, the sharing of views, and a new understanding of democracy that is able to cope with pluralism, conflict, and complexity.

Sybille De La Rosa's contribution points out the importance of revising and reformulating liberal concepts of representation from a cosmopolitan point of view. She identifies a liberal but traditional concept of representation (understood as the representation of interests) in Archibugi's work on cosmopolitanism, and then argues that the challenge is to find the Eurocentric shortcomings of traditional concepts and to create new concepts (drawing, for example, on the ideas of Iris Marion Young and Nadia Urbinati) that point out how representation could be understood in order to build part of a critical cosmopolitism. In this way she arrives at an understanding of representation that is centred around the idea of the possibilities of expression and an agonistic but dialogic process of intercultural communication.

For Spiros Makris, answers to at least some of the questions raised in this volume—questions about the disjuncture between political reality and the cosmopolitan ideal—can be found through a careful reading of the works of Derrida. He thus provides us with an analysis of Derrida's own words, in the form of direct quotations, which he applies to the problem at hand. In particular, Makris debates Derrida's concept of hospitality and the idea of the *city of refuge*. He argues that it should not be taken as a proposal for a simple reform of international law, but that it should be understood as a challenge to Kantian state-centric cosmopolitanism and as a starting point for a project of self-transcendence. The Kantian cosmopolitan vision, he argues, is marked by the contradiction between the ideal of an unconditional hospitality and a limitation on any right to residence. In contrast, Derrida offers the idea of hospitality as creative political activity that strives towards the transcendence of national identities, practices, and institutions.

CONCLUSION

The chapters contained in this volume do not promise to provide answers to the cosmopolitan question, but they do demand that we consider the question itself more carefully than we may have done in the past. While each chapter is sympathetic to the cosmopolitan ideal, each is also critical of its historical association with colonialism and Western imperialism, the legacy of which is deeply rooted in the structures of everyday life. By drawing on critical social theories—the critical theory of the Frankfurt School, feminism, postcolonial and decolonial theories, postmodernism, deconstruction, and so on—the contributors to this volume hope to revitalize the cosmopolitan debate by injecting into it a fresh sense of urgency and a renewed and relevant politics. In that respect, the volume is incredibly timely: The cosmopolis of the twenty-first century is a place defined primarily by its borders, and it is at those borders that wars are fought, basic rights are denied, and Arendt's conditions of right-lessness prevail. Any attempt to better understand those borders, and the cosmopolitan ideal in general, is surely welcome.

NOTE

1. With some exceptions, such as Bhabha's concept of the 'third space' (Bhabha 1994) and Spivak's concept of learning (Spivak 2004).

BIBLIOGRAPHY

Appiah, K. A. (2006). *Cosmopolitanism: Ethics in a World of Strangers*. London: Penguin.
Archibugi, D. (2003). *Debating Cosmopolitics*. London: Verso.
———. (2009). *The Global Commonwealth of Citizens: Toward a Cosmopolitan Democracy*. Princeton: Princeton University Press.
——— and Held, D. (eds.) (1995). *Cosmopolitan Democracy: An Agenda for a New World Order*. Cambridge: Polity Press.
Arendt, H. (1998). *The Human Condition*. Chicago: University of Chicago Press.
Bauman, Z. (2002). *Society under Siege*. Cambridge: Polity Press.
Beck, U. (2000). 'The Cosmopolitan Perspective: Sociology of the Second Age of Modernity' in *British Journal of Sociology* 51, 1, 79–105.
———. (2006). *The Cosmopolitan Vision*. Cambridge: Polity Press.
——— and Beck-Gernsheim, E. (2002). *Individualization*. London: Sage.
——— and Grande, E. (2007). *Cosmopolitan Europe*. Cambridge: Polity Press.
——— and Sznaider, N. (2006). 'Unpacking Cosmopolitanism for the Social Sciences: A Research Agenda' in *British Journal of Sociology* 57, 1, 1–23.
Bhabha, H. K. (1994). *The Location of Culture*. London: Routledge.
Brown, G. W. and Held, D. (eds.) (2010). *The Cosmopolitanism Reader*. Cambridge: Polity Press.
Dahl, R. (1971). *Polyarchy, Participation and Opposition*. New Haven: Yale University Press.
Delanty, G. (2009). *The Cosmopolitan Imagination: The Renewal of Critical Social Theory*. Cambridge: Cambridge University Press.
——— (ed.) (2012a). *Routledge Handbook of Cosmopolitanism Studies*. London: Routledge.
———. (2012b). 'Introduction: The Emerging Field of Cosmopolitanism Studies' in Delanty (2012a) *op cit*.
———. (2012c). 'The Idea of Critical Cosmopolitanism' in Delanty (2012a) *op cit*.
——— and Inglis, D. (eds.) (2010). *Cosmopolitanism: Critical Concepts in the Social Sciences*. London: Routledge.
De La Rosa, S. (2012). *Aneignung und interkulturelle Repräsentation*. Bielefeld: Springer VS-Verlag.
Gadamer, H-G. (2004). *Truth and Method*. London: Bloomsbury Academic.
Heater, D. (1996). *World Citizenship and Government: Cosmopolitan Ideas in the History of Western Political Thought*. London: Macmillan.

Held, D. (1995). *Democracy and the Global Order: From the Modern State to Cosmopolitan Governance.* Cambridge: Polity Press.

———. (2003). *Cosmopolitanism: A Defence.* Cambridge: Polity Press.

———. (2010). *Cosmopolitanism: Ideas and Realities.* Cambridge: Polity Press.

Hensby, A. and O'Byrne, D. J. (2012). 'Global Civil Society and the Cosmopolitan Ideal' in G. Delanty (ed.) *Routledge Handbook of Cosmopolitanism Studies.* London: Routledge.

Inglis, D. (2012). 'Alternative Histories of Cosmopolitanism: Reconfiguring Classical Legacies' in G. Delanty (ed.) *Routledge Handbook of Cosmopolitanism Studies.* London: Routledge.

Kögler, H. H. (2007). 'Roots of Recognition—Cultural Identity and the Ethos of Hermeneutic Dialogue' in C. Kanzian (ed.) *Cultures: Conflict-Analysis-Dialogue: Proceedings of the International Wittgenstein Symposium.* Kirchberg: Austria.

Mignolo, W. (2000). *Local Histories / Global Designs: Coloniality, Subaltern Knowledge, and Border Thinking.* Princeton: Princeton University Press.

———. (2001). 'The Many Faces of Cosmo-polis: Border Thinking and Critical Cosmopolitanism' in *Public Culture* 12, 3, 721–48.

——— and Schiwy, F. (2003). *Transculturation and the Colonial Difference. Double Translation* in T. Maranhao and B. Streck (eds.) *Translation and Ethnography: The Anthropological Challenge of Intercultural Understanding.* Tucson: University of Arizona Press.

Nussbaum, M. (1997). 'Kant and Stoic Cosmopolitanism' in *Journal of Political Philosophy* 5, 1, 1–25.

O'Byrne, D. J. (1997). 'Working-Class Culture: Local Community and Global Conditions' in J. Eade (ed.) *Living the Global City: Globalization as Local Process.* London: Routledge.

———. (2003). *The Dimensions of Global Citizenship: Political Identity beyond the Nation-State?* London: Frank Cass.

———. (2005). 'Globalisation, Cosmopolitanism and the Problem of Civil Society: Some Introductory Remarks' in J. Eade and D. J. O'Byrne (eds.) *Global Ethics and Civil Society.* Burlington, VT: Ashgate.

———. (2013). 'Dealing with Disasters in an Age of Globalized Sentiment: Testing the Boundaries of the Cosmopolitan Ideal' in *Perspectives on Global Development and Technology* 12, 283–97.

Rumford, C. (ed.) (2006). *Cosmopolitanism and Europe.* Liverpool: Liverpool University Press.

———. (2008). *Cosmopolitan Spaces: Europe, Globalization, Theory.* London: Routledge.

Spivak, G. C. (2004). 'Righting Wrongs' in *South Atlantic Quarterly,* 103, 2/3, 523–81.

Taylor, C. (1985). *Understanding and Ethnocentricity* in Taylor, C. (ed.) *Philosophy and the Human Sciences.* Philosophical Papers, Bd.2, Cambridge, 116–33.

Zolo, D. (1997). *Cosmopolis: Prospects for World Government.* Cambridge: Polity Press.

———. (2002). *Invoking Humanity: War, Law and Global Order.* London: Continuum.

I

The Debate on Cosmopolitanism and Connected Discourses

ONE

Humanity, Rights, and the Ideal of a Global Critical Cosmopolitanism

Amos Nascimento

Globalization brings important challenges and opportunities for a Critical Theory of cosmopolitanism. In this chapter I discuss this issue according to four steps. The first is to establish a dialogue with contemporary disciplinary perspectives that provide interesting and sophisticated accounts of cosmopolitanism. Many of these approaches, however, are limited due to their selective focus and lack of clear normative criteria to define what counts as a critical perspective. The second step considers the German tradition of Critical Theory because it speaks more directly of human rights as criteria for cosmopolitan endeavors and offers a robust interdisciplinary framework to articulate various approaches that contribute to *critical cosmopolitanism*. Yet, this tradition is not global enough because its claims are generally bound to European idiosyncrasies. Therefore, a third step examines authors who share the intentions of Critical Theory but expand its framework by revealing these biases and addressing a diversity of human rights issues related to Africa, Asia, Latin America, and the Middle East, thus leading us toward a *global critical cosmopolitanism*. In the process of mapping this variety of positions, we progressively realize that cosmopolitan theories must not only account for the challenges and opportunities of globalization but also affirm the plurality of human identities, experiences, and contingencies. Accordingly, a new ideal for a Critical Theory of cosmopolitanism must be sensitive to the voices of children, women, the poor, ethnic identities, and excluded groups in different geographic locations. In summary, therefore, I hope to show that a global critical cosmopolitanism needs to

13

be inclusive and global enough, so that it can be experienced as a truly *cosmopolitan* cosmopolitanism.

What is cosmopolitanism? This old concept has experienced a recent resurrection and is being applied in various ways in contemporary philosophy, sociology, political science, international relations, literature, anthropology, law, and global studies. Undoubtedly, this concept continues to be applied because it speaks directly to the contemporary challenges and opportunities of globalization. On the one hand, recent global challenges have been related to the weakening of nation-states, the creation of multilevel political structures, the spread of chronic poverty, the volatility of financial markets, greater political instability, ongoing international conflicts, transnational environmental problems, and the need to mitigate the impacts of climate change, among other issues. On the other, opportunities have arisen in relation to the recognition of a plurality of identities, the emergence of multicultural societies and new forms of individual and collective agency, increasing communication and interaction among cultures, the affirmation of contextual values and perspectives, the expansion of accessibility to education, and the promotion of human rights. The concept of cosmopolitanism has been used in direct relation to each one of these aspects.

As a result of this variety, we now have different labels to specify the kind of cosmopolitanism at stake. We speak of moral cosmopolitanism, legal cosmopolitanism, political cosmopolitanism, economic cosmopolitanism, cultural cosmopolitanism, rooted cosmopolitanism, and many other forms. However, as we proceed with these analytical differentiations and focus on particular aspects of global processes, there is always a risk of getting lost amidst this complexity. There is a danger of failing to recognize the connections among the many forms of cosmopolitanism. On the one hand, mainstream legal or political approaches often disregard the underlying moral claims that legitimize their call for the establishment of new cosmopolitan institutions; on the other, positions that explicitly consider moral claims to equality and universality pay little attention to the agents who raise these claims and the contexts in which they emerge. Therefore, there is a danger of not being cosmopolitan enough. There is the peril of not being critical. In light of this scenario, we need to reaffirm the importance of a global critical cosmopolitanism. What is global critical cosmopolitanism?

The answer to this question requires a comprehensive view capable of identifying and sorting out what is fundamental or relevant amidst a variety of definitions of cosmopolitanism and the multiple possibilities brought about by globalization. In what follows, I begin to answer this question by mapping contemporary discussions on this subject.

THE CONTEMPORARY VARIETY OF COSMOPOLITANISMS

Gerard Delanty has recently proposed the development of cosmopolitan studies as an interdisciplinary project that might offer answers to the questions I asked above (2012). Hence, he would be a good starting point. As he focuses on the idea of a 'cosmopolitan imagination,' he attempts to define a critical enterprise that dialogues with contemporary issues and maps the various applications of cosmopolitan studies. To bring this variety to a common denominator, he relates them to ongoing globalization processes. For example, he concedes that 'global forces have become more and more visible and take a huge variety of forms, from economic and technological to cultural and political', so that they need to be addressed by a critical normative perspective. For him, this is the task of a critical cosmopolitanism that does not simply rely on political philosophy, but includes the contributions of social sciences and moral theories in order to address four components of a cosmopolitan imagination: cultural pluralism and heterogeneity, global-local relations, negotiation of territorial borders, and the reinvention of a political community around global ethics. A particularly useful aspect is his conception of the interaction of plural values and an ethical ideal as a 'site of tensions', because this has an interactive character that addresses the complex variety of cosmopolitanisms I indicated earlier (Delanty 2009:7, 15, 51–68, 79). Yet, in this approach, individuality and, therefore, issues related to freedom, autonomy, and the very conditions for 'imagination' disappear from sight. Who is the agent to which we ascribe a cosmopolitan imagination? Individual intentionality is certainly related to the imaginative process and fundamental to many forms of freedom and agency that need to be protected in relation to cultural identities, imposition of global structures upon local contexts, and the exercise of power over political communities. Moreover, the task of promoting or protecting this individuality requires a consideration of legal issues that are absent in Delanty's view.

Ulrich Beck presents a *social theoretical approach* in order to criticize the traditional sociological focus on nationalist frameworks and address particular challenges related to the European experience. He describes the challenges of a world-risk society and proposes a more global outlook in a program that goes from a *Cosmopolitan Manifesto* (1998, reprinted in Brown and Held 2010) through a *Cosmopolitan Europe* (Beck and Grande 2007) to a *Cosmopolitan Vision* (2006). In this process, he defines 'cosmopolitanization' as a 'reflective' attitude that promotes de-territorialized interactions. Such interactions create movements whose agents emerge 'from within' and expand nonlinearly toward non-national democratic institutions that deserve the label 'cosmopolitan' (2006: 81–86, 99f). Beck is convincing in his critique of sociology and in his account of social practices. His conception of a 'cosmopolitanization from below', involving movements of civil society; a 'cosmopolitanization from outside', involving global politics; and a 'cosmopolitanization from above', involving supranational institutions is very helpful, for it describes dynamic social processes that occur at various levels and cut across several contexts (Beck and Grande 2007: 157–61).

However, he seems less clear in providing a more compelling definition of what is *prescriptive* in cosmopolitanization. Not all movements that emerge from below are critical. For example, transborder individual actions of terrorism or the action of transnational corporations that exploit peoples and natural resources in different locations need to be criticized. What are the criteria that allow us to identify and qualify these actors? Without such criteria, we would not be able to differentiate individual tourists from refugees or so-called 'terrorists' from legitimate political activists. Beck does mention the need to recognize the plurality of the external others, but it is not clear on what grounds this endeavor should rest. Should we open borders or be responsive to any claims for rights? Because Beck has neither asked nor answered questions such as these, he does not seem to provide a sufficiently critical standard to evaluate the cosmopolitan processes he describes.

There are many other positions in political theory, especially those based on the tradition of 'liberal cosmopolitanism', which offer a much clearer response to questions of freedom and justice. Building on the legacy of John Rawls's political liberalism, they insist on the importance of establishing new institutions to promote human rights and cope with the reality of globalization (Freeman 2006). At the same time they combine this with a form of moral egalitarianism, so that individual autonomy is maintained as a core normative demand. Interesting examples in this proposal for global justice are Simon Caney's *Justice beyond Borders* (2005), Kok-Chor Tan's *Justice without Borders* (2004), and many others who defend a new form of global governance with the purpose of protecting persons' basic rights. Caney argues for a 'humanity-centered' cosmopolitan political morality based on the premise that some of Rawls's principles of distributive justice are expandable to the global level and can be applied universally to *all* individuals, independently of morally arbitrary characteristics. This requires a global normative framework that he defines as *cosmopolitan justice* (2005).

In relation to this debate, many other positions emerge and propose a variety of categories. There is talk of 'moral and institutional' (Beitz 1999 and 2009; Tan 2004; Pierik and Werner 2010), 'thick and thin' (Held 2010: 75), and 'weak and strong' forms of cosmopolitanism (Miller 2007: 24–31). Scheffler uses the terminology of 'extreme and moderate' cosmopolitanism to contrast the strong normative requirement to justify obligations and commitments in light of a global cosmopolitan principle with the more accommodating view that relaxes this demand and excludes certain special obligations from this requirement (Scheffler 1999: 255–76). In these cases, we observe a growing tension between ideal normative requirements and the real conditions for their application at the individual level. For instance, David Miller depicts moral cosmopolitanism as incompatible with existing legal and political frameworks at the national level (Miller 2007). This way of perceiving the tension between norms and facts has contributed to an ongoing polarization rather than an articulation of these various positions.

Mathias Risse attempts to articulate these differences by understanding them as different 'grounds of justice' (2012: 1–17), but his proposed framework is defined as *global justice* because he sees little use for the word 'cosmopolitanism' (2012: 9–10). He prefers the term 'pluralist internationalism' and opposes cosmopolitans for not viewing 'the state as having moral significance in a theory of justice' (2013: 1038), but ends up having to wrestle with cosmopolitanism because what he proposes is very compatible with the idea of democratic political cosmopolitanism (2012: 82–84; 2013: 1057–59). He appears to be concerned more with the label, not necessarily with the content of what is characterized as 'cosmopolitan'. There are cosmopolitan theories that make room for state agency in global justice, studies that warn about the danger of weak states, authors who avoid state-centric approaches, and positions that focus on institutions in order to question the pitfalls of a Westphalian concept of state.

Thomas Pogge has made an attempt to distinguish and articulate these points by combining moral and political theory in a way that, in his view, could address more directly the concrete challenges of global poverty, global health, and global (human) rights. In discussing these issues, he characterizes a tension between 'moral and legal cosmopolitanism' that is at play at the level of institution building (2008: 175) and relates duties and obligations to the current repertoire of human rights. For Pogge, responding to global challenges and promoting human rights implies the commitment to build the necessary structures that can implement ideal cosmopolitan norms. This clear distinction between individual and institutional levels as well as between the moral and legal demands of cosmopolitanism is very helpful, but there are issues with the institutional limitations drawn by Pogge. One can agree that beyond the merely individual, interactional, and egalitarian aspects of cosmopolitanism, there needs to be a more concrete duty to assist in the establishment of institutions that safeguard human rights as well as a duty to become concretely involved in eradicating poverty and promoting global health. However, Pogge limits global obligations to institutions in such a way that he explicitly says that an individual case of violence against a woman or other particular crimes involving certain groups would remain outside the scrutiny of human rights frameworks (2008: 57–58). Although his conception of human rights accounts for *individuals* as bearers of rights (2008: 175), the individual dimension is weakened in the realm of cosmopolitan duties and responsibilities because it is tied mainly to how individuals participate in institution building within the framework of a nation-state, not so much on how they interact with others. For instance, in his account of poverty, Pogge leaves out the agency of individuals and communities in poor regions or weak states, where institutions do not exist or do not function properly. He seems to see these actors mainly as objects of the charity and solidarity of agents in rich countries who should promote a just global order, and not so much as subjects of a bottom-up process through which individuals and groups claim their right to participate in the opportunities created by globalization.

A reference to global institutions surely requires a consideration of cosmopolitanism in relation to transnational processes discussed in the realm of international relations theory, which can be seen in Mervyn Frost (1986), Andrew Linklater (1998), and Molly Cochran (1999). These authors defend a cosmopolitan approach from the charges coming from realism, Marxism, and pragmatism and appeal to postmodern or poststructural antifoundationalist views in order to include a consideration of different actors that transcends the nation-state. Cochran mentions the need to account for contingencies that reveal who are the agents in cosmopolitan interactions and to question the structures that domesticate them. It is on this basis that she criticizes the marginalization of women in international relations theory and cosmopolitanism. Ultimately, she sides with Richard Rorty's pragmatist views on contingency and solidarity, hoping that its combination with feminism can be useful by integrating gender issues in the cosmopolitan agenda (Cochran 1999: 146–67, 220–30).

Another attempt to integrate postmodern and poststructural theories into a conception of cosmopolitanism in international relations can be seen in Beardsworth, who describes the wide spectrum of cosmopolitanism and contrasts it with realism, Marxism, and postmodernism. He concludes that political liberalism can better address the respective political, economic, and cultural challenges presented by these positions. Interestingly, Beardsworth proposes a *differentiated universalism* in international relations which, in his view, is true to 'the more general fact that the practical implementation of cosmopolitan ideas is necessarily layered' (2011: 231). He definitely includes the plural dimension of globalization, but universality appears to be much particularized in this way. Conceptions of the universal in international relations theory have been invariably connected to imperialism, colonialism, and other negative forms of universalism (Koskenniemi 2001), so cosmopolitan projects in this area require more attention to cultural particularities. However, universal norms that transcend particularities are needed as well (Nascimento 2013); otherwise, we run the risk of projecting our biases as universal. An alternative route would be to see universality emerging from the recognition of plurality, so that instead of defining the content of universalism in advance, this universalism could be seen as the result of a process through which different particular communities make propositions and come to an agreement on core values. To be sure, Beardsworth's intention is to distinguish between national, regional, and global institutional levels in order to offer the possibility of articulating them within a universal approach while maintaining that social agents can be embedded in various contexts (2011: 159). However, he neither accounts for the identity of the agents in these contexts nor defines what would count as a universal agreement derived from interactive relations. His differentiated universalism appears very compatible with the unilateral affirmation of power and self-interest by different nation-states, but this seems to be at odds with the demands of moral universality. Therefore, other conditions are necessary in order to avoid this conflict.

Parallel to these proposals, there remains a tension between liberal and communitarian approaches to global challenges. This tension has been addressed by many, but I will focus on feminist positions that bring a more radical perspective of contingency.

Gillian Brock criticizes Rawls but upholds the idea of impartiality. Based on a thought experiment, she adapts Rawls's account of the 'original position' to propose a needs-based minimum floor principle to guarantee equality from the outset (2009: 45f; see also Gould 2004). She then expands this model by applying it globally to issues of poverty, humanitarian intervention, and working conditions (2009: 45f, 232). Interestingly, she considers a needs account more basic than a human rights or a capabilities approach because, in her view, this account addresses material needs more directly and early enough—both as concrete conditions to equality and as quasi-institutional instances to promote global justice. However, in being impartial, she does not provide enough information about who is involved in this process. She thus repeats the same problem Allen Buchanan identifies in Rawls's *Law of Peoples* (Martin and Reidy 2006: 150f.): The agents involved in real and just global interactions remain as abstract as the individuals of her fictional point of departure. Therefore, her project lacks a concrete human component as the agent and subject of concrete needs and global justice.

Toni Erskine criticizes Rawls as well, but explores the contrast between a communitarian 'embedded cosmopolitanism' and a liberal 'impartialist cosmopolitanism' based on Rawls (2008: 39–42, 51f). In her defence of the embedded perspective, she adopts Walzer's communitarianism and Gilligan's feminist ethics to conclude that community is a structure more flexible than liberal and realist theories assume (2008: 170–75). I agree with Erskine that community should not be identified with the state but be open to various levels of individual agency, even in the extreme case she presents: combatant enemies who should be treated as members of 'overlapping communities' (2008: 2009). This concept is helpful, but because she affirms that 'moral commitments cannot be derived from our "common humanity"' (2008: 176), she ends up falling into a form of communitarian particularity that contradicts the dimension of universality required by moral cosmopolitanism.

What can we learn from these positions? So far, we can see that this variety of theories helps us identify critical dimensions that ought to be addressed when talking about cosmopolitanism. However, it is obvious that some aspects are missing in one particular position while given by another. Thus we can see that sociological descriptions of the current social situation are important to help us navigate globalization, but stronger normative references seem to be missing. Similarly, moral egalitarianism is strong normatively, but taken alone it can neither deliver institutional structures capable of implementing human rights and promoting global justice nor be specific enough to identify the agents involved in constructing and benefitting from these institutional structures. Yet, although institutional and practical approaches try to address this problem, they manage to cause double damage: They weaken the normative dimension and are blind to contextual circumstances—this explains why they are often accused of simply projecting liberal biases to the global arena. Also, positions that have a strong institutional component rely almost exclusively on the nation-state, despite the fact that challenges of globalization have weakened national structures and led to the creation of subnational, international, transnational, and supranational structures that render state-centric approaches obsolete. We have also seen interactive and relational models of cosmopolitanism, proposals for bottom-up movements identified as 'cosmopolitanism from below', and attempts to define universalism in ways that make it compatible with cultural plurality.

It is easy to conclude that these forms of cosmopolitanism are not cosmopolitan enough because something fundamental is always missing in what they offer. Each one of these positions addresses specific issues with great sophistication, but none seem to be global enough. There is a dual sense of 'global' here: The positions are not interdisciplinary enough, and they are not sufficiently open to cultural and geographic diversity. Hence, they are not critical enough. The specific aspects they highlight are important and should not be considered in isolation but rather in terms of complementarity. In any case, the different perspectives discussed so far could be seen as part of a division of labor through which various disciplines and perspectives work on addressing specific aspects such as the role of individuals, their interactions within communities, the relation to states, and the fact that globalization brings challenges and opportunities to these processes. What, then, is this common issue to which they could contribute? How is this related to the question concerning critical cosmopolitanism?

COSMOPOLITANISM AND CRITICAL THEORY

So far we simply have an overview of the 'varieties of cosmopolitanism'. What kind of cosmopolitanism deserves the adjective 'critical'? And among them, which one can help us in our endeavor? To address these questions, let us turn to a critical tradition that has its origins in Germany and will help us answer the above questions in relation to a conception of Critical Theory that has been central to debates about cosmopolitanism. This tradition relies on a particular European tradition that has its beginnings in Immanuel Kant, continues through the Frankfurt School, and influences many contemporary authors such as Jürgen Habermas, David Held, Matthias Lutz-Bachmann, and Jim Bohman, who identify themselves as heirs of this school of thought. To be sure, this is one among many theories available, but I will focus on this one because it provides one of the most robust frameworks for the discussion about cosmopolitanism. This indicates not only a historical continuity in critical approaches to cosmopolitanism but also the continuous expansion of Critical Theory as it includes explicit reflections on globalization.

First, we need to see Immanuel Kant's definition of cosmopolitanism as a corollary to his *critical idealism*, which is surely central to current debates on this subject today. His views are presented in several ways and in different texts and notes. In his short essay of 1784, 'Idea for a Universal History from a Cosmopolitan Point of View', he talks about a 'condition of world citizenship' (*weltbürgerliche Lage*) (*AA VIII*: 27 in Kant 1902f.). In lectures given in 1793–1794, which were later published as the *Metaphysics of Morals Vigilantius*, he speaks of 'world patriotism and local patriotism' (*Vaterlandsliebe*), adding that 'both are required of the world citizen' (*AA XVII* 2.1: 673–74; Kleingeld 2011; G. Brown 2009). In the essay 'On the Common Saying: "This May be True in Theory but It Does not Apply in Practice"', he advocates a federative world-republic (*AA VIII*: 289), an idea that is justified in ethico-political terms in *Religion Within the Limits of Reason Alone* (*AA VI*: 94; Lutz-Bachmann 2005). In his tract of 1795, *Toward Perpetual Peace*, Kant defends a right of humanity (*das Recht der Menschheit*) and insists that individual autonomy, equality, and republicanism beyond the limits of the modern nation-state would constitute the core of a right of world citizenship (*Weltbügerrecht*). He not only recognizes that individuals move between states (traders visit different countries, and persons have cultural interests about different regions) but also states—in the third definitive article of *Perpetual Peace*—that 'world citizenship rights should be limited to the conditions of general hospitality'. This culminates in Kant's *Doctrine of Right* (*Metaphysische Anfangsgründe der Rechtslehre*), where world citizenship is presented as a cluster of different legal aspects that go from the individual to the global level (§ 62). Yet, the normative criterion for a critical cosmopolitanism is provided by the ethical demand of 'respect' (*Achtung*) for other humans and the condition of 'hospitality' (*Hospitalität*).

What does *hospitality* mean? Does it mean that we have an obligation to any stranger or that territorial limits should be abolished? At first, this criterion seems to say that individuals should be free to move as global citizens in different parts of the world—thus affirming a value that is compatible with liberal individual rights and may serve as a norm to assess situations of oppression. However, this minimalist formula does not account for the need to establish structures that enable this free movement. Neither does it account for the situation of immigrants, asylum seekers, refugees, and other actors who move across borders. Kant implicitly says that, if someone can claim hospitality, then someone else has the duty to offer it. Based on what? Is this granted by the state, or could this be based on an individual's moral virtue? Although Kant's cosmopolitanism initially focuses on individual world citizenship as the condition for membership in an extensive community, he also acknowledges that world citizenship has to be guaranteed as a right by national states, which can also exercise some kind of limitation in granting access to their territory. As globalization weakens the power of states and questions territorial sovereignty, the question about subnational and supranational instances as promoters of world citizenship becomes very important. Kant, however, does not have much to offer on these issues; obviously during his lifetime, he could not be aware of globalization processes.

It is also important to remember that Kant uses the idea of a right to world citizenship to demarcate a new realm that cannot be identified with either comparative law or with a global state, but requires cosmopolitan law (*jus cosmopoliticus*) as an ideal, yet to emerge in terms of a global republican structure—a point Kant does not explain sufficiently, except by saying this ideal is a 'negative surrogate'. In any case, this results in the design of a legal system with different levels that would correspond to national law (*Staatsrecht*) and international or comparative law (*Völkerrecht*) that, in turn, would correspond to the traditional 'law of peoples' (*jus gentium*) and a law of world citizenship (*Weltbürgerrecht*) based on a world republic (Lutz-Bachmann and Bohman 1996).

There are many other aspects to Kant's cosmopolitanism, and Pauline Kleingeld offers a detailed account of them (2011). She reads Kant in light of six varieties of cosmopolitanism in eighteenth-century Europe, especially Germany (Kleingeld 1999: 505; 2011: 1–12). Kleingeld shows that there is an intrinsic plurality in Kant's project, including an interdisciplinary account of moral, political, legal, cultural, economic, and even romantic forms of cosmopolitanism—that is, the ideal of humanity united by faith and love (1999: 506; 2011: 18, 128, 179f, 197–99). Yet, it is obvious that his position needs to be criticized and updated in many respects.

Second, this critique and updating is offered by Jürgen Habermas in his identification of cosmopolitanism with the normative criteria of human rights. His initial reading of Kant's cosmopolitanism can be traced back to *The Structural Transformation of the Public Sphere* (1962) but is reappraised in 'Kant's Idea of Perpetual Peace, with the Benefit of Two Hundred Years' Hindsight' (1996), before being expanded in publications such as *The Crisis of the European Union: A Response* (2011). Addressing the shortcomings in the Kantian position, Habermas insists on juridification processes, the primacy of rights (1992), and the pursuit of global constitutionalism (1998) as basic conditions for critical cosmopolitanism. In his writings on this subject, Habermas is vehement about the need to understand cosmopolitanism as the juridification and institutionalization of human rights at the global level. Yet, he also realizes that the creation of regional supranational spheres can be a step towards this goal.

Important in Habermas's discussion is his emphasis on the normativity of human rights. Because he defines *human rights* and *human dignity* as co-originary (*gleich-ursprünglich*), he brings together two complex aspects. On the one hand, human dignity (*Menschenwürde*) is a controversial term that can be related to either a religious metaphysics or to empiricist genetic engineering (2001). In *The Future of Human Nature*, Habermas is concerned with the conflict between religious views and medical practices such as preimplantation genetic diagnosis, genetic interventions, and embryo research, which affect the authentic self-understanding of autonomous persons (2001: 60). To address this conflict, he proposes a 'species ethics' (*Gatttungsethik*) as the intersubjective way of seeing human dignity as a person's self-understanding as a member of a community of the human species (2001: 59–60, 66, 99). On the other hand, human rights (*Menschenrechte*) are understood as a way of transitioning from the universalization claim of morality to the more concrete realm of political deliberations and legal procedures that define a person's self-understanding in terms of constitutional rights. With this subtle formulation, Habermas is able to affirm that no one would have the right to affect the future autonomy of another person—except for therapeutic purposes— otherwise we would be considering other humans as means, not ends. Thus, the connection and mutual delimitation among ethics, politics, and law is internal to the very concept of human rights, and at the same time it offers a wider framework to integrate a variety of approaches to cosmopolitanism.

In 'The Concept of Human Dignity and the Realistic Utopia of Human Rights' (2011), Habermas states that '"human dignity" is not only a classificatory expression, an empty placeholder, as it were, which lumps a multiplicity of different phenomena together, but the moral "source" from which all of the basic rights derive their sustenance' (2011: 16). We can interpret this statement as saying that *human* could be read as an abbreviation for 'human dignity' while *rights* refer to the juridification of whatever authors and addressees define as human—provided this definition is set by means of a politically oriented constitutional process based

on the exercise of both communicative freedom and communicative power. Consequently, moral elements proper to a discourse ethics are
morphed into rights discourses and may eventually become positive law
through democratic political measures that need to recognize all humans
as possessing the same status (2011: 23–27). Surely, law adds a further
step to guarantee individuality and the absolute value of the person (*der
absolute Wert der Person*) in non-metaphysical terms (2011: 33), but it is
important to remember that legal processes are also political and deliberative. For Habermas, it is the exercise of free communication and engaged participation that provides a critical dimension to human rights.
The very concept of human rights expresses, therefore, the complementarity of legal, political, and moral precepts that ought to come together
in critical cosmopolitanism. Habermas's contribution is to establish a
stronger internal link between the moral, political, and legal dimensions
of both humanity and rights while upholding the indissociability of the
terms constituting the concept of *human rights*. He provides us with general communicative principles to connect a variety of cosmopolitan concepts and contexts, but the details on how these principles are applied
more concretely in various areas are left to other authors who complement his theory.

Third, for instance, we can take David Held as an example of a critical
and democratic political approach to global governance. Developed in
partnership with Daniele Archibugi, this project aims at moving beyond
the sociological, political, and legal approaches we have seen. Held attempts, first, to identify, describe, and analyse the challenges of globalization (Held and McGrew 2003); second, to develop a whole program to
address global challenges to both the nation-state and the interstate system in terms of an institutionalization process (Archibugi and Held 1995;
Archibugi, Held, and Köhler 1998); and third, to link these initiatives to
the normative guidance of deliberative democratic practices at the global
level (2010). Upon realizing the limits of national frameworks, he em-
braces the cosmopolitan alternative wholeheartedly. In Held's view,
these challenges are to be addressed by means of a program that rethinks
democracy and establishes new structures beyond the nation-state (1995;
see also Held in Lutz-Bachmann and Bohman 1997: 235–51). This yields
what Held sees as a 'thick' form of cosmopolitanism defined as 'the ethical and political space which sets out the terms of reference for the recognition of people's equal moral worth, their active agency and what is
required for their autonomy and development' (2010: 49). Out of this
definition he derives autonomy and impartiality as two metaprinciples,
which are complemented by eight principles: equal worth and dignity,
active agency or self-determination, personal responsibility and accountability, consent or participation in non-coercive political processes, collective decision making through voting, inclusiveness of people affected by
establishing more democratic decision making and subsidiarity of deci-

sions, refraining from harming others, and promotion of sustainable development.

Many critics note that Held arrives somewhat too hasty to a list of prescriptions about the constitution of a new global order, thereby contradicting the participatory measures he proposes. For instance, he provides lists of issues related to politics, finance, security, the environment, and, above all, democratic representation. What is attractive in Held and Archibugi is the role of civil society as part of a multilayered institutional structure, but they seem to reduce cosmopolitanism to the idea of a multilevel self-governance without paying attention to the concrete individual and collective processes that occur at these various levels (Archibugi 2008: 85f.). After realizing that they rely too heavily on institutional frameworks such as the United Nations without accounting for the concrete individual and collective agents involved in various global processes, they began to redefine the project of cosmopolitan democracy in order to make it open-ended and more sensitive to collective agency (Archibugi and Held 2011).

Fourth, Matthias Lutz-Bachmann and Jim Bohman have developed a joint project in dialogue with these positions. Lutz-Bachmann's point of departure is the view that recent global developments require a new definition of the relationship between ethics and politics, a definition that should also take into account recent debates in the area of human rights and, thus, consider new developments in the realm of law (Lutz-Bachmann and Niederberger 2009; Lutz-Bachmann, Köhler, Brunkhorst 1999). New events such as the terrorist attack on the World Trade Center and the Pentagon in September 2001, the impact of cross-border terrorism, the changes observed in the structure of future military conflicts—especially the new recurrence of wars—are changing the realities of world politics, so that old structures (including the United Nations) appear as incapable of addressing global trends. On the one hand, there is a continuous tension between the idea of a global politics and the threat of a super-state or an imperialistic world policy (Lutz-Bachmann and Bohman 2002). On the other, there are local actors, regional contingencies, and new forms of belligerent conflicts that are not yet fully grasped by existing legal structures. Therefore, Lutz-Bachmann proposes a turn back to Kant's views on 'perpetual peace' (Lutz-Bachmann and Bohman 1997) and affirms that political philosophy now needs to evolve from a 'philosophy of the *polis*'—that is, as a theory of a politically oriented individual State—to a 'philosophy of *cosmopolis*'—or a cosmopolitan 'philosophy of international relations' that needs to reflect upon its own foundations (Lutz-Bachmann 2014: 10). At this point, he gives less emphasis on the legal aspect—although he does provide an important historical reconstruction of concepts of ethics and law in the European context (Lutz-Bachmann, Wagner, Fidora 2010) and insists on the importance of the Magna Charta.

Jim Bohman starts from the premise that humanity and the plurality of rights are fundamental aspects necessary for a critical cosmopolitanism (Bohman 2007: 101f.). However, he sees that recent discussions about human rights have given much more emphasis to the meaning of *rights* than to the meaning of *human*, because references to human worth, human dignity, human needs, or human capabilities are deemed too metaphysical or weak to provide a stable legal foundation for the universality of human rights. Bohman relies on Karl Jaspers and Hannah Arendt to provide an insightful distinction between humanness and humanity so as to better qualify the status of what is 'human' in human rights. He also accounts for the plurality of political communities, which he identifies as *dêmoi* with localized deliberative processes, but his focus is on the self-understanding of modern democracy at the global level. If we insist on this plurality, other distinctions may emerge. For instance, this prompts a discussion on universality. Moreover, it requires a justification of the inalienability of human rights in light of numerous challenges—such as the appeal to metaphysics or the imperialistic imposition of certain cultural norms. Although Bohman is aware of these many challenges, these core issues remain unaddressed and unresolved.

In any case, Jim Bohman and Matthias Lutz-Bachmann provide a strong case for the globalization of philosophy and the development of a critical cosmopolitan view more attuned to the connection between ethical, political, and legal principles and to the tension between human universality and plurality. However, they have developed broad programmatic sketches but not yet provided more concrete links to legal, political, and moral aspects that could be grasped by a robust definition of critical cosmopolitanism.

At this point, we can summarize what we have learned from Critical Theory. Based on the proposed critical framework and the possibilities presented by the authors in this tradition, we can verify whether the plural conditions and identities characteristic of a global society are being recognized in a given position and whether their corresponding human rights are being safeguarded without disregarding the *human* component of such rights. Recent cosmopolitan positions based on liberalism have a tendency to insist on the epistemic dimension of individual rights and downplay the humanity of those who claim or bear such rights with the claim that this would affect impartiality (Kymlicka 1995; Rawls 1999; Brock 2009). This is why the critical tradition from Kant through Habermas to Lutz-Bachmann and Bohman is relevant here. Despite a certain initial insistence on juridification and postnational constitutionalism, critical theorists have recognized that issues such as human dignity had been neglected. Still, the 'human' component and its plural dimensions need a much better clarification. What counts as human? To address this question, we ought to continue in our search for a more critical and inclusive form of cosmopolitanism that not only discusses the moral, political, and legal issues related to globalization, but also understands the cultural and political processes that are compatible with the affirmation of the universality and plurality of humanity. A critical form of cosmopolitanism needs to articulate more clearly the challenges and opportunities of globalization and at the same time recognize the historical and cultural conditions under which cosmopolitan ideals are applied.

TOWARD A GLOBAL CRITICAL
THEORY OF COSMOPOLITANISM

When talking about a critical cosmopolitan approach, we cannot be limited to a European view or to the German context. It is important to specify more clearly who are the global agents and processes involved in cosmopolitan interactions. Therefore, a critical cosmopolitanism needs to be truly global and include some aspects that have been neglected by the German tradition of Critical Theory and cosmopolitanism. Due to the limits identified in the positions we have seen so far, we need to move beyond the examples above and take into consideration other approaches that offer a wider historical or cultural perspective. How can we *globalize* Critical Theory? To answer this question, we need to consider a series of recent publications that overcome the limits of previous positions and map new discursive elements constitutive to a global critical cosmopolitanism.

An initial approach towards a more global critical position can be labelled *cultural cosmopolitanism* and takes feminist, postcolonial, postmodern, and communitarian theories and practices into account. This label can be used to characterize various authors who take a courageous look at controversial issues and tell us who are affected by them (Breckenridge et al. 2002; Vertotec and Cohen 2002; Appiah 2006; Cheah 2006; Van Hooft and Vandekerckhove 2011). Seyla Benhabib has contributed to this endeavor in various publications, especially in *The Rights of Others: Aliens, Residents, and Citizens* (2004) and *Dignity in Adversity: Human Rights in Troubled Times* (2011). In his book *Cosmopolitanism: Ethics in a World of Strangers*, Appiah addresses the question of a culturally rooted cosmopolitanism (2006). Martha Nussbaum has developed interesting views on cosmopolitanism in articles such as 'Kant and Cosmopolitanism' (1997) and books such as *For Love of Country? A Debate on Patriotism and Cosmopolitanism* (1996), while also developing her 'capabilities approach' in *Frontiers of Justice: Disability, Nationality, Species Membership* (2006) and other publications. Eduardo Mendieta differentiates between various forms of cosmopolitanism and defends 'cosmopolitanism from below' as an alternative to Eurocentric cosmopolitanism (2007, 2014). In 'The Many Faces of Cosmo-polis: Border Thinking and Critical Cosmopolitanism' (2001) Walter Mignolo expands and radicalizes this position by stressing the need to question the situation of coloniality imposed upon those located in the global South, especially in Latin America. All these are complementary positions that help us make the case for a more global critical cosmopolitanism.

First, Seyla Benhabib emphasizes the concreteness and situatedness of humans, especially women, which leads to her proposal for another kind of cosmopolitanism that rejects the metaphysical, epistemic, and cultural limits in Kant, Habermas, and Held. In her writings, Benhabib has certainly both criticized and made use of postmodern and feminist categories that question a limiting conception of cosmopolitan rights that blindly accept the power of state-centric institutions and their imposition of very limiting citizenship conditions for the granting and exercise of rights (Benhabib et al. 2006: 171–75). In her view, rights are not dispensations from state structures, but rather a legitimate and inalienable aspect of individual and collective agency. Individuals and groups are bearers of cosmopolitan rights and have, therefore, the possibility of questioning the imposed limits of the nation-state and moving beyond such limits. She proposes an alternative cosmopolitanism that ought to recognize the rights of 'concrete others' — such as immigrants, refugees, asylum seekers, and others — who deserve hospitality at the local and global levels. This position is developed progressively in various publications.

In *Situating the Self: Gender, Community, and Postmodernism in Contemporary Ethics* (Benhabib 1992), she turns to postmodernism to consider its critique of homogeneity and totalitarianism, but at the same time she questions postmodern views on rationality and normativity. She also questions communitarianism for similar problems, especially due to the danger of totalitarian exclusion of individuals (1992: 71–82). Moreover, she critiques the 'generalized other' depicted in liberal ethics and proposes a consideration of a 'concrete other' based on Gilligan's feminist revision of Kohlberg's theory of moral development (1992: 164–70; Erskine 2008: 150–80). As she establishes a dialogue with Linda Nicholson, Nancy Fraser, Judith Butler, and other feminist thinkers, Benhabib concludes that feminism is part of the broader transformations that have questioned modernity and affirmed a 'situated criticism' (1992: 225–28). Although she distances herself from the postmodern 'retreat from utopia' (1992: 228–30), this does not impede Benhabib from espousing the recognition of differences and diversity (2002). This point informs her feminist reading of cosmopolitanism, similarly to other authors who defend a feminist cosmopolitanism such as Erskine's proposal for an 'embedded cosmopolitanism' (Erskine 2008: 39–42) and Ulrike Vieten's views on gender and cosmopolitanism (Vieten 2012: 1–11).

A more explicit connection between feminism and cosmopolitanism can be read in Benhabib's *The Rights of Others: Aliens, Residents, and Citizens* (2004). After reevaluating Kant's cosmopolitanism and the international human rights regime, Benhabib applies the framework of Critical

Theory to identify a 'disaggregation of citizenship,' as exemplified by cases of tensions with immigrants in Europe. These are seen as generalized others, but she also recognizes the concrete others exemplified by Muslim women wearing a scarf in France or in Germany, who enter the public sphere to claim their rights and identities (2004: 171–76, 183–202). In *Another Cosmopolitanism: Hospitality, Sovereignty, and Democratic Iterations* (Benhabib et al. 2006), she shows how this attention to gender and alterity sheds light on cosmopolitanism. She continues to side with Habermas's Critical Theory, but acknowledges that his views on cosmopolitanism do not provide an account of gender inequality, 'bounded communities,' and non-citizens, thus failing to enlarge the scope of what counts as human: 'Because the discourse theory of ethics articulates a universalist moral standpoint, it cannot limit the scope of the *moral conversation* only to those who reside within nationally recognized boundaries; it views the moral conversation as potentially including all of *humanity*' (Benhabib et al. 2006: 18, emphasis in original).

To indicate how these various subjects contribute to an alternative form of cosmopolitanism, Benhabib borrows the term 'iteration' from Derrida to show that when discriminated individuals insist on affirming their identity, contingencies, and claims—as the Muslim women in Europe did—they exercise 'democratic iterations' that augment the '*meaning of rights claims*' and promote the '*growth of the political authorship by ordinary individuals*' (Benhabib et al. 2006:49, emphasis in original). Expanding on the principle of communicative freedom in *Dignity in Adversity: Human Rights in Troubled Times* (2011), she insists that cosmopolitan norms can move society towards more compliance with human rights. However, she adds that change cannot be limited to states, but must include bottom-up processes involving individuals and groups that express themselves in a public communicative framework by means of a 'jurisgenerative politics.' Promoting cosmopolitanism and human rights is a process of raising claims that need to be reiterated, made visible and audible, so that change in the repertoire of rights may eventually happen.

Second, in two books, *The Ethics of Identity* and *Cosmopolitanism: Ethics in a World of Strangers*, Kwame Anthony Appiah addresses the question of a culturally rooted cosmopolitanism (Appiah 2005: 213–72 and 2006: 81, 143–47). This is his alternative to a naïve form of political universalism that has yielded colonialism, imperialism, and totalitarianism. He warns that 'when we seek to embody our concern for strangers in human rights law and when we urge our government to enforce it, we are seeking to change the world of law in every nation on the planet' (Appiah 2006: 82). However, imposing one singular and universalistic project across nations and cultures has many side effects. This applies even when we deal with the case of contemporary slavery. Appiah shows that 'international treaties define slavery in ways that arguably include debt bondage; and debt bondage is a significant economic institution in parts of South Asia' (Appiah 2006: 82). Opposing this practice in terms of a universal law that is blind to cultural differences may offend 'people whose income and whose style of life depend upon it' (Appiah 2006: 82). He thus concludes that if cosmopolitanism is understood solely as the enforcement of international law and approached as an absolute, it could well lead to more harm than good.

At this point one may ask, how is a global critical cosmopolitanism possible at all? Appiah responds that cultures have been able to change from within and adapt their norms throughout the centuries. For example, *dignitas* was an honor bestowed upon the elites, but then *human dignity* emerged as a transformative concept to include all humans, in a process that involved multiple factors, not simply external imposition (Appiah 2006: 137–38). Cultures have internal resources that can be prompted to motivate these transformations. It is possible to say the same about cannibalism or head-hunting, which were once acceptable in some cultures and were progressively banned by them. Nonetheless, it is important to note that this does not happen in isolation as Appiah seems to present, but through intercultural interactions and conflicts that expose traditional views to alternative values. Upon reflection or based on pragmatic reasons, changes from within may occur, but this cannot be a metaphysical wish or a deterministic process. Hence, we need to engage in a more purposive intercultural communication for this progressive change to occur.

Third, Martha Nussbaum is not necessarily identified with the feminist front, but can be included here due to her work on cosmopolitanism and women's issues. She not only offers a reconstruction of cosmopolitanism in Stoic philosophy (1996, 1997) but also connects this historical tradition to contemporary debates on human development. On the one hand, her studies on cosmopolitanism help us identify the origins of cosmopolitanism in the Greek cynic, Diogenes of Sinope, who is now acknowledged as being one of the first to express the idea of being a citizen of the cosmos (Nussbaum 1997; Ruin 2008: 40; E. Brown 2010). Asked by the Athenian citizens about his origin, belonging, and allegiance, Diogenes simply answered that he was a cosmopolitan—*cosmopolites*. As Nussbaum explores the passage from Cynicism to Stoicism and provides a detailed reading of the tradition that goes from Zeno through Seneca to Cicero, she reminds us of the Stoic conception of humans as citizens of two communities: 'The local community of our birth and the community of human argument and aspiration' (Nussbaum 1997: 29). On the other hand, she criticizes contemporary patriotism and highlights the human dimension at play in global human rights, including the role of emotions, the dimension of sexuality, and the recognition of disabilities (Nussbaum 1996, 2004b).

Nussbaum then focuses on the inclusion of women and peoples with disability. Some authors have identified her with liberal theories on individual rights, but she has proposed important corrections and additions to these theories. Beyond her reconstruction of cosmopolitanism in Stoic and Kantian philosophy (Nussbaum 1996, 1997), she questions the limits of the liberal discourses emphasizing 'rights'. As an alternative, she insists on the need to highlight the human dimension at play in global human rights (Nussbaum 2004b). She starts with the assumption that humans are not necessarily equal, but have differences that need to be recognized and compensated in certain situations, so that all humans have the right to pursue their full potential as humans. To say, for example, that women are de facto equal to men is to disregard centuries of oppression and to pretend that a simple nominal equalization would be able to repair this damage. Similarly, we cannot merely affirm that all humans are equal when we discriminate against people with disabilities. As Nussbaum explains, focusing on discourses, 'the language of rights has a moral resonance that makes it hard to avoid in contemporary political discourse. But it is certainly not on account of its theoretical and conceptual clarity that it has been preferred. There are many different ways of thinking about what a right is, and many different definitions of "human rights"' (2001: 97–98). Along these lines, Nussbaum questions, first, whether only individuals have rights. Other entities, families, and ethnic, religious, and linguistic groups may claim rights as well. Second, she also questions the correlation between duties and rights, and asks what, specifically, rights entitle us to. This answer may refer to goods, processes, goals, and other variables. For all these uncertainties and difficulties, she concludes, third, that the language of rights is limited. As an alternative, she develops her 'capabilities approach' and proposes that human rights include the rights to life, bodily health, senses and imagination, emotions and friendship, and play and control over one's environment (2001: 96–101). For her, 'capability must be the goal' because it helps us better define occluded elements that make us humans (2001: 105). She does not deny the importance of rights, but insists on the need to make room for basic human capabilities.

Fourth, in *Global Fragments*, Mendieta states that the affirmation of difference, fragments, and multiplicity 'cannot be read as condoning a frivolous and insouciant form of postmodernism,' but at the same time he concludes that 'postmodernity, when appropriately matched up, arranges in a constellation of related concepts and must yield insights into the geopolitics of contemporary societies' (Mendieta 2007: 7, 64, 59–77). This means that both the critique of universalism and the radical affirmation of one's particularity have to be understood as a critique of the move of stepping outside a particular local context in order to impose universalism. A claim to universality without any mediation runs the risk of becoming particularism. Therefore, if an approach to cosmopolitan ideals beyond metaphysical and epistemic impositions is still possible at all, it will have to pay attention to the contextual, local, and personal dimension. This claim surely appears contradictory. How can we be cosmopolitan and affirm the personal, local, communitarian, or heterogeneous dimension? Avoiding these aspects could be understood as an echo of the classical cosmopolitan metaphysics. Postmodern authors rightly point to this discrepancy by denouncing and then correcting the problems of such views. Instead of a metaphysical authority, they claim, one has only the contingency of particular events. Communitarians would certainly enlarge the chorus of those who oppose this form of cosmopolitanism. Instead of a subjective and individualistic moral obligation based on legal responsibility and allegiance to a nation-state, they expand the spectrum to include particular or neglected collectivities—including women, ethnic minorities, the poor, and victims of gender discrimination. According to the particularistic challenge to cosmopolitanism, upholding a critical position is not a matter of rationality, right, or responsibility, but rather an exercise in sensitivity, sensibility, and solidarity towards humanity. These ideas may seem controversial, but they are progressively finding echo in contemporary debates on cosmopolitanism (Mendieta 2007: 7–13; Mendieta and Elden 2011; Mendieta 2014: 119–38). In accounting for this variety, Eduardo Mendieta differentiates between civic, critical, and dialogic forms of cosmopolitanism, which radicalize the dimension of diversity and take subalternity into account (2007, 2014). He therefore defends a global cosmopolitanism from below as 'a version of cosmopolitanism that is grounded, enlightened, and reflexive, which corrects and supersedes Kant's own Eurocentric cosmopolitanism' (2014: 119).

Finally, Walter Mignolo complements and radicalizes this approach because he stresses the situation of coloniality and those who suffer under this situation. In his essay 'The Many Faces of Cosmo-polis: Border Thinking and Critical Cosmopolitanism' (Cheah and Robbins 1998; Mignolo 2001: 721–48), his point of departure is the implicit Eurocentrism of cosmopolitan projects and the need to call attention to differences that are left aside by classic authors such as Vitoria, Kant, Marx, and other defenders of modern forms of cosmopolitanism. Accordingly, he differentiates between three kinds of cosmopolitan projects related to modern colonialism: 'The first of these designs corresponds to the sixteenth and seventeenth centuries, to Spanish and Portuguese colonialism, and to the Christian mission. The second corresponds to the eighteenth and nineteenth centuries, to French and English colonialism, and to the civilizing mission. The third corresponds to the second half of the twentieth century, to U.S. and transnational (global) colonialism, and to the modernizing mission' (Mignolo 2001: 725). The metaphysical cosmopolitanism of the Christian mission can be traced back to Augustine, but Mignolo highlights its theologico-political upgrade in Vitoria's concept of a universal (planetary) circle (*orbis universalis*). The civilizing mission (*mission civilisatrice*) was promoted by the French and British empires as well as the colonial projects carried out by Holland, Belgium, and Germany. Here

Mignolo shows how the cosmopolitan right (*ius cosmopoliticum*) became international law and culminates in Kant's world citizen law. Following Dussel and Eze, Mignolo reads Kant from the perspective of coloniality and reminds us of Kant's prejudices and racism regarding Amerindians, Africans, and South Europeans (1993; 2001: 733–35). In a move akin to the deconstructionist and postmodern approaches, Mignolo attempts to demarcate the *locus enuntiationis* of these overarching discourses and propose a form of critical cosmopolitanism that recognizes differences, acknowledges the fatal outcomes of the missionary and civilizing or modernizing global designs, and reveals the silenced voices and forgotten histories that were victims of these processes (1995, 1999).

Mignolo connects postmodernism, cosmopolitanism, and human rights very much in consonance with what we have seen so far, but he gives names and locates those affected by cosmopolitan projects. As he states, 'Vitoria and Kant anchored cosmopolitan projects and conceptualizations of rights that responded to specific needs: for Vitoria, the inclusion of the Amerindians; for Kant, the redefinitions of person and citizen in the consolidation of the Europe of nations and the emergence of new forms of colonialism. The *United Nations Declaration of Human Rights* that followed World War II also responded to the changing faces of the coloniality of power in the modern/colonial world' (2001: 736). The condition of coloniality and sensitivity to differences allow Mignolo to identify a series of contradictions and oppressive structures that resulted in the violent repression of initiatives by indigenous peoples, provoked the Zapatista movement in Mexico, and resulted in other social movements that implicitly reveal limitations in contemporary human rights discourses. His proposed alternative is critical and dialogic, emerging from the various spatial and historical locations of the colonial difference: 'Critical and dialogic cosmopolitanism as a regulative principle demands yielding generously ('convivially' said Vitoria; 'friendly' said Kant) toward diversity as a universal and cosmopolitan project in which everyone participates instead of "being participated"' (2001: 743; Mendieta 2007: 10–12). Mignolo coins the term 'diversality' to characterize this diversity as a universal or cosmopolitan project. I prefer the term 'global plurality', as it indicates the transition from multicultural and intercultural plurality to a global universality expressed by cosmopolitan ideals.

What seems to bring these authors together is the expression of solidarity with minorities and strangers who are displaced or dislocated beyond the borders of acceptability as well as beyond the limits of legally, politically, or economically institutionalized structures of particular nation-states and supranational structures. Mendieta summarizes many of these positions, saying that 'this grounded, placed, rooted, and patriotic cosmopolitanism acknowledges the contingency and fragility of the kinds of institutions that enable our enacting cosmopolitanism or cosmopolitan iterations' (2014: 136–38).

As we can see from these contemporary authors, the discussion on cosmopolitanism is directly related to globalization processes and the need to affirm and respect human contingencies, particularities, and differences. In this process, these authors progressively address the question about individual rights, which are then expanded not as exclusive entitlements to citizens of particular nation-states but as human rights and universal human ideals. These views on cosmopolitanism, world citizenship, and global human rights discourses clearly question the sole emphasis on rights, the legal order, or international law under the aegis of economic globalization. They connect these juridical processes to moral claims, political deliberations, and cultural contingencies so as to give voice to those affected and excluded by the negative aspects of a blind positivistic juridification. They downplay the epistemic dimension in order to highlight the complementarity of the human dimension. In so doing, they reveal and affirm the plurality of human perspectives. In all these authors, there is an attempt to enlarge the scope of what counts as human and what rights they claim. The scope is enlarged by their effort to be truly global and by their insistence in bringing different voices and perspectives to the discussion about critical cosmopolitanism. This global and multicultural perspective is compatible with a critical ideal of cosmopolitanism, and, hopefully, it can help us answer the questions we have asked so far.

CONCLUSION

The challenges and opportunities of globalization provide an important opportunity for a Critical Theory of cosmopolitanism. However, we were able to identify various blockades that impede the attainment of this goal.

First, many current views on cosmopolitanism provide a detailed analysis of specific aspects involved in this task, but fail to provide a critical perspective because they neither see the big picture nor recognize the various agents involved in global processes. Several contemporary disciplinary perspectives provide interesting and sophisticated, but partial, accounts of legal, moral, and political cosmopolitanism, and therefore fall short of offering a robust ideal for critical cosmopolitanism.

Second, the German tradition of Critical Theory offers a robust understanding of critique that is interdisciplinary and, therefore, capable of articulating complementary approaches. Initial insights in this direction can be found in Immanuel Kant, especially when he tries to connect the moral and political aspects implicit in world citizenship. Jürgen Habermas provides an important updating of Kant's ideas and relates cosmopolitanism more directly to human rights, establishing an internal connection between rights and humanity by articulating morality and law by means of a deliberative politics. This is expanded even more by James Bohman and Matthias Lutz-Bachmann, who complement Habermas's views by adding the dimension of plurality and global politics. However, this critical tradition is not yet global enough, because it bases its claims mainly on the German tradition or the North Atlantic context.

Third, due to the shortcomings of these previous views, we then turned to recent authors who are expanding the critical framework by showing global issues affecting diverse contexts such as Africa, Asia, Latin America, and the Middle East, thus yielding new understandings of cosmopolitanism. This growing group of authors is clearly establishing connections among cosmopolitanism, globalization, and the plurality of human identities, experiences, and contingencies, thus providing the conditions for a more global critical cosmopolitanism. Through this new approach, a new perspective emerges, which accounts for the contemporary debate, establishes a dialogue with Critical Theory, and hears the voices of women, the poor, ethnic minorities, people with disabilities, and other groups in different geographic locations.

Based on this overview of contemporary debates on cosmopolitanism, we can conclude that the task of establishing a global critical cosmopolitanism is daunting, but its conditions are relatively simple: A critical cosmopolitanism needs to be global and inclusive enough. It is under this condition that a Critical Theory can be truly cosmopolitan. The many positions we were able to review indicate that we are not there yet, but are moving forward toward a critical ideal. We are in the middle of a process that has yielded many perspectives. Once we are able to establish the global critical ideal of more inclusiveness, maybe it could be called *cosmopolitan cosmopolitanism*.

BIBLIOGRAPHY

Appiah, K. A. (2005). *The Ethics of Identity*. Princeton, NJ: Princeton University Press.

———. (2006). *Cosmopolitanism: Ethics in a World of Strangers*. New York: W.W. Norton.

Archibugi, D. (2008). *The Global Commonwealth of Citizens: Towards Cosmopolitan Democracy*. Princeton, NJ: Princeton University Press.

——— and Held, D. (1995). *Cosmopolitan Democracy: An Agenda for a New World Order*. Cambridge: Polity Press.

——— Held, D. (2011). 'Cosmopolitan Democracy: Paths and Agents' in *Ethics and International Affairs* 25/4 (December 2011): 433–61.

———, Held, D., and Köhler, M. (eds.) (1998). *Re-imagining Political Community*. Cambridge: Polity Press.

Beardsworth, R. (2011). *Cosmopolitanism and International Relations Theory*. Cambridge: Polity Press.

Beck, U. (1998). *The Cosmopolitan Manifesto*. Cambridge: Polity Press.

———. (2006). *The Cosmopolitan Vision*. Cambridge: Polity Press.

——— and Grande, E. (2007). *Cosmopolitan Europe*. Cambridge: Polity Press.

Benhabib, S. (1992) *Situating the Self: Gender, Community, and Postmodernism in Contemproary Ethics*. London: Routledge.

———. (2002). *The Claims of Culture: Equality and Diversity in the Global Era*. Princeton: Princeton University Press.

————. (2004). *The Rights of Others: Aliens, Residents, and Citizens*. Cambridge: Cambridge University Press.

———— with J. Waldron, B. Honig, and W. Kymlicka. (2006). *Another Cosmopolitanism: Hospitality, Sovereignty, and Democratic Iterations*. Tanner Lectures, edited by R. Post. Oxford: Oxford University Press.

————. (2011). *Dignity in Adversity: Human Rights in Troubled Times*. Cambridge: Polity Press.

Beitz, C. (1999). 'Social and Cosmopolitan Liberalism'. *International Affairs* 75/3, July, 125–40.

————. (2009). *The Idea of Human Rights*. Oxford, UK: Oxford University Press.

Bohman, J. (1996). *Public Deliberation: Pluralism, Complexity, and Democracy*. Cambridge, MA: MIT Press.

————. (2007). *Democracy across Borders: From Dêmos to Demoi*. Cambridge, MA: MIT Press.

Breckenridge, C. et al. (eds.) (2002). *Cosmopolitanism*. Durham, NC: Duke University Press.

Brock, G. (2009). *Global Justice: A Cosmopolitan Account*. Oxford: Oxford University Press.

Brown, E. (2010). 'Die Erfindung des Kosmopolitanismus in der Stoa' in Matthias Lutz-Bachmann et al. (Hrsg.) *Kosmopolitanismus: Zur Geschichte und Zukunft eines umstrittenen Ideals*. Weilerswist: Velbrück, 9–24.

Brown, G. (2009). *Grounding Cosmopolitanism: From Kant to the Idea of a Cosmopolitan Constitution*. Edinburgh: Edinburgh University Press.

Buchanan, A. (2006). 'Taking the Human Out of Human Rights' in Rex Martin and David Reidy (eds.) *Rawls's Law of Peoples: A Realistic Utopia?* Oxford: Oxford University Press, 150–68.

Caney, S. (2005). *Justice beyond Borders*. Oxford: Oxford University Press.

Cheah, P. (2006). *Inhuman Conditions: On Cosmopolitanism and Human Rights*. Cambridge, MA: Harvard University Press.

———— and Robbins, B. (eds.) (1998). *Thinking and Feeling Beyond the Nation*. Minneapolis: University of Minnesota Press.

Cochran, M . (1999) *Normative Theory in International Relations: A Pragmatic Approach*. Cambridge: Cambridge University Press.

Delanty, G. (2009). *The Cosmopolitan Imagination: The Renewal of Critical Social Theory*. Cambridge: Cambridge University Press.

———— (ed.) (2012). *Routledge International Handbook of Cosmopolitan Studies*. London: Routledge.

Erskine, T. (2008). *Embedded Cosmopolitanism: Duties to Strangers and Enemies in a World of Dislocated Communities*. Cambridge: Cambridge University Press.

Freeman, S. (2006). 'The Law of Peoples, Social Cooperation, Human Rights, and Distributive Justice' in *Social Philosophy and Policy* 23/1, January, 23–61.

Frost, M . (1986). *Towards a Normative Theory of International Relations*. Cambridge: Cambridge University Press.

Gould, C . (2004). *Globalizing Democracy and Human Rights*. Cambridge: Cambridge University Press.

Habermas, J. (1962). *Strukturwandel der Öffentlichkeit*. Frankfurt: Suhrkamp.

————. (1992). *Faktizität und Geltung: Beiträge zur Diskurstheorie des Rechts und des demokratischen Rechtsstaats*. Frankfurt a.M.: Suhrkamp.

————. (1996). *Die Einbeziehung des Anderen*. Frankfurt: Suhrkamp.

————. (1998). *Die postnationale Konstellation*. Frankfurt: Suhrkamp.

————. (2001). *Die Zukunft der menschlichen Natur*. Frankfurt: Suhrkamp.

————. (2011). *Zur Verfassung Europas: Ein Essay*. Berlin: Suhrkamp.

Held, D. (1995). *Cosmopolitan Democracy: An Agenda for a New World Order*. Cambridge: Polity Press.

———. (1997). 'Cosmopolitan Democracy and the Global Order: A new agenda' in Lutz-Bachmann, M. and Bohman, J. (eds.) *Perpetual Peace.* Cambridge, MA: MIT Press, 235–51.

———. (2010). *Cosmopolitanism: Ideals and Realities.* Cambridge: Polity Press.

Held, D. and McGrew, A. (eds.) (2003). *The Global Transformations Reader: An Introduction to the Globalization Debate.* Cambridge: Polity Press.

Kant, I. (1902f.) *Gesammelte Schriften* [Hrsg. von der Königlichen Preussischen Akademie der Wissenschaften—*Akademieausgabe*] Berlin: W. de Gruyter.

Kleingeld, P. (1999). 'Six varieties of Cosmopolitanism in late 18th century Germany' in *Journal of the History of Ideas* 60/3, 505–24.

———. (2011). *Kant and Cosmopolitanism: The Philosophical Ideal of World Citizenship.* Cambridge: Cambridge University Press.

Koskenniemi, M . (2001). *The Gentle Civilizer of Nations: The Rise and Fall of International Law: 1870–1960.* Cambridge: Cambridge University Press.

Kymlicka, W. (1995). *Multicultural Citizenship: A Liberal Theory of Minority Rights.* Oxford: Clarendon Press.

Linklater, A . (1998). *Transformation of Political Community.* Cambridge: Polity Press.

Lutz-Bachmann, M. (2005). 'Das "ethische geimeine Wesen" und die Idee einer Weltrepublik. Der Beitrag der *Religionsschrift* Kants zur politischen Philosophie internationaler Beziehungen' in Städler, M. [Hrsg.] *Kants 'Ethisches Gemeinwesen'.* Berlin: Akademie Verlag.

———. (2014). 'The Idea of Human Rights and the Realities of World Politics: A reflection on the relationship between Ethics and Politics' in Lutz-Bachmann, M. and Nascimento, A. (eds.) (2014) *Human Rights, Human Dignity, and Cosmopolitan Ideals.* Surrey: Ashgate, 9–21.

——— and Bohman, J. (eds.) (1997). *Perpetual Peace.* Cambridge, MA: MIT Press.

——— and Bohman, J. [Hrsg.] (2002). *Weltstaat oder Staatenwelt?* Frankfurt: Suhrkamp.

——— and Niederberger, A. [Hrsg.] (2009). *Krieg und Frieden im Prozess der Globalisierung.* Weilerswist: Velbrück.

———, Fidora, A., and Wagner, A. [Hrsg.] (2010). *Lex and Ius.* Stuttgart: formanholzboog.

———, Köhler, W., and Brunkhorst, H. [Hrsg.] (1999). *Recht auf Menschenrechte: Menschenrechte, Demokratie und internationale Politik.* Frankfurt: Suhrkamp.

———, Niederberger, A., and Schink, P. [Hrsg.] (2010). *Kosmopolitanismus: Zur Geschichte und Zukunft eines umstrittenen Ideals.* Weilerswist: Velbrück.

——— and Nascimento, A. (eds.) (2014). *Human Rights, Human Dignity, and Cosmopolitan Ideals.* Surrey: Ashgate.

Martin, R. and Reidy, D. (eds.) (2006). *Rawls's Law of Peoples: A Realistic Utopia?* Oxford: Oxford University Press.

Mendieta, E. (2007). *Global Fragments: Globalizations, Latinoamericanisms, and Critical Theory.* Albany: State University of New York Press.

———. (2014). 'From Imperial to Dialogical Cosmopolitanism' in Lutz-Bachmann, M. and Nascimento, A. (eds.) (2014). *Human Rights, Human Dignity, and Cosmopolitan Ideals.* Surrey: Ashgate, 119–38.

——— and Elden, S. (eds.) (2011). *Reading Kant's Geography.* Albany: State University of New York Press.

Mignolo, W . (1993). 'Colonial and Postcolonial Discourses: Cultural Critique or Academic Colonialism?' in *Latin American Research Review* 28/3, 120–34.

———. (1995). *The Darker Side of Renaissance. Literacy, Territoriality and Colonization.* Ann Arbor, MI: Michigan University Press.

———. (1999). *Local Histories, Global Designs: Coloniality, Subaltern Knowledges, and Border Thinking.* Princeton, NJ: Princeton University Press.

———. (2001). 'The Many Faces of Cosmo-polis: Border Thinking and Critical Cosmopolitanism' in *Public Culture* 12/3, 721–48.

Miller, D. (2007). *National Responsibility and Global Justice.* Oxford: Oxford University Press.

Nascimento, A. (2013). *Building Cosmopolitan Communities: A Critical and Multidimensional Approach*. New York: Palgrave MacMillan.

Nussbaum, M. (1996). 'For Love of Country' in Cohen, J. and Nussbaum, M. (eds.) *For Love of Country? A Debate on Patriotism and Cosmopolitanism*. Boston: Beacon Press.

———. (1997). 'Kant and Cosmopolitanism' in Lutz-Bachmann, M. and Bohman, J. (eds.) *Perpetual Peace*. Cambridge, MA: MIT Press, 25–57.

———. (2001). *Women and Human Development: The Capabilities Approach*. Cambridge: Cambridge University Press.

———. (2004a). 'Duties of Justice, Duties of Material Aid: Cicero's Problematic Legacy' in Strange, S. and Zupko, J. (eds.) *Stoicism: Traditions and Transformations*. Cambridge: Cambridge University Press, 214–49.

———. (2004b). *Hiding From Humanity: Disgust, Shame, and the Law*. Princeton, NJ: Princeton University Press.

———. (2006). *Frontiers of Justice: Disability, Nationality, Species Membership*. Cambridge, MA: Harvard University Press.

Pierik, R. and Werner, W. (eds.) (2010). *Cosmopolitanism in Context: Perspectives from International Law and Political Theory*. Cambridge: Cambridge University Press.

Pogge, T. (2008). *World Poverty and Human Rights: Cosmopolitan Responsibilities and Reforms*. Cambridge: Polity Press.

Rawls, J. (1999). *The Law of Nations*. Cambridge, MA: Harvard University Press.

Risse, M. (2012). *On Global Justice*. Princeton, NJ: Princeton University Press.

———. (2013). 'A Précis of On Global Justice, with Emphasis on Implications for International Institutions' in *Boston College Law Review* 54/3, 1037–61.

Ruin, H. (2008). 'Belonging to the Whole: Critical and "Heraclitical" Notes on the Ideal of Cosmopolitanism' in Lettevall, R. and Linder, M. K. (eds.) *The Idea of Kosmopolis: History, Philosophy and Politics of World Citizenship*. Flemingsberg: Södertörns högskola, 31–50.

Scheffler, S. (1999). 'Conceptions of Cosmopolitanism' in Utilitas 11, 255–76.

Tan, K-C. (2004). *Justice without Borders*. Cambridge: Cambridge University Press.

Van Hooft, S. and Vandekerckhove, W. (eds.) (2011). *Questioning Cosmopolitanism*. Dordrecht: Springer.

Vertotec, S. and Cohen, R. (eds.) (2002). *Conceiving Cosmopolitanism: Theory, Context, and Practice*. Oxford: Oxford University Press.

Vieten, U. (2012). *Gender and Cosmopolitanism in Europe: A Feminist Perspective*. Surrey: Ashgate.

TWO

A Feminist Cosmopolitanism

Relational or Non-Relational?

Angie Pepper

Feminists from a variety of theoretical backgrounds have long been engaged in a sustained and fruitful critique of contemporary theories of
social justice. This feminist critique has challenged prevailing theories for
being, among many other things, too abstract,[1] too individualistic,[2] inat-
tentive to gender,[3] based on defective conceptions of personhood,[4] and
for drawing a strict dichotomy between public and private spheres.[5]
However, there has been little feminist contribution to the debate concerning *global* distributive justice—a debate that has flourished in contemporary political philosophy for the last forty years.[6] This is not to
suggest that feminists are not concerned with questions of global justice.
Indeed, there are many feminists working on issues of global concern
such as gender injustice, oppression, the feminization of poverty,[7] human
rights,[8] multiculturalism and women's rights,[9] and the denigration of the
environment,[10] to name but a few. Rather, my claim is that there has been
little feminist engagement with the dominant perspectives in the contemporary debate on global justice.

It is my contention that we cannot hope to develop adequate theories
of global justice without paying attention to gender inequality and oppression more broadly. Thus, feminist contributions are essential, just as
they have been for improving our theorising about social justice, to improving our thinking on matters of global distributive justice. This position has recently been articulated by Alison Jaggar (2014) and others who
suggest that a truly *global* cosmopolitanism "must be sensitive to the

voices of children, women, the poor, ethnic identities, and excluded groups in different geographic locations" (Nascimento, this volume).

Having suggested elsewhere that feminists ought to be cosmopolitans about global justice (Pepper 2014), in this paper I will argue that feminists should be *non-relational* cosmopolitans about global justice. My argument is structured as follows: I begin by setting out the distinction between relational and non-relational forms of cosmopolitanism before moving on to consider some of the undesirable consequences of relational accounts. Following this I suggest that there are existent feminist arguments that support and strengthen the challenge to relational accounts. Lastly, I consider why some feminists might be thought to favour relational forms of cosmopolitanism, and I demonstrate, by examining a care theoretical approach to personhood, why such feminist theorists would be better served by non-relational approaches. Ultimately I argue that relational cosmopolitanism problematically renders duties and entitlements of justice contingent on the existence of particular relationships and thereby has the potential to exclude vulnerable individuals from the scope of justice—an outcome that is unacceptable from both a cosmopolitan and feminist perspective.

RELATIONAL AND NON-RELATIONAL APPROACHES TO GLOBAL DISTRIBUTIVE JUSTICE

Cosmopolitan approaches to global distributive justice fall, broadly speaking, into two camps: relational and non-relational. Relational accounts ground justice in features of relationships, association, and shared institutions (Beitz 1975, 1999; Mollendorf 2002; Pogge 1989, 1992, 2002). By contrast, non-relational accounts ground justice in some feature or features of human beings (Barry 1995, 1999; Caney 2005, 2009; Nussbaum 2000, 2006). The fundamental difference between these two ways of grounding justice is that for relational accounts, duties of justice are contingently grounded on the existence of certain relationships, whereas for the non-relational theorist, duties of justice are not conditional on our relationships with others but are instead rooted in our humanity.

Consider the following example. In our world, Earth, the relational cosmopolitan maintains that we have duties to our fellow human beings because we are all locked into the same global economic, institutional, and social scheme. Accordingly, for the relational cosmopolitan, we have a cosmopolitan duty of justice to tackle any injustice arising from our shared scheme of interaction and interdependence. By contrast, the non-relational cosmopolitan thinks that '[o]ne has obligations of justice to others because they are fellow human beings—with human needs and failings, and human capacities for, and interests, in autonomy and well-being—and facts about interdependence do not, in themselves, determine the scope of distributive justice' (Caney 2009: 391). Thus, for the non-relational cosmopolitan, *all* humans on Earth are entitled to have their needs and interests counted when we are trying to determine a fair pattern of distribution, regardless of whether all humans do in fact participate in a shared global scheme.

Now imagine that astronomers discover another world that is populated with human beings. On this other world—let us call it Dearth—humans are suffering from the effects of extreme poverty: malnutrition, starvation, and disease. Moreover, imagine that scientists on Earth develop new technologies that allow us to transport goods to Dearth. Do we, on our relatively prosperous world, have a duty of justice to redistribute resources to those on Dearth? That is, do we have stringent and legitimately enforceable duties to those on Dearth, which correlate with the rights of Dearth's citizens, to distribute resources that they are *owed* as a matter of justice?

Though both relational and non-relational cosmopolitans agree that there are duties of justice that are global in scope, by imagining two planets populated by humans, we can see how the two perspectives diverge. For a relational cosmopolitan, it seems that we owe the inhabitants of Dearth very little, if anything, as matter of justice. These two worlds are not interdependent, there are no institutions shared between the two, and there is little social interaction between the inhabitants of each world. Since individuals on Earth share no relations with those on Dearth, those on Earth owe nothing, as a matter of justice, to those on Dearth.

A non-relational cosmopolitan, on the other hand, will be committed to the idea that we do in fact have duties of justice to people on Dearth because, like us, they are human, and it is their humanity that grounds duties and entitlements of justice. It remains to be seen what such cosmopolitan duties would entail, and it is perfectly consistent with a cosmopolitan approach that our duties to those on Dearth be considerably weaker, or in some way less demanding, than our duties to fellow inhabitants on Earth. Setting these issues aside, the take-home point is that for a non-relational cosmopolitan, what is owed to those on Dearth is a matter of justice and not merely the weaker demands of a humanitarian morality.

THE MORAL RELEVANCE OF SOCIAL
AND ECONOMIC INTERACTION

One compelling objection to relational accounts focuses on the moral relevance of social and economic interaction. As noted above, those who advocate relational accounts argue that duties of justice only arise when certain relationships hold between individuals. Often the kinds of relationships that are held to be important are those that come about when individuals engage in schemes of social interaction and interdependence. However, following Caney, it strikes me that when we think about distributive justice, 'it is difficult to see how and why the fact that one group of people is linked by interaction should impact on their entitlements' (2005: 111).

Caney asks us to imagine two individuals living in separate systems of interaction (2005: 111). Recall Earth and Dearth. Individuals on Earth have knowledge that Dearth and its inhabitants exist, and, conversely, individuals on Dearth have knowledge of Earth and its inhabitants. However, there is no interaction between them. Now, consider Mollie, who lives on Earth, and Millie, who lives on Dearth. Mollie and Millie are identical in their abilities, efforts, and needs, and yet Mollie receives sufficient benefits for her participation in Earth's prosperous institutional arrangements to have a decent standard of living, while Millie, because Dearth's global order cannot meet the basic needs of its members, does not. Since Mollie and Millie are identical with respect to their abilities, efforts, and needs, the only difference between them is that Mollie had the luck of being born into a prosperous world while Millie did not. Like Caney, I too find it difficult to see why Mollie is justly entitled to more, and I have a hard time seeing the situation as fair. [11]

To be clear, the non-relational view insists that when there is more than one human being, it is appropriate to ask whether the situation is just or not. This does not mean that circumstances will always be sufficient to generate duties and entitlements of justice. For example, if inhabitants of Earth were unaware of the existence of Dearth, or if they had no means of fulfilling any redistributive duties, then the situation would not be marked by injustice. In this scenario, the disparity between the two worlds should be considered merely unfortunate. I am assuming that 'ought' implies 'can', where 'can' means that it is both physically and psychologically possible. Hence, it would be meaningless to claim that the citizens of Earth have a duty of justice to those on Dearth when they have either no knowledge of the existence of the other world, or no means of fulfilling that obligation. Nevertheless, it is important to note that the duties and entitlements of individuals on both worlds are subject to revision. If circumstances change such that the inhabitants of Earth become (a) aware of those on Dearth, and (b) have the technology to redistribute resources, then duties of justice would be generated.

With this in mind, recall that Mollie lives on the prosperous planet Earth where most inhabitants are aware of the plight faced by inhabitants on Dearth, and that, furthermore, there is technology available to distribute resources to Dearth. As noted earlier, what distinguishes Mollie's situation from Millie's is that she was born into a prosperous scheme while Millie was not. Thus, the burden now lies with the relational cosmopolitan to show that this fact—the fact that Millie and Mollie belong to different interactional schemes—is morally relevant to determining the scope of justice. However, this task poses a problem for relational accounts because the logic internal to cosmopolitanism, which most relational cosmopolitans endorse, undermines the relational perspective (Caney 2005: 111–12). Most are agreed that when thinking about justice, we should not let our thinking be influenced by morally arbitrary features of our world. Cosmopolitans have been keen to emphasize that just as a person's sex, race, class, physical attributes, and conception of the good should not affect their entitlements, neither should the matter of where one is born. This is a fundamental cosmopolitan thesis. None of us chooses the country into which we are born, and so the fact of where one is born is irrelevant to our reasoning about justice (Caney 2001: 115; Pogge 1989: 247; Nussbaum 1996: 133).

However, as Caney argues, if we think that the fact of where one is born is irrelevant to our moral thinking about questions of distributive justice, then why should we consider the scheme of interaction to which one is a member morally relevant? That is, 'can someone not equally persuasively argue that "one's life prospects or one's access to opportunities" should not depend on "morally arbitrary considerations" such as which associational scheme one is born into?' (Caney 2005: 112). The problem with relational cosmopolitanism is that it commits one to the view that two similar individuals born into separate schemes of interaction do not have duties of justice to one another, nor can they make claims on one another, even when one is impoverished and the other is not. But this is in conflict with a key cosmopolitan premise: People should not be penalized because of the circumstances of their birth (Caney 2005: 112).[12]

THE DANGER OF MAKING JUSTICE CONTINGENT ON RELATIONSHIPS

Let us for a moment ignore the charge of theoretical inconsistency, and grant that some form of interaction is necessary to ground duties of distributive justice. In this section I draw out the implications of being committed to such a view. I begin by considering why making justice contingent on certain relations is problematic from the perspective of entitlement-bearers, before going on to argue that the consequences for duty-bearers are also theoretically unattractive.[13]

One outcome of the relational picture is that some individuals may potentially be denied entitlements to goods that they had previously been entitled to. The cases I have in mind differ from the example involving Earth and Dearth. Here I am interested in cases where relations have dissolved and individuals have become isolated from the scheme of interaction. For example, imagine Authentia, a state that has a government pursuing isolation in order to preserve cultural purity. Further imagine that the government manages to successfully isolate its citizens from the rest of the global economic and social order. The borders are closed, allowing no one in (though the right to leave is protected), the import and export of goods is prohibited, and little or no communication is permitted between those inside and those outside of state boundaries. Now, prior to isolation, the state, and therefore the individuals constituting the state, were part of the global economic order. As members of the global scheme, Authentians were entitled, as a matter of justice, to certain goods, and they had certain duties of justice to others. However, at the point at which Authentia successfully withdraws from the global economic order, Authentia's citizens can no longer make legitimate justice-based claims on those residing outside of the state, and non-compatriots, incidentally, no longer have a duty of justice to Authentians.

One might argue that there is no injustice here since Authentia has chosen to isolate itself from the global economic order. However, it seems uncontroversial to note that the decisions of those in power do not always reflect the views or interests of the general population. Moreover, we can further imagine that though Authentia does not intentionally violate its citizens' human rights, it may fail (through lack of resources or an ineffective scheme of distribution) to secure a decent standard of living for all of its citizens. What should trouble us about this case is that, on the relational account, the citizens of Authentia are not eligible, because of the state's successful separation from the global scheme, to have anything more than their basic rights respected out of a weaker commitment to humanitarian morality. This seems particularly problematic given that the fundamental needs and interests of the Authentians remain the same both prior to, and after, the separation of their state from the global scheme. While Authentians are entitlement-bearers before separation, their claims on others outside of Authentia no longer hold once the state withdraws from the global order—even when the state in which they live fails to secure for them a decent standard of living.

Let us now consider a different case. Imagine another state, Abundia, where citizens enjoy a prosperous scheme of interaction. Abundia cooperates with other states in the global economic order, and its awareness of the dire poverty faced by those in other societies, coupled with its ability to redistribute resources, means that for both relational and non-relational cosmopolitans the citizens of Abundia have a duty of justice to redistribute resources to those doing less well. However, the relational cosmopolitan holds that Abundians only have this duty if Abundia participates in a global scheme of interaction and interdependence. This means that Abundia's duty to those less fortunate could be dissolved if the state successfully managed to withdraw from the global order. The chief concern here is that on the relational view, it is possible for agents to absolve themselves of duties of justice simply by refusing to cooperate or interact in the right ways. That is, they can change their status as duty-bearers and in so doing avoid the claims of others less fortunate. This strikes me as deeply inadequate.

Relational accounts, then, are problematic both from the perspective of entitlement-bearers and duty-bearers. Those who fall outside of the global scheme of interaction cannot be legitimate entitlement-bearers. This means that excluded individuals cannot make legitimate claims on others to have their basic needs and interests met because they fail to stand in the correct justice-grounding relations. In addition, prosperous countries/individuals can freeze out resource-poor countries from the global scheme of interaction, or they themselves can withdraw in order to dissolve distributive duties of justice to less fortunate individuals.

The relational cosmopolitan might, at this point, respond by arguing that my examples are too fanciful. Indeed, many cosmopolitans hold that the level of interconnectedness at the global level makes it nigh on impossible for a government to completely isolate the state from the global order (Held 1995). But, even if we accept this, there remains something deeply unsatisfying about the claim that justice holds because our social world happens to be structured in the correct way, especially when we can so easily imagine it being structured otherwise.

FEMINISM, RELATIONAL COSMOPOLITANISM, AND THE PROBLEM OF EXCLUSION

On the basis of the forgoing discussion, it seems sensible to suggest that a feminist cosmopolitan should adopt a non-relational account in order to avoid internal inconsistency and unpalatable theoretical implications. Though I take these to be compelling reasons in support of my claim that feminists should adopt non-relational versions of cosmopolitanism, there are some feminist considerations that lend additional support to the preceding concerns. My aim here is to employ existing feminist arguments to strengthen the preceding critique and to further demonstrate that feminists ought to be non-relational cosmopolitans about global justice.

Feminists have sought to ensure that theories of justice encompass all those affected by the realm of the political. In particular, feminists have critiqued mainstream theories for neglecting the experiences of women and other oppressed social groups and for excluding such groups from their theorizing altogether (MacKinnon 2006; Nussbaum 1999, 2000; Okin 1980, 1989, 1994). Thus, one feminist goal has been to ensure that the scope of justice captures all persons, and to challenge theories of social justice that arbitrarily exclude those who do not fit the dominant model of a subject of justice or member of the moral community.

This feminist commitment to inclusion can be seen in continued efforts to include, or challenge the exclusion of, disability in political theory. In her critique of social contract theorists, Martha Nussbaum notes that the tradition of social contract theory, ranging from historical theorists such as Hobbes, Locke, and Kant to contemporary theorists like Rawls and Gauthier, fails to adequately account for the disabled. Broadly speaking, social contract theory makes use of a thought experiment involving freely contracting parties in an initial choice situation (pre-political authority) to determine which constitutions, laws, or principles could or would be agreed upon to regulate our institutional arrangements. Nussbaum traces the inability of the social contract tradition to accommodate disability to two deeply held commitments: 'the idea that parties to the social contract are roughly equal in power and ability, and the related idea of mutual advantage as the goal they pursue through cooperating rather than not cooperating' (Nussbaum 2006: 68). Theories shaped by these commitments inevitably have difficulty accommodating disability because many disabled people (owing to the extent of their impairment and/or because of how society is structured) are not equal in power and ability, and some (owing to the extent of their impairment and/or because of how society is structured) cannot cooperate in a scheme for mutual advantage.[14] Being committed to the idea that contracting parties in the initial choice situation are rough equals, who cooperate for mutual advantage, hinges on the assumption that the parties are representatives of 'normal' citizens. This is problematic from the point of view of social justice because the needs and interests of all those who do not fit the paradigm of 'normality' do not factor into the contracting parties' reasoning, neither do they inform the conception of justice agreed upon.

I take it that a key factor in the exclusion of those with disabilities from the initial choice situation is that they are deemed unable to cooperate with others in a scheme for mutual advantage. This seems suggestive of a relational approach to social justice because the scope of justice extends to include all those engaged in the cooperative scheme. Hence, such approaches are relational because duties and entitlements of justice are generated between those who stand in particular cooperative relationships with one another, or, in other words, mutually advantageous cooperative relationships. The difficulty for many people with disabilities is that they may (owing to the extent of their impairment and/or because of how society is structured) not be able to cooperate in ways that are deemed mutually advantageous to other members in the scheme, or they may not be able to cooperate at all. Consequently, many people with disabilities are viewed as unable to stand in the correct justice-grounding relationship of cooperation for mutual advantage, and are, therefore, beyond the scope of justice.

The challenge that disability poses for social contract theory suggests that this theory cannot provide us with a viable theoretical framework for conceptions of justice. A theory of social justice ought to encompass all actual citizens, not just the theoretical ideal of a citizen. Moreover, principles of social justice ought to be informed by the perspectives of all citizens, not merely those of the nondisabled. Thus, as Nussbaum argues, social contract theory is politically inadequate because the disabled 'are not being treated as full equals of other citizens; their voices are not being heard when basic principles are chosen' (2006: 15). This is a question of scope. The proper subjects of justice are those represented by parties in the initial choice situation. All those who are not represented fall outside of the scope of justice, and their needs and interests can only be factored in at a later stage.

These points demonstrate how equality generally, and not just the equality of women specifically, is of central importance to the feminist agenda. Attempts to undermine the equality of individuals on the basis of arbitrary factors such as sex, race, and disability have been challenged time and again. It is this deep-rooted commitment to substantive equality which suggests that a non-relational cosmopolitanism is more compatible with feminist goals than relational accounts.

As we saw in the previous section, when the duties and entitlements required by justice are made contingent on holding certain relationships, it is possible that some individuals will lose their claims on others. That is, individuals who exist outside of the appropriate scheme of institutions or interaction will be beyond the scope of justice, and on social contract theories of social justice, it is possible for individuals to stand outside of the scope of justice because they cannot cooperate with others in mutually advantageous ways. Given the commitment to the equality of women to men, and the more general commitment to equality between all individuals, this should be of concern to feminists. Individuals who fall outside of the scope of justice are not thought of as being the full moral equals to those considered to be within its bounds. Moreover, their exclusion tells us that they are not regarded as the proper subjects of justice.

I take all this to suggest that relational theorists will have a harder time meeting the demands of those committed to both the moral and substantive equality of all humans. Relational cosmopolitanism permits a situation in which two human beings—similar in need, interests, and capacity—can be unequal in both moral worth and in their status as the proper subject of justice when the only difference between them is the scheme of interaction in which they live out their lives. This possibility conflicts with the feminist commitment to substantive equality which challenges all barriers that undermine a person's equal political and moral status. A theoretical perspective which allows that the place of one's birth can affect one's moral status and entitlements is plainly incompatible with a feminism that seeks to preserve the equal moral worth of all.

A FEMINIST OBJECTION TO NON-RELATIONAL COSMOPOLITANISM

One might argue that while I have provided some feminist arguments for thinking that non-relational cosmopolitanism is to be preferred to relational cosmopolitanism, there is a long history of feminist thought that suggests the contrary. In particular, I have in mind the ethics of care tradition which is motivated by the fact that all of us are, for significant periods of our lives, dependent on others. Each of us is dependent on others in the initial stages of our lives, and across a lifetime we are likely to require, and enjoy, care from others in a variety of ways. For some, the role of care will be crucial to their ongoing survival, and they will be highly dependent on others throughout the course of their lives. These undeniable facts about the human condition make care, for the care ethicist, a (if not *the*) fundamental value. Consequently, care theorists reject the normative priority given to individuals in much of contemporary political philosophy and instead take caring relationships as primary because such relationships are 'normatively prior to the individual's well-being' (Held 2006: 102).

At first glance the ethics of care looks to be more compatible with relational cosmopolitanism than with the non-relational approaches that I have been arguing for. Relational cosmopolitans are keen to emphasize human interdependence at the global level; they argue that we are all enmeshed in a global network of relationships; they acknowledge that some relationships are problematic because they render already disadvantaged people vulnerable to further abuses; and they stress the need to foster better relationships with one another and seek to eliminate the harms that the privileged do to the world's worst off. Importantly, relational cosmopolitans reject the statist picture of international politics that takes states as independent, self-sufficient units, because to accept such a picture would be to hold a false view of the actual world in which we live. Given that care theorists are also keen to emphasize the interdependence of individuals, the importance of relationships, and the importance of fostering good caring relationships, and that they reject the view of persons as independent, self-sufficient beings, there looks, initially, to be a lot that the care theorists would find appealing in relational accounts.[15]

Though relational accounts appear to have much in common with the ethics of care tradition, it is my contention that the aims of care theorists would be better met by a non-relational approach. To show this I will consider Eva Kittay's work (2001, 2005) on the moral status of the severely cognitively impaired. Grounding her position in an ethics of care, Kittay argues that the category of personhood should be extended to encompass individuals with severe cognitive impairments. The conception of personhood put forward by Kittay is relational, and her reasons for favouring a relational approach suggest that relational cosmopolitanism would better reflect some of her concerns. However, as I will argue, a relational view has problematic consequences and renders the moral status of the severely cognitively impaired insecure in ways that a non-relational approach does not.

It is often argued, or implied, in moral theory that those with severe cognitive impairments stand outside of the moral community because they lack certain crucial capacities that are necessary for moral reasoning. Kittay rejects the idea that personhood can be fixed solely on the basis of certain capacities and instead argues that duties and entitlements of justice are generated by the human relationships that we engage in. Since many human beings with severe cognitive impairments engage in human relationships, they should be considered persons. This thought is captured in the following:

> We do not become a person without the engagement of other persons—their care, as well as their recognition of the uniqueness and the connectedness of our human agency, and the distinctiveness of our particularly human relations to others and of the world we fashion. (Kittay 2001: 568, emphasis added)

For Kittay, then, personhood is constituted by the scheme of human relationships that individuals find themselves embedded in.[16] On this account, 'persons' are created by the interpersonal network of human relationships. That is, without the network of human social relations there would be no persons. Kittay notes that many of the most profoundly cognitively impaired are capable of saying a few words, engaging with others, and being responsive to the world around them and, hence, on her account they are persons.

It is clear that Kittay's position is seemingly more compatible with relational cosmopolitanism than with non-relational cosmopolitanism. Moreover, because non-relational cosmopolitanism grounds duties and entitlements of justice in features of human beings, there is good reason to suspect that Kittay, and others who hold similar relational views, will find non-relational positions unappealing. However, building on the arguments made thus far, I contend that we should be wary of attempts to ground duties and entitlements of justice in certain relationships because the claims of certain individuals may be undermined when the correct relationship fails to hold.

The lives of many severely cognitively impaired people, both historically and at present, are blighted by rejection and negligence on the part of their families and the communities into which they are born. Indeed, it is a sad truth that globally many of these individuals receive little more than the human contact necessary to keep them alive and it would be difficult to argue that they are engaged in networks of human relationships in any meaningful sense.[17] Moreover, across the globe it is all too common for those born with severe physical and/or mental impairments to not be given the requisite care for survival. Kittay suggests that a person is a being who has the 'uniqueness and the connectedness of their human agency' recognized by others, but in a world in which disability is stigmatized I worry that this condition of personhood may be too demanding since there is much evidence to suggest that many disabled people are not recognized in these ways.[18]

Kittay would hold that the personhood of these humans is not in question despite the failure on the part of others to recognize their status as persons. Thus I believe her aims would be better met by emphasising the *capacity* of the severely cognitively impaired to engage in human relationships, rather than on them actually being engaged in human relationships. By focusing on the capacity to engage in certain relations with other persons, it makes no difference whether those relations are actualized, and thus people do not lose their status as persons just because they have been socially excluded or are deemed to be unworthy of care.

Kittay may try to argue against me here. She suggests that social relations are not ad hoc relationships requiring two fully conscious agents:

> By a 'social relation' I mean a place in a matrix of relationships embedded in social practices through which the relations acquire meanings. It is by virtue of the meanings that the relationships acquire in social practices that duties are delineated, ways we enter and exit relationships are determined, emotional responses are deemed appropriate, and so forth. A social relation in this sense need not be dependent on ongoing interpersonal relationships between conscious individuals. (Kittay 2005)

Given this understanding of a social relation, Kittay could argue that my challenge misses the mark because her account does not require that persons stand in actual relations with one another. While there may be failures of care for certain individuals, and though some individuals cannot be said to be engaged in human relations in any meaningful sense, this does not change their status as persons. I take it that the thought is roughly that social practices give meaning to social relations in some way. When certain individuals are socially excluded, isolated, and left generally uncared for, the failure can be located in a breakdown in our understanding of what is appropriately required in those relationships. So the severely cognitively impaired who are isolated, neglected, and excluded from socially meaningful relationships may still count as persons just in virtue of being embedded in a social world that gives particular meaning and understanding to our relationships.

It is difficult to ascertain precisely what Kittay means here, but she does provide us with an example that helps to illuminate her account. For Kittay the parents of an anencephalic child may care for their child and feel that the child has suffered a loss even though the child is incapable of engaging with them (2005: 109–10). The reason for this is that they remain, in spite of the tragedy of the situation, parents to the child, and the social network within which they live determines that their responses are appropriate to the parent-child relationship. A social relation, in this case the parent-child relationship, is given meaning by the social practices of the community, and so even in cases where there is no longer an ongoing interpersonal relationship or where the relationship is dysfunctional, there is still a set of appropriate and inappropriate behaviours and attitudes associated with that relationship.

But Kittay's account has troubling consequences. Although the situation for some of the world's cognitively and physically impaired has improved, there is no society today that fully protects the basic rights of, and secures substantive equality for, those with disabilities:

> In every region in the world, in every country in the world, persons with disabilities often live on the margins of society, deprived of some of life's fundamental experiences. They have little hope of going to school, getting a job, having their own home, creating a family and raising their children, enjoying a social life or voting. For the vast majority of the world's persons with disabilities, shops, public facilities and transport, and even information are largely out of reach. (United Nations Department of Economic and Social Affairs et al. 2007)

Since people with physical and cognitive impairments are frequently stigmatized and discriminated against, making their status as persons contingent on social attitudes is a politically risky theoretical strategy. There are pervasive negative stereotypes and discriminatory social attitudes towards disability in most societies. Unfortunately it is not uncommon for those with physical and mental impairments to have their agency undermined, and to be regarded as morally and politically unequal to the nondisabled. Given the prevalence of harmful attitudes towards those with disabilities, it is not obvious that the network of human relations into which people with disabilities are born will be sufficient to secure their personhood.

Recall that on Kittay's picture, social practices shape the network of human relationships into which an individual is born, and they give meaning to our social relations. Thus, our social practices in some sense define our social relations, giving them meaning and marking out appropriate and inappropriate behaviours associated with those relationships. Moreover, our social practices determine the duties that we have to one another in virtue of the particular relations that we share. If we grant that in general the cognitively and physically impaired are subject to negative and discriminatory social attitudes that rely on implicit assumptions about the inferiority of those with disabilities, then we have good cause to be sceptical about Kittay's account to secure personhood for the severely cognitively impaired.

Though social practices may determine the meaning of, say, child/
parent, wife/husband, teacher/pupil, employer/employee relationships,
there is little to suggest that the socially determined meanings of these
relationships will be the same for those with disabilities as they are for
those without disabilities. In fact, given the prevalence of negative attitudes towards disability, it seems likely that there will be an alternative
set of social meanings for relationships involving those with disabilities,
and those meanings will determine an alternative set of associated behaviours and duties.

This is well illustrated in WHO's *World Report on Disability* (2011). The
report suggests that negative social attitudes are manifested in the relationships between disabled people and healthcare workers, teachers, em-
ployers, and family members (WHO 2011: 262). A good example of how
this works is in the education of disabled children:

> Negative attitudes are a major obstacle to the education of disabled
> children. In some cultures people with disabilities are seen as a form of
> divine punishment or as carriers of bad fortune. As a result, children
> with disabilities who could be in school are sometimes not permitted to
> attend. A community-based study in Rwanda found that perceptions
> of impairments affected whether a child with a disability attended
> school. Negative community attitudes were also reflected in the lan-
> guage used to refer to people with disabilities.
>   The attitudes of teachers, school administrators, other children, and
> even family members affect the inclusion of children with disabilities in
> mainstream schools. Some school teachers, including head teachers,
> believe they are not obliged to teach children with disabilities. (WHO
> 2011: 216)

Here we can see how social practices and attitudes shape an alternative set of meanings for relationships involving disabled people. In this
case, the teacher/pupil relationship can differ radically when it involves a
disabled pupil. The above statement indicates that social attitudes to disability can lead to the exclusion of disabled children from the teacher/
pupil relationship altogether. When there are negative attitudes and hostility towards disability, disabled children may not be considered the
right kind of beings who can be pupils. And, importantly, the duties that
teachers have as teachers may not extend to disabled children. Thus, the
negative social attitudes and practices affect the nature of the relationships that disabled people can have, and may, in certain contexts, undermine their agency, equal moral worth, and ultimately their status as persons.

Generally, the social meaning of human relationships is contextual
and in constant flux. Thus, there are countless examples where social
attitudes and practices have defined particular social relations in ways
that are harmful to members of particular social groups. Not all that long
ago, British social attitudes and practices associated with the wife/hus-

band relationship put married women in a position of political and economic vulnerability.[19] In a society where 'a man's home is his castle' in which he is to rule over his wife and children, where domestic violence is widespread, where women have no say politically, and where it is only right and proper that the husband controls the family income, on what grounds could it be claimed that the meaning of social relations secures the status of women as the full equals to men? Moreover, it is not clear that those living in the society just outlined would be prepared to concede that women are in fact persons.[20] The trouble with Kittay's account is that an individual's status as a person is tied to how society perceives them. If you happen to be a member of a socially marginalized group, about whom negative stereotypes and attitudes are prevalent, then there is no guarantee that you will be recognized as a person, and it is unlikely that the meaning of social relations can help to secure that status for you.

Though Kittay is at pains to stress that relationships are pivotal to the concept of personhood, I have suggested that the capacity to be in certain relationships with other persons would better secure the status of the severely cognitively disabled as persons. Not only do I think that grounding personhood in capacity would more successfully achieve Kittay's aims, but I also believe that this suggestion is not completely at odds with her view. At times Kittay herself implies that it is the capacity to be in certain relationships with other persons that is crucial to personhood:

> I propose that being a person *means having the capacity* to be in certain relationships with other persons, to sustain contact with other persons, to shape one's own world and the world of others, and to have a life that another person can conceive of as an imaginative possibility for him- or herself. (Kittay 2001: 568, emphasis added)

Although relationships do in many important ways come to constitute who we are as people, it seems to me that without the capacity to be in certain relations with others, it is doubtful that a human being could meaningfully engage with other persons in ways that seem essential to Kittay's definition. If a human being lacks the capacity to engage in distinctively human relations with other persons, then they seemingly do not qualify for personhood, since the capacity for engagement in distinctively human relationships with other persons is essential for such relationships to get off the ground.

Thus, the important thing is not that a person stands in particular relationships with others, but that he or she has the capacity to do so. It should also be clear that having the capacity to be in certain relationships with others is indicative of a non-relational approach. A conception of personhood grounded in capacity, irrespective of whether that capacity is rationality or the capacity to engage in certain relationships, is non-relational since it fixes personhood in some feature of individuals. Unlike relational views, it does not require that human beings stand in certain relations to others before they count as persons. Despite Kittay's attested commitment to a relational view of personhood, there is room in her account to ground her conception of personhood on a human capacity rather than on human relationships.

Consequently, I hope to have demonstrated that Kittay's position, and the views of others who argue similarly, should not be seen as incompatible with the non-relational cosmopolitan perspective that I have been advancing here. Moreover, I think that in order to more accurately reflect the capacities of the severely cognitively impaired, and avoid the worry that some cognitively impaired individuals may not be owed anything on grounds of justice because society fails to view them as beings capable of certain kinds of valuable relationships, Kittay would be better off adopting a non-relational view. On this view, what confers someone the moral status of a person, and thus secures them the status of a being entitled to goods as a matter of justice, is the *capacity* to be in certain relationships with other persons.

CONCLUSION

In this paper I have argued that there are good reasons for both feminists and cosmopolitans to abandon relational approaches to global justice in favour of those that are non-relational. Having argued that relational cosmopolitanism is inconsistent with a core cosmopolitan commitment, I then spelt out some of the problematic consequences of adopting a relational approach. I suggested that there are two sides to the dangers of making justice contingent on certain relationships: (1) individuals may lose their just entitlements when the relationship, for whatever reason, cannot be sustained; and (2) individuals may absolve themselves of their duties of justice by disengaging from relationships.

Following this I considered Nussbaum's argument that social contract theory is an inappropriate model for securing justice for those with physical and cognitive impairments. My aim was to show that there is an existing feminist critique of relational theories of justice. Moreover, I suggested that this critique supports my earlier conclusion that relational cosmopolitanism problematically renders justice contingent on the existence of particular relationships, and this should give feminists further reason to be wary of such approaches. Finally, I argued that though one might think that certain strands of feminist thought, particularly the ethics of care, might in fact be more compatible with relational accounts, there are good reasons to doubt this. To demonstrate why, I considered the work of Kittay as someone who is rooted in the ethics of care tradition and who has articulated a view that looks to be relational in nature. I argued that Kittay's relational approach suffers from problems similar to those outlined earlier, and that her goal of protecting the moral status of those with severe cognitive impairments would be better met by adopting a non-relational approach to moral personhood, and, indeed, a non-relational form of cosmopolitanism.

In general, I hope to have shown how approaching the contemporary philosophical debate on global distributive justice from a feminist perspective can help us to develop a more critical and inclusive cosmopolitanism. That is, by applying a feminist analysis to the existing literature, we can shape accounts of distributive justice that genuinely protect the world's most vulnerable people. What is more, it should by now be clear that feminists and cosmopolitans alike must reject relational approaches to global justice in order to avoid placing the needs and interests of some of the world's most vulnerable people beyond justice's reach.

NOTES

1. This objection can be found in the following: Benhabib (1987, 1992); Held (2006); MacKinnon (1989); Young (1990).
2. See, for example, Benhabib (2002); Held (2006); Jaggar (1983); Kittay (1999, 2005); Young (1990).
3. See, for example, Nussbaum (2003, 2006) and Okin (1989, 1996, 2005a).
4. Eva Kittay (1999, 2001, 2005, 2009).
5. For instance, Elshtain (1993); Landes (1998); Okin (1989); Pateman (1989); Young (1986).
6. Martha Nussbaum is one of the few feminist theorists working in this area, and she has written extensively on women and global justice. Nussbaum both critiques contemporary theories of global justice for their inattention to gender and advocates the capabilities approach as an alternative (2000, 2004, 2006). Similarly, though not to the same degree, Iris Marion Young (2000, 2006) situates herself in the contemporary global justice debate when she discusses global democracy, self-determination, and global responsibility. Also, see Onora O'Neill (1990), who has emphasized the importance of making women's inequality central to our theorising about global justice.
7. See Jaggar (2009, 2013) and Okin (2003).
8. See, for example, Bunch (1994); MacKinnon (2006); Okin (1998); Parekh (2008); Reilly (2009).
9. For instance, Benhabib (2002); Okin (1998, 2005b); Phillips (2007, 2010).
10. Ecofeminists, for instance, see the domination of women and nature as interconnected and attempt to address the global exploitation and denigration of our planet by calling for sustainable development that is ecologically sound, non-patriarchal, and non-exploitative (Mies and Shiva, 1993; Eaton and Lorentzen, 2003).
11. It should be noted that to my knowledge Caney does not himself discuss a 'two-worlds' scenario. Thus, although I believe the conclusions that I draw here follow from his view, he might have other reasons for resisting the idea that the inequality between Millie and Mollie is an unjust one.
12. This is not intended to be a full discussion about the possibility of making interaction relevant to our moral thinking about distributive justice. Indeed, despite what I have said here, it might turn out that institutional frameworks and schemes of interaction are morally relevant when it comes to, say, determining the *content* of the principles of justice. However, I have tried to suggest that when we consider the *scope* of justice, relational cosmopolitans who attempt to restrict the scope of justice to institutional/interactional schemes do so contrary to the logic of cosmopolitanism.

13. I borrow the terms 'duty-bearer' and 'entitlement-bearer' from Caney (2005) as a useful way of highlighting that distributive justice is concerned both with what people are entitled to and what duties they have to others.

14. It is also worth noting that there are not in fact any human beings who can fulfill these two commitments fully over the whole course of a human lifetime. Nussbaum points this out when she suggests that a theory of social justice must recognize that nondisabled people also have periods of their lives where they are entirely dependent on others (as in infancy), and that many suffer from temporary impairment and disability (2006:99).

15. One might object that to even suggest a possible allegiance between care theory and any type of cosmopolitanism is misguided. Since care theorists reject the language of rights and justice, so the objection could go, their views are fundamentally incompatible with theories of distributive justice. I think that this objection falsely represents much of the recent work in care ethics. Many care theorists now agree that justice is an important value but disagree about the weight attributed to it in our moral thinking. Given this, it would be wrongheaded to argue that a care theorist could not, or would not want to, endorse an approach to questions of global distributive justice.

16. Though I am sympathetic to many of Kittay's arguments, I remain unconvinced about the plausibility of her conception of personhood, and thus this discussion should not be taken as a wholehearted endorsement of her view. The crucial point is that regardless of whether one takes her view to be convincing, her aims would be better met by a non-relational account over the relational one that she at times seems to favour.

17. As noted in the United Nations Children's Fund (UNICEF) report *The State of the World's Children: Children with Disabilities*, 'in many countries, responses to the situation of children with disabilities are largely limited to institutionalization, abandonment or neglect' (2013: 1).

18. See, for example, the World Health Organisation's (WHO) *World Report on Disability* (2011) and the British Equality and Human Rights Commission's (EHRC) *Hidden in Plain Sight—Inquiry into Disability-Related Harassment* (2011).

19. I do not mean to imply that the institution of marriage in the UK no longer results in gender inequality, only that things were considerably worse in, say, the eighteenth century, for women's status as persons than they are now.

20. See William Blackstone's portrayal of eighteenth-century English law where he describes how marriage alters the legal status of women by subsuming the wife's personhood into that of the husband and suspending the 'very being or legal existence of the woman . . . during the marriage' (Blackstone, 1775: 442).

BIBLIOGRAPHY

Barry, B. (1995). *Justice as Impartiality*. Oxford: Clarendon Press.
———. (1999). 'Statism and Nationalism: A Cosmopolitan Critique' in I. Shapiro and L. Brilmayer (eds.) *Global Justice*, NOMOS, New York: New York University Press, 12–66.
Beitz, C. (1975). 'Justice and International Relations'. *Philosophy and Public Affairs* 4, 4, 360–89.
———. (1999) *Political Theory and International Relations* (2nd ed.). Princeton, NJ: Princeton University Press.
Benhabib, S. (1987). 'The Generalized and the Concrete Other: The Kohlberg-Gilligan Controversy and Feminist Theory' in S. Benhabib and P. Cornell (eds.) *Feminism as Critique*. Cambridge: Cambridge University Press.
———. (1992) *Situating the Self: Gender, Community, and Postmodernism in Contemporary Ethics*. New York: Routledge.
———. (2002) *Claims of Culture: Equality and Diversity in the Global Era*. Woodstock, Oxfordshire: Princeton University Press.

Blackstone, W. (1775). *Commentaries on the Laws of England—In Four Books.* Oxford: Clarendon Press.

Bunch, C. (1994). 'Strengthening Human Rights of Women' in M. Nowak (ed.) *World Conference on Human Rights Vienna 1993: The Contributions of NGOs Reports and Documents.* Vienna: Manzsche Verlags und Universitatsbuchhandlung.

Caney, S. (2001). 'Cosmopolitan Justice and Equalizing Opportunities'. *Metaphilosophy* 32, 1–2, 113–34.

———. (2005). *Justice beyond Borders: A Global Political Theory.* Oxford: Oxford University Press.

———. (2009). 'Cosmopolitanism and Justice' in T. Christiano and J. Christman (eds.) *Contemporary Debates in Political Philosophy.* Oxford: Wiley-Blackwell, 387–407.

Eaton, H., and L. A. Lorentzen. (2003). *Ecofeminism and Globalization: Exploring Culture, Context, and Religion.* Lanham, MD: Rowman & Littlefield Publishers Inc.

Elshtain, J. B. 1993. *Public Man Private Woman: Women in Social and Political Thought* (2nd edition). Princeton: Princeton University Press.

Equality and Human Rights Commission. (2011). *Hidden in Plain Sight—Inquiry into Disability-Related Harassment.* Manchester: Equality and Human Rights Commission.

Held, D. (1995). *Democracy and the Global Order: From the Modern State to Cosmopolitan Governance.* Stanford, CA: Stanford University Press.

Held, V. (2006). *The Ethics of Care: Personal, Political, and Global.* Oxford: Oxford University Press.

Jaggar, A. M. (1983). *Feminist Politics and Human Nature.* Lanham, MD: Rowman & Littlefield Publishers Inc.

———. (2013). 'Does Poverty Wear a Woman's Face? Some Moral Dimensions of a Transnational Feminist Research Project'. *Hypatia,* early view—article first published online: 10 January 2013 (n/a), 1–18.

——— (ed.) (2014). *Gender and Global Justice.* Cambridge: Polity Press.

Kittay, E. F. (1999). *Love's Labor: Essays on Women, Equality and Dependency.* London: Routledge.

———. (2001). 'When Care is Just and Justice is Caring: The Case of the Care for the Mentally Retarded'. *Public Culture* 13, 3, 557–79.

———. (2005). 'At the Margins of Moral Personhood'. *Ethics* 116, 100–31.

———. (2009). 'The Ethics of Philosophizing: Ideal Theory and the Exclusion of People with Severe Cognitive Disabilities' in L. Tessman (ed.) *Feminist Ethics and Social and Political Philosophy: Theorizing the Non-Ideal.* Netherlands: Springer, 121–46.

Landes, J. B. 1998. *Feminism, the Public and the Private.* Oxford: Oxford University Press.

MacKinnon, C. (1989). *Toward a Feminist Theory of the State.* Harvard: Harvard University Press.

Mies, M., and V. Shiva. (1993). *Ecofeminism.* London: Zed Books.

Mollendorf, D. (2002). *Cosmopolitan Justice.* New York: Westview Press.

Nussbaum, M. (1996). 'Reply' in *For Love of Country?* Boston: Beacon.

———. (1999). *Sex and Social Justice.* New York: Oxford University Press.

———. (2000). *Women and Human Development: The Capabilities Approach.* Cambridge: Cambridge University Press.

———. (2003). 'Rawls and Feminism' in Samuel Freeman (ed.) *The Cambridge Companion to Rawls.* Cambridge: Cambridge University Press, 488–520.

———. (2004). 'Women and Theories of Global Justice: Our Need for New Paradigms' in Deen K. Chatterjee (ed.) *The Ethics of Assistance: Morality and the Distant Needy.* Cambridge: Cambridge University Press, 147–76.

———. (2006). *Frontiers of Justice: Disability, Nationality, Species Membership.* Cambridge, MA: Harvard University Press.

Okin, S. M. (1980). *Women in Western Political Thought.* Princeton, NJ: Princeton University Press.

———. (1989). *Justice, Gender and the Family.* New York: Basic Books.

———. (1994). 'Political Liberalism, Justice, and Gender'. *Ethics* 105, 1, 23–43.

———. 1996. 'The Gendered Family and the Development of a Sense of Justice' in Edward S. Reed, Elliot Turiel and Terrance Brown (eds.) *Values and Knowledge*. Mahwah, NJ: Lawrence Erlbaum Associates Inc.

———. (1998). 'Feminism, Women's Human Rights, and Cultural Differences'. *Hypatia* 13, 2, 32–52.

———. (2003). 'Poverty, Well-Being, and Gender: What Counts, Who's Heard?' *Philosophy and Public Affairs* 31, 3, 280–316.

———. (2005a). '"Forty Acres and a Mule" for Women: Rawls and Feminism'. *Politics, Philosophy and Economics* 4, 2, 233–48.

———. (2005b). 'Multiculturalism and Feminism: No simple Question, No Simple Answers' in A. Eisenberg and J. Spinner-Halev (eds.) *Minorities Within Minorities*. Cambridge: Cambridge University Press.

O'Neill, O. (1990). 'Justice, Gender and International Boundaries'. *British Journal of Political Science* 20, 4, 439–59.

Parekh, S. (2008). 'When Being Human Isn't Enough: Reflections on Women's Human Rights' in P. Des Autels and R. Whisnant (eds.) *Global Feminist Ethics*. Lanham, MD: Rowman & Littlefield Publishers, 139–54.

Pateman, C. (1989). *The Disorder of Women: Democracy, Feminism and Political Theory*. Cambridge: Polity Press.

Pepper, A. (2014). 'A Feminist Argument Against Statism: Public and Private in Theories of Global Justice'. *Journal of Global Ethics* 10, 1, 56–70.

Phillips, A. (2007). *Multiculturalism without Culture*. Princeton, NJ: Princeton University Press.

———. (2010). *Gender and Culture*. Cambridge: Polity Press.

Pogge, T. (1989). *Realizing Rawls*. Ithaca: Cornell University Press.

———. (1992). 'Cosmopolitanism and Sovereignty'. *Ethics* 103, 1, 48–75.

———. (2002). *World Poverty and Human Rights*. Oxford: Polity.

———. (2005). 'Real World Justice'. *The Journal of Ethics* 9, 1/2, 29–53.

Reilly, N. (2009). *Women's Human Rights*. Cambridge: Polity Press.

United Nations Children's Fund. (2013). *The State of the World's Children: Children with Disabilities*. New York: UNICEF Press (accessed 21 July 2014), www.unicef.org.uk/Documents/Publication-pdfs/sowc-2013-children-with-disabilities.pdf.

United Nations Department of Economic and Social Affairs et al. (2007). 'From Exclusion To Equality: Realizing the Rights of Persons with Disabilities' (accessed 2 July 2014), www.ipu.org/PDF/publications/disabilities-e.pdf.

World Health Organisation and the World Bank. (2011). *World Report on Disability*. Geneva, Switzerland: WHO Press.

Young, I. M. (1986). 'Impartiality and the Civic Public: Some Implications of Feminist Critiques of Moral and Political Theory'. *Praxis International* 5 (4):381.

———. (1990). *Justice and the Politics of Difference*. Princeton, NJ: Princeton University Press.

———. (2000). *Inclusion and Democracy*. Oxford: Oxford University Press.

———. (2006). 'Responsibility and Global Justice: A Social Connection Model'. *Social Philosophy and Policy* 23, 1, 102–13.

II

The Challenges of Intercultural Communication

THREE

Finding the Universality beyond Language and Culture

Comparative Political Theory and the Cosmopolitanism of Wang Yangming and Immanuel Kant

Sae-Hee Lee

WHAT IS COSMOPOLITANISM IN THE PURSUIT OF PRACTICAL UNIVERSALISM?

Although many scholars have advocated different cosmopolitan visions, the core element on which all cosmopolitans agree is the idea that we have universal duties to all human beings. This means that all human beings have a duty to protect other human beings, including ourselves, as an end, simply because we are human beings. This simple fact, however, is often undermined, dismissed as idealistic or utopian. Human beings' history, however, gives evidence that the cosmopolitan idea of deontological ethics applied to the entire human being may not truly be an unattainable ideal, as its detractors think; the problem is in the assumption that it is not possible or feasible.

Consider that time in mankind's history when we first formed tribal unions and then developed them into tribal nations. Even today, cosmopolitanism is expressed in the concept of the 'united' nations. Just as the ancient (ethnic) clans in any given region united and created one nation-state because of the struggle for survival, similar cosmopolitan ideas have the same significance in the twenty-first century: the survival of mankind in a stressful time, faced with worldwide problems such as 'deepening

economic interdependence, worsening environmental degradation, proliferating transnational threats, and accelerating technological change'
(Patrick 2014: 58). This is only one simple but grand reason for us to step
back from the system of nationalism and try to look at the world as a
composite of every national clan in a global village. This thesis, then,
aims to show that the excuse of cultural difference is no longer a significant factor to advocate one-sided cosmopolitanism. There is no radically
different ethics which is particularly relevant to the East and the West,
respectively.

It is true in a sense that cosmopolitanism is often regarded as the
concept of globalization since there are various international or even so-
called universal bodies like the United Nations (UN), and it seems to be
working. However, cosmopolitanism has a different character, or it might
not be a concept which can be comparable to 'globalization'. While one of
the main characteristics of globalization shows 'overlapping networks of
power and interaction' among nation-states (Held 2003: 466), cosmopolitanism emerges as a result of questioning the phenomenal reality of globalization. In other words, whereas globalization is an empirical reality
for which people find material and tangible evidence from pole to pole,
cosmopolitanism represents a conceptual 'signpost' to guide the globalization of human interaction in order to promote better global conditions
and to mitigate conflicts. That is to say, when we find cosmopolitan aspiration from different languages and cultures, we ought to have a firm
sense of cosmopolitan aspiration's purpose as a superordinate concept
and verify whether those cosmopolitan aspirations from political language comply with the common ground of the world's cosmopolitan
aspiration. To do so, we translate and interpret each political language
which is based on certain culture, history, and political behaviour, and so
we confirm that there is no radically different ethic attached to a certain
culture. Through this we find a legitimacy to set a grand cosmopolitan
consensus on the matter of global governance. It can be microscopic and
time-consuming, and so becomes a heavy process; however, this is the
only practical way to reveal the textual evidence of universalism and to
check cultural cosmopolitan arguments which could cause unnecessary
political turmoil between countries.

COMPARATIVE POLITICAL THOUGHTS

Of all the culturally specific cosmopolitan approaches, this paper compares only Kantian cosmopolitanism with Confucian cosmopolitanism,
focusing on the similarities between their conceptual semantics. The analysis is drawn from today's major challenges to cosmopolitan dialogues:
the increasing difficulties both in achieving cooperation and opening global dialogue between different national interests (Delanty and He 2008).

Since cosmopolitan discourses have encountered a need to overcome major political and cultural divisions, the attempt to find conceptual common ground linking different literatures is expected to have academic implications in bringing together the otherwise dispersed and adrift global dialogue.

So far, many elements provide a broad outline of universal cosmopolitanism between Kantian and Confucian cosmopolitanism; however, they do not yet fully reduce differences between cultures or political orientations. This is because cosmopolitanism itself often causes a rejection of either the universality of philosophical concepts or the significance of hierarchically ordered principles, such as morality and justice (Freeden and Vincent 2013: 14). As Freeden and Vincent further explain, there is 'the very denial of the possibility of meaningful comparison' (2013: 14). In the past a Chinese public intellectual, Tu Weiming, had also presented this argument, claiming 'the mentality of the modern West is dramatically opposed to the Chinese habits of the heart' (Tu 1996). That is, we might infer that he believes that the Chinese habitual cultural and socio-political languages and their modes of expression are different from those of the West. Nonetheless, one notable point from his remark is that the 'heart' of language, which conveys the core meaning of the socio-political language, may not vary regardless of cultural differences. Therefore, my aspiration is to find the core of political language from each culture and focus more on practical universality, which is the one based less on cultural rationality, and beyond textual principal, so as to ultimately bring different perspectives on cosmopolitanism into one single paradigm.

It is important to clarify the methodology underpinning this paper. First of all, this section briefly considers the definition of comparative political thought as a methodological approach and identifies its potential strengths and weaknesses. Then, the specific analytic approach of this paper is explained, and the difficulties of, and obstacles to, the method of comparison are explored. Comparative political thought has been an expanding field of inquiry for political science in the last two decades. It finds its values in reflecting upon 'the status and meaning of political life no longer in a restricted geographical setting but in the global arena' (March 2009: 531). According to Fred Dallmayr (drawing on Heidegger, Gadamer, and Derrida), 'the point of comparative political theory, is precisely to move towards a more genuine universalism, and beyond the spurious "universality" traditionally claimed by the Western canon and by some recent intellectual movements' (2004: 253). In other words, the methodology for comparison, especially when the texts relate to non-Western contexts, enables non-Western perspectives to enter into familiar political debates in the context of the universal problems impeding the desire for 'living together'. In this manner, this paper particularly employs two main analytic approaches. The first approach is a strict exegesis in an attempt to understand Confucianism's cosmopolitan aspects by directly analyzing the Confucians' use of words, their logical structures, and the relation between various aspects of their philosophies. To be sure, this approach can be extremely useful not only in highlighting key similarities of cosmopolitan logic within the Confucians' literatures, but also in providing a synoptic reading of the works of the Eastern philosophers. The second approach is to reconstruct the typical forms of cosmopolitanism extracted from the Eastern and Western literatures. This is a constructivist's angle, which seeks to decontextualize cosmopolitanism from each speech culture and then to establish a coherent and defensible argument: that there is 'no radically different ethics'. It is not then critical to establish the relation between these two approaches and its' significance. When the comparison of thought is being conducted, one cannot access the other's context directly, since one's context and processes of thought are transmitted through one's own culturally embedded language. In this regard, comparative political thought as a methodological approach is a mode of 'interpretation of cultures' (Dallmayr 2004: 249), which is critical for this paper. Nevertheless, its motivation, justification, and, more importantly, central purpose are not merely to focus on opening a dialogue for non-Western perspectives. While many non-Western advocates are inclined to have value-neutral perspectives when engaging with the distinctive patterns of political thought and speech found in one specific culture, Andrew March criticizes non-Western perspectives for failing to understand 'similar analogues or equivalent certain concepts established across space and time' (2009: 544). Indeed, March claims that, although non-Western perspectives in comparative political theory may uphold certain non-Western discourses which have been excluded from an arbitrary Western canon, they often give too much weight to representing a certain culture and civilization. This is because non-Western perspectives conduct comparison mainly in relation to the concepts or standards of Western perspectives, rather than by actively addressing their own normative beliefs and truths that may have a universal impact. Considering this issue of comparison, rereading Confucianism will be first conducted in a manner of engaging self-critics, avoiding vagueness and internal self-contradiction.

REREADING CONFUCIANISM

Beginning with a brief introduction to Confucianism, the core concept can be identified as *jen* (仁), translated as 'humanism' or 'benevolence', which is applied most consistently to any forms of morality in Confucianism (Wawrytko 1982). The message of the *Analects* is to give substance to four main teachings: self-cultivation (修身), management of domestics (齊家), governance of the state (治國), and creation of a prosperous and peaceful world (平天下) (Singerland 2003). Kongzi argues that these four main teachings are related to each other, because one man cannot be only himself, but must himself be a father or son in a family, the ruler or the ruled in a state, and a human being along with other creatures in the universe (Ivanhoe 2002). This is the same context as Marcus Cicero's 'concentric circles of belonging', in which human beings establish various forms of self-identity (Cicero 1999). Cicero says the first circle in which an individual finds one's identity is drawn from one's own immediate family, and then it further expands its scope to one's neighbours and one's fellow countrymen (Nussbaum 2010: 31). The overarching idea of the concentric circles of belonging is to remember that our placement is not intrinsic but incidental, and so 'the most fundamental allegiance is to what is human' (Nussbaum 2010: 31). Thus, Cicero's concentric circle, which is an inclusive concept, is in line with what Kongzi is trying to say: a respect for human being. Kongzi further emphasizes the behaviour expected of individuals in any form of social community necessary for that community to become harmonious. This is because, for Kongzi, following traditional rituals represents the showing of respect for others; however, it is different from following traditional rituals blindly. Claiming that the principles of humanism lie in social interaction among people, Kongzi asserts that human beings, as social beings, can only develop humanity within social relations. This further implies that, as a human being, one develops one's relationships with others, thereby complying with one's social obligation, and eventually attaining a flexible and relational social identity. Furthermore, his consistent argument is that humanism is 'relative' because humanism is about how to balance one's desires with those of others. Nonetheless, Kongzi's teachings do not explain why an individual ought to cultivate him or herself so as to balance his or her needs with those of a total stranger. For cosmopolitans, this is a critical counterargument against Kongzi: The society to which one belongs is the outer of the concentric circles of belonging; therefore, when the society to which one belongs is removed, there is no longer a circle of relationships to explain why one would be dedicated to self-cultivation towards the world.

Mengzi, however, a hundred years after Kongzi died, developed Kongzi's limited collectivism. Mengzi interprets humanism from a fundamental perspective. He derives the meaning of humanism from human nature—not from human inclination, impulse, or instinct, but from compassion. Mengzi distinguishes the former attributes from the latter. This is because, Mengzi argues, one cannot attain the ideal merely by copying the actions that are attributed to them, which is how Mengzi develops Kongzi's ideas of following traditional rituals. Rather, he believes that one's benevolent mind can be found in one's innate nature as a human being. Mengzi argues that human beings are born to desire goodness. However, individuals' desire for 'pleasure' affects their human nature and masks their innate desire for goodness—in other words, nascent morality. To make sense of human nature, Mengzi gives a metaphoric example of a child about to fall into a well.

> When men suddenly see a child about to fall into a well, they all have feelings of alarm and distress, not to gain friendship with the child's parents, nor to see the praise of their neighbors and friends, nor because they dislike the reputation of 'lack of benevolence' if they did not rescue him. From such a cause, we see that a man without the feeling of compassion is not a man. (Chai 2001)

Mengzi strongly believes that this benevolent mind is something common to all human beings. However, it is important to mention that he also does not say that human beings are good, but that they are born with an inclination towards goodness. Here, one counterargument—that human beings' desire to be good varies from person to person—often confuses Mengzi's whole point of goodness. Mengzi claims that the moral sense impelling us to care about others is only a potential aspect, and not an immediate fact (Ivanhoe 2002: 25). Indeed, the implication is that Mengzi's concept of goodness is not about human nature; rather, it is possibly that goodness occurs in the moment, when human beings can do good when it is necessary. In this manner, Mengzi not only understands Kongzi's four main teachings as expressing an essential moral value, but adds more implications about human beings, claiming that they have the potential inclination towards good. In short, human beings have the ability to notice goodness. Therefore, Mengzi, building on Kongzi's demand for 'self-cultivation', contends that human beings ought to find their goodness, the moral sense that all human beings potentially have (Ivanhoe 2002).

So far, the ideas of Kongzi and Mengzi are shown to be still limited to the normative principles of an anthropocentric world, consisting of one's family, society, and state. Wang Yangming extends the Confucians' particular communal vision of humanism to push towards an 'anthropocosmic' world (Roetz 2008; Ivanhoe 2002: 21). That is, owing to the influence of Buddhism during the Zhou dynasty, Wang brings a metaphysical understanding of the relationship between the empirical human world and nature: the metaphysics of presence. Here, his word *nature* does not necessarily indicate the physical laws of nature, and this makes Wang's ideas distinct from Kant's metaphysical moral foundation. According to Ivanhoe, both Buddhists and Confucians assume that the world consists of two distinct realms: the empirical world and the metaphysical world. The difference between Buddhists and Confucians (especially Wang himself) is that, while Buddhism tends to see the metaphysics of the world as 'empty', that is, 'characteristic of all reality as entailing the emptiness of the self', Confucians see the 'pattern' or 'principle' which lies 'beneath each and every aspect of reality as constituting the essential nature of the self' (Ivanhoe 2002: 23). In other words, Wang fills the Buddhists' 'emptiness' with the concept of 'principles'. Principles, according to Wang, are not influenced by any physical law of nature or any causal relationship, but exist as ends in themselves. In Confucian terms, this is called *Li* (理). It might be said that Wang adds a teleological understanding of nature: Wang's idea of 'one body' (一體) explains that all creatures of the world are related to each other at the fundamental level, according to this principle. Thus, the physical law of nature becomes part of the principle of metaphysics; hence, the empirical human world is also part of the metaphysical principle.

Nevertheless, on the distinction between human beings and other creatures, Wang says that 'human beings are uniquely capable of refining the quality of their "physical nature" and thereby allowing their underlying "original nature" to shine through' (Ivanhoe 2002: 23). It becomes critically important to grasp and appreciate this idea of nature in order to understand the Confucians' moral foundation, which subsumes the ideas of moral worth from Kongzi and Mengzi. This is because by giving a meaning to the metaphysical world, Wang finds a universal moral principle beyond a local, communal morality. That is, first of all he states as his premise the universal connection between all things of the world by the metaphysical principle. Nevertheless, human beings, as distinctive creatures who have a capacity to find their 'original nature', become one, a unity, compared with other creatures. Therefore, the foundation of morality that Wang enunciates is not only concentrated on one's local community for the sake of one's physical communal relationships, but must also extend its arena to include all human beings.

KANT'S *A PRIORI* CONSTRUCTION AND THE CONFUCIANS' *LI*

First of all, the concept of *Li*, which Wang has claimed to be the fundamental principle of nature, has the same meaning as the *a priori* constructions of Kant. More specifically, the logical connection between the metaphysical realm and the empirical realm of the world which Kant and Wang explain is evidently the same. This is drawn from the idea that both the concept of Li and the a priori system are established to understand the role of nature. In addition, as was pointed out earlier in the first section of the analysis, both Li and a priori are referred to as the location of universal morality. To begin with Wang's understanding of Li, he speaks about it as nature's teleological role, in contrast to physical nature. However, this does not mean that Li exists 'in some realm apart from the actual world and from there decrees its structure' (Ivanhoe 2002: 23). Rather, the function of Li is to provide patterns and principles for the empirical world. In other words, the physical law of nature, like the law of gravity and the law of energy conservation, is imagined as a particular

phenomenon that is determined by Li and so able to be manifested (Ivanhoe 2002: 23). Here, we might say, Li is like a basis for all given things of
the world, but achieves its ends not through any other laws, but by providing patterns and principles for things and events (Ivanhoe 2002;
Needham 1956: 473–74). This is well represented in Wang's message:

> Because of pattern or principle (Li), there is naturally a relative impor-
> tance. Take, for example, the body which is one. We use our hands and
> feet to protect our head and eyes, but does that mean we are prejudiced
> and regard the hands and feet as less important? We do this because it
> accords with pattern or principle. (Wang 1963: 276)

Wang says every component of an individual's body corresponds to
the principle of the human body. However, he does not mean the principle of the human body in the sense of a physical law of nature. Instead of
discussing the function of hands and feet compared to other parts of the
human body, for instance, he emphasizes that the components of the
human body coexist in accordance with the law of harmony. If this view
is expanded to the context of individuals and the history of human beings, it can be understood that Wang acknowledges that the experiences
of human beings correspond to the law of harmony. This is how Wang's
understanding of metaphysics has its teleological aspects. That is, it can
be understood that Wang's argument points out that Li becomes a necessary complement to understanding the progress of human beings. He
also proposes it in association with his view of early Confucian moral
ideas such as 'righteousness', 'rites', 'benevolence', and 'filial piety'.
Many Confucians argue that these moral ideas are to be viewed as specific expressions of Li. However, Wang insists that 'truth has no form', but
exists as an end to provide an impetus for progress (Wang 1916: 95). Li
exists to explain how all creatures of the world interact with one another,
and their phenomenal order is assigned to them so as to respect their
function and their place; therefore, Li should enable them to work together and maintain a harmonious cosmos (Ivanhoe 2002).

Kant's problematic theory of history follows a similar understanding
of this naturalistic teleology. It is found in one of his prominent works,
Perpetual Peace: A Philosophical Sketch:

> Perpetual peace is guaranteed by no less than the great artist Nature
> herself. The mechanical process of nature visibly exhibits the purposive
> plan of producing concord among men, even against their will and
> indeed by means of their very discord. (Reiss 1970: 108)

Although this naturalistic teleology seems to contradict Kant's assertion that a priori principles of human reason are independent, Kant continues to describe the intention of nature, or 'providence', as a guiding
force in the history of human beings (Reiss 1970: 108). In *Perpetual Peace*,
what he says about the intention of nature is that human beings are

supposedly driven by the purpose of nature to attain a civil society in which universal justice can be administered. In other words, human beings are forced to relate to one another socially, but they are continuously threatened by their tendency to fall into discord. However, human beings are driven by 'the purposive plan of producing concord among men'; therefore, they are 'guaranteed to use all means' for its inevitable construction until a cosmopolitan matrix is ultimately procured (Brown 2013: 38). This can have significantly dangerous ramifications, especially of destructive war among men. However, as Karl-Otto Apel points out, Kant's implication in presupposing the metaphysics of morality behind human existence and its relation to human rationality can be perfectly logical only if it is possible to derive a moral purpose from it (Apel 1997). This point—that Kant makes sense of the link between the metaphysical a priori construction and the idea of human reason—is examined more thoroughly in the next section. The point in this section is that the empirical human world cannot be fully explained without establishing the a priori experience of human beings, because without that experience, there is no guiding principle that compels human beings to make progress. In this regard, both Wang's delineation of Li and Kant's a priori constructions entail a teleological analysis. However, neither philosopher implies that this analysis achieves a dominant position, in the sense of presenting a fatalistic view. Here, it means that Kant does not consider the history of human beings as a mere phenomenal progression; instead, by establishing the a priori experiences of human beings, he attempts to understand the realm beyond the empirical world, a realm which makes human beings pursue a 'perpetual peace' throughout the history of humanity's attempts to resolve conflicts among men. Unlike fatalists, who would first presume and then inductively imagine the history of human beings as a given thing, Kant's intention is not to speak conclusively about the determinism of human history, but to understand the process of pursuing perpetual peace. This is the moment at which both Kant and Wang would agree upon the impalpable teleology of nature.

KANT'S RATIONALITY OF HUMAN BEINGS AND THE CONFUCIANS' PURE KNOWING

Although a discussion of the world beyond the realm of empirical experience would help to explain the demanding morality that provides a guiding principle to the human world, both Kant and Wang insist that the world itself, wherein the guiding principle lies, is not 'self-sufficient for the purpose of explanation' (Reiss 1970: 17; Wang 1916). In other words, the guiding principle does not exist anywhere other than in humanity's empirical world. This is because, both Kant and Wang acknowledge, human beings are conditioned to be subjective beings, which means that they comprehend things in the world only in accordance with their experiences. Reiss explicitly reveals this by reading Kant's political writings: 'We can never explain the world as it appears to us merely by reference to experience' (Reiss 1970: 17). If this is the case, how do we then make sense of the idea of a priori experience as a guiding principle? Both Kant and Wang derive the answer from the idea of reason: They see the human mind as a lawgiver. To find the logic of morality and its relation to human reason requires much effort and time. Therefore, this section addresses only a few points that are critical to finding an intersection between Wang and Kant. First, a conversation between Wang and his friend elucidates the link between the universal principle and the idea of the human mind; that is, those human beings who have the capacity of reason are lawgivers.

> The Teacher was roaming in Nan-chen. A friend pointed to flowering trees on a cliff and said, '[You say] there is nothing under heaven external to the mind. These flowering trees on the high mountain blossom and drop their blossoms of themselves. What have they to do with my mind?' The Teacher said, 'Before you look at these flowers, they and your mind are in the sense of silent vacancy. As you come to look at them, their colors at once show up clearly. From this you can know that these flowers are not external to your mind'. (Wang 1963: 222)

What we can understand from this passage is that the 'silent vacancy' between things and the human mind implies that things do not carry any element that is given meaning by human beings. This means that, as Ivanhoe explains, 'without principle, the universe would have no shape at all, and without the conscious aspect of this principle, our pure knowing, its shape would not be known' (Ivanhoe 2002: 26). Hence, this is the point on which Kant, Wang, and Apel would agree: that human beings, as lawgivers, need to assign a meaning to things in the world so that the capacity of human reason can enable us to understand the external world. This conscious aspect of the principle is what Wang describes as the human mind, while Kant names it 'human reason'. In Kant's critical writings, the *Critique of Practical Reason* (Kant 1956) and the *Fundamental Principles of the Metaphysics of Morals* (Kant 2005), *feeling* is an objective form of human reason which applies to all human beings, while *understanding* is a subjective form of human reason which applies to an individual. For example, the feelings of human beings respond to the physical law of nature, such as pleasure, inclination, preference, or pain. This is universally applied to all human beings. It can be more easily understood from the case of an individual who is hit by a stone falling from the sky. It is natural for him to feel pain, and, later, he will know that if he sees a stone falling towards him again, he should try to avoid it. This is how Kant would say human reason corresponds to the physical law of nature; universal *phenomenon*. Unlike feeling, understanding represents dianoetic human reasoning, which is capable of establishing a mathematical understanding of natural science or other system of reasoning. From this, Kant confirms that human beings have a capacity for reason which enables them to understand the external world. With this in mind, it is now necessary to investigate how Kant and Wang defend the concept that human beings' minds (or reasoning faculties) can proclaim the existence of universal morality prior to their experiences. To explain this, first Wang combines the idea of 'one body', which implies the underlying unity of the universe, with the idea of human beings' spontaneous compassion.

> The mind may be compared to a mirror. The mind of the sage is like a bright mirror, the mind of the ordinary man like a dull mirror. (Wang 1916: 93)

Wang figuratively compares the mind of human beings to a 'mirror' to explain his concept of 'pure knowing' and its relation to the ideas of morality. Wang says that the mind of a person is like a mirror which accurately reflects every situation it encounters. Wang admits that 'none of its reflections are its own', because the reflections in the mirror are passively reflected from the external forces, external images, or impressions (Ivanhoe 2002: 25). However, he clarifies this in his suggestion that its reflections provoke a response to each situation 'in the appropriate manner'; not according to one's desires, wishes, or preferences, but according to the original nature—the mind in itself which forms 'one body' with the universal principle (Ivanhoe 2002: 25). In other words, Wang sees the human mind as originally (fundamentally) equivalent to the universal principle that gives guidance as to how to respond in 'the appropriate manner'. Then, the 'dust of the earth', which refers to selfish desire, is added to the mirror, the human mind (Wang 1963: 94). And to allow one's original nature to shine through, Wang therefore tells us to 'sweep' the dust away and 'to follow the order and act' (Wang 1963: 94). This remark raises a critical question for him (Wang 1963: 94): 'If effort is expended in causing the mirror to reflect while the glass is still dull, how can one succeed?' This means that Wang feels challenged to solve the contradiction between human beings' rootedness in the empirical world and their independent (or determinate) free will. Kant also encounters this critical challenge and provides 'a practical reason' to solve the antinomy of human reason.

One of the four main themes of Kant's 'Antinomies of Pure Reason' (1956), which can be compared to Wang, is the third theme, the antinomy of freedom. This discusses how human beings, who are bound to the physical force of nature independently, will independently choose to follow a metaphysical moral duty which may be contrary to the physical law of nature (Klemme 2010). In other words, Kant says, 'a rational action', which is different from an action that stems from human instinct or desire, refers to an action which is determined by duty (or *Sollen*) (Kant 1956). Then, a particular form of human reasoning which is conscious of moral duty regulates the individual's action, directing it not to follow the individual's preference or inclination but to follow what the individual ought to do. This is what Kant famously enunciates as 'practical reason'. In particular, Kant considers an issue of moral duty or moral principle which necessarily entails a normative (or compulsory) action. However, as was investigated above, human feeling and human understanding also entail consequential action, a fact which draws out an interpretation, so that Kant claims that feeling and understanding, as 'theoretical reflections', represent human reasoning in the explanation and prediction of conditional imperatives. This means, according to Wallace, that 'looking backward to events that have already taken place, it asks why they have occurred; looking forward, it attempts to determine what is going to happen in the future' (Wallace 2009). When put together, what Kant tries to say is that, unlike human feeling or understanding, which entails human beings' actions, under the condition of the causal principle a 'practical reason', which requires human actions to follow a universal principle, does not entail any causal principle. It sounds as if Kant intends to say that conducting a moral action and, at the same time, recognizing the moral principle have a single unitary status, meaning that moral action is synonymous with understanding the moral principle. However, this does not mean that the moral principle is equivalent to the moral action; instead, it is more likely that he is proposing that moral principle and moral action create their *own* causal principle. We choose the right thing because it is the right thing to do.

In a similar vein to that followed by Kant's logic of 'practical reason', Wang gives a didactic message: 'knowledge is the beginning of practice; doing is the completion of knowing' (Wang 1916: 55). In other words, if one's mind comprehends the universal principle, this must entail an action. Wang fully elaborates by describing the case of the child about to fall into a well, a situation which was proposed by Mengzi. That is, when a child is about to fall into a well, an individual who sees this potential accident and feels compassion will perform an action according to the projected reflections of the universal principle, which is to protect the child. However, this is different from a person's knowing about cold or pain. The knowledge of feeling cold and pain also drives the person to perform an action which tells him to avoid it. However, Wang's demanding universal moral principle requires a 'united' task, which means that an individual's action ought to consider the whole of humanity. The result, or consequence, of the person's practice does not end with (or is not limited to) himself; rather, his practice further considers the other's pain and cold as if he feels that pain as his own (Wang 1916). Wang's assertion that human beings have pure knowing, in Ivanhoe's interpretation, gives us a straightforward explanation of how an individual expresses universal humanism: 'The morally cultivated person forms one body with Heaven, Earth and all things. He feels their pain and imperfections as his own, and he does so because they are all aspects of a single universal mind' (Ivanhoe 2002: 27). Indeed, Wang elaborates, the moral duty of human beings entails compulsory moral action, and this duty accords with the universal moral principle which is conceptualized by human beings. This, in turn, can be regarded as having the same intention as Kant when Kant proclaims his belief in human beings' practical reason in order to 'secure the validity of the moral law' (Klemme 2010: 12). Therefore, for both Kant and Wang, in treating the point that human beings have 'practical reason' (Kant's term) or 'pure knowing' (Wang's term), human reasoning entails the principle of the freedom (free will) and autonomy of human beings. Furthermore, this particular human reasoning is the evidence for defining 'humanity' (*Menschheit*) and 'human character' (*Persönlichkeit*) (O'Neill 1989).

TOWARD A COSMOPOLITAN CONDITION

The analysis section attempted to determine whether the fundamental ethical concepts at the heart of two different cultural settings are actually identical to each other. The main findings from the comparison of the writings of Kant and the Confucians can be simplified into two themes. First, the classical canons from Western and Asian civilizations both regard human beings as a primary concern of normative ethics. Second, both are concerned with the necessary distinction between the empirical realm, in which human beings perform their actions, and the metaphysical realm, which provides a guiding principle to lead human beings to achieve a harmonious society. That is, there is no fundamentally (or radically) different ethics in a theoretical sense: Both insist that humans as rational beings have the capacity to use their *practical reason* to help them approach a concept of universal morality in order to regulate their actions whenever they may otherwise infringe upon others' inherent and intrinsic human *value*, and both argue that this universal morality can be regarded as an end in itself. This in turn provides a basis for respecting all human beings equally, regardless of their nationality, ethnicity, or gender, in any circumstances. Hence, finding common ground in the fundamental normative morality expressed within two different cultural settings has significant implications for international relations in terms of creating the possibility of reconstructing contemporary global dialogue. In other words, as Freeden and Vincent point out, in culture-specific approaches, while the possibility of comparison tends to focus on 'prioritizing the core indigenous culture in general' (Freeden and Vincent 2013: 13), the most important task of contemporary global governance is to focus on the pursuit of grander social visions, looking for the common ground and linking threads in order to find a way out from each one's tenacious own point of world politics. Besides, in a comparative mode, the focus of interest of a global dialogue which advocates multiple cosmopolitan perspectives seems to become 'the rhetorical devices ratcheting up the intensity' of global speech culture towards each different 'chord' that depends on local beliefs and ideologies (Freeden and Vincent 2013: 20). Therefore, this paper, following Freeden and Vincent's approach, has attempted to seek 'critical distance from our own positions and preferences, not only from those of others' (Freeden and Vincent 2013: 12–20), and to do so, it has particularly focused on the comparison of 'conceptual morphology' in each of the selected literatures: Kantian cosmopolitanism and Confucian cosmopolitanism. Thus, the results found through meaningful comparison become noteworthy because they imply that the similarities between different cultural settings can provide a chance to understand the core moral concepts embedded in cultural-political differences. That is, the results reveal that the contemporary cosmopolitan discourses have been focused on an *instrumental* universalism, not a *practical* (commensurate with the Kantian term) universalism which cosmopolitanism ought to pursue. Nevertheless, to some extent it must be true that the recognition of cultural differences makes it possible to open up a more positive global dialogue in terms of searching for an adequate methodology to attain a cosmopolitan community. In this regard, critical cosmopolitan thinkers who advocate multiple cultural perspectives might intend to address universalism for the sake of inviting these perspectives to participate in the discourse of cosmopolitanism. This is also supported by Kymlicka's argument that, since 'a particular culture in which one is raised and lives provides the context for one's choices and actions', culture becomes a powerful subject to explain and predict how others' political behaviour would be directed (Kymlicka 1995: 82–84). Kymlicka's argument does not guarantee others' respect for one's own indigenous cultural perspective. It is because one's own cultural value conflicts with others'. Tu asks, 'How can we expect others to respect our way of life, if we disregard what they themselves regard as meaningful and worthwhile?' (Tu 2008: 329). Nevertheless, with an intention to offer an alternative global paradigm, what Tu thinks should be questioned is highly problematic either to critical cosmopolitan perspectives or even to the general discussion of cosmopolitanism itself. Even though he asks this question in the context of international relations, we can draw an underpinning critical implication from it: a question as to whether the state can be the public expression of a shared cultural practice existing to protect cultural sovereignty. Tu, who consistently proposes 'a much needed communal critical self-consciousness', argues that the Neo-Confucian values have cultural competence as a 'soft power' (moral persuasion in Tu's expression), and that this implies the existence of 'multiple modernities' which aspire to promote universal justice (Tu

2008: 330). Tu's self-assertive assumption, which is phrased as a suggestion, well represents the trend of the global transformation 'from the
politics of domination to the politics of communication, networking,
negotiation, interaction, interfacing, and collaboration' (Tu 2008: 330).
However, he confirms the realists' view on international relations, which
is to speak of a specific culture's sovereign identity. Here, it is assumed
that Tu attempts to see the state as the receptacle of a socio-political,
moral community which allows it a legitimate claim on the principles of
nonintervention and respect. By doing so, he considers that the state
conforms to the principle of self-determination. Nevertheless, what he
misses is the understanding that, as Murray insists, 'the state is not an
appropriate moral referent in the first place' (Murray 1997: 163). In other
words, the state is a problem-solving mechanism created under the necessity of providing security for people; therefore, states as political
frameworks are permitted only 'derivative value' (Brown, 1992). No nation-state or cultural community can itself represent the source of universal justice, because those cultures and forms of socio-political practice are
mediums for carrying fundamental moral values which are universally
inherent in human beings. In a similar vein, Beitz also argues that 'states
cannot be the sources of ends in the same sense as are persons', because
the raison d'être of states is to establish and advance the ends of a group
of people who share practices and institutions, and thereby provide a
ground for people 'to act on the categorical imperative' (Beitz 1979:
52–55; Brown 1992). Hence, this point emphasizes that no supreme or
representative institutions can expropriate the universal right of human
beings. In short, a culture which organizes itself internally and externally
sets boundaries in order to distinguish it from others, and so cannot be
regarded as the primary means of practicing universal justice before
searching for universal humanity (Murray 1997).

Nevertheless, the role of culture, which provides human beings' social
relationships and further constitutes individual identity, cannot be entirely neglected, because culture provides particularistic values, such as 'the
loyalties and affiliative sentiments characteristic of membership in cultural or national groups' (Beitz 1994: 129–30). In a bid to create a cosmopolitan condition, the global cultural dialogue attempts to advocate for international ethics by claiming the participation of multiple cultural perspectives. In one sense, this is regarded as an attempt to promote a universal
structure of cosmopolitanism. However, in the motive to approach universalism from a cosmopolitan point of view, there seems to be a gap
between moral cosmopolitanism and institutional cosmopolitanism. This
is because, as Beitz says, 'if it is a fact that membership in a distinct
political community has value for the members of that community, then,
[to advocate a universal condition] on a cosmopolitan view, this fact
should matter for practical reasoning' (1994: 129–30). That is, his assumption leads us to realize that, if the contemporary global dialogue volun-

teers for a cosmopolitan view, humanity as the end itself ought to be regarded as a primary referent object not only for its political implication but also for its socio-cultural aspects, rather than for distinguishing inevitably different cultural practices. Here the point is that, while the principle of cosmopolitanism and its universal morality always posits humanity as the end in itself, in the center of a demanding universal morality, contemporary global cultural dialogue projects a certain group of people as a body to approach to ask for respect. Therefore, theoretically speaking, we need to focus not on a superficial universalism, which invites multiple cosmopolitanism and so draws attention from cultural particularism, but on a practical universalism, which sets a common ground for cultural particularism in order to help us to find a common goal for humanism. Achieving a practical universalism in the pursuit of a cosmopolitan common ground inevitably leads us to compare fundamental moral values embedded in the cultural discourses of each community. Thus, regardless of different cultural settings, we install human beings as a primary concern for cosmopolitanism in the true sense of the term *universalism*.

CONCLUSION: A CONTINUED
COSMOPOLITAN ENTHUSIASM

What I have attempted to demonstrate in this paper is simply that comparative cosmopolitanism—looking at different cultural settings—can make a useful contribution to contemporary cosmopolitan debates. The role of cosmopolitanism is like a 'signpost' to show international relations which way to go. However, the 'sign' (or the symbol) of cosmopolitanism often confuses us, or even complicates matters more than is necessary. This is because the amorphous character of cosmopolitanism and its demand for universality are almost impossible for us to understand as one fixed form. To some extent, while there is a need to respect the cultural and political orientation of each nation-state, the very denial of the possibility of meaningful comparison misses out on the highest purpose of cosmopolitanism, which is to establish international ethics in an attempt to attain a social vision of international community. In other words, contemporary debates, in a bid to accomplish a just global dialogue, have proved that culture-oriented global dialogue pursuing multiple approaches to international ethics reduces the core ethical values which are assumed to be shared by human beings, regardless of the culture to which they belong. Consequently, the point in question is that in their attempts to associate cultural-political approaches with the advocacy of universal respect, those conducting these debates have revealed that their point of view masks the highest ethical value of cosmopolitan humanity. That is, those making efforts to reify indigenous cultural traditions use 'culture'—which is supposed to enable human beings to advance their ends—as an instrument to justify suggesting universal respect for each culture and political orientation and, furthermore, also defend human beings' adherence to specific cultures. Therefore, in order to move towards a more genuine universalism, the aim of this research task has been to explore how different cultural and political communities have their own moral values which can lead us towards international ethics. In this exploration, classical texts from both the West and the East have been compared and rearticulated to find universal moral components which enable human beings to ground their position in the center of cosmopolitan dialogue. The findings, in turn, provide us with significant insights for an approach to international ethics. Specifically, the formal and normative ethics demonstrate that there is no radically different ethics, and that, if this fact is acknowledged, there is a chance for understanding other culturally and politically different communities. In this regard, through making meaningful comparison of different cultural settings, this paper has intended to imply the attainability of genuine universalism which allows us to circumvent many of the problematic 'spurious' approaches to universalism. None of this, of course, is to say that its approach possesses any necessary validity—the construction of a systematic validation and defence of its assumptions is a task beyond the scope of this paper—or to deny that multicultural dialogue, along with critical cosmopolitanism, remains in need of reform. Instead, this paper suggests one possible avenue for further research, and that academic endeavors should engage in a more profound comparative analysis to understand the contextualized, substantive issues that each political society has encountered. In other words, comparing the core indicators of political thoughts embedded in each culture would lead us to understand how each cultural filter has operated and been transmitted in the nature of politics. Once rearticulated, we can fully understand how each different speech culture and its transmission process causes divergence among different societies. Although conducting meaningful comparison in a bid for constructing a semantic approach is a demanding task, it is worthwhile if it can arrive at a genuine meaning of universalism through understanding one another.

BIBLIOGRAPHY

Apel, K-O. (1997). 'Kant's Toward Perpetual Peace as Historical Prognosis from the Point of View of Moral Duty' in J. Bohman and M. Lutz-Bachmann (eds.) *Perpetual Peace: Essays on Kant's Cosmopolitan Ideal.* Cambridge, MA: MIT Press, 79–111.
Beitz, C. (1979). *Political Theory and International Relations.* Princeton: Princeton University Press.
———. (1994). 'Cosmopolitan liberalism and the state system' in C. Brown (ed.) *Political Reconstructing in Europe—Ethical Perspectives.* London: Routledge.

Brown, C. (1992). *International Relations Theory—New Normative Approaches*. London: Harvester Wheatsheaf.

Brown, W. G. and Held, D. (eds.) (2010). *The Cosmopolitanism Reader*. Cambridge: Polity Press.

Brown, G. (2013). *Grounding Cosmopolitanism: From Kant to the Idea of a Cosmopolitan*. Edinburgh: Edinburgh University Press.

Chai, S. (2001). 'Neo-Confucian Cosmopolitanism and Chinese Perception of World Order: A Study of Wang Yangming's Virtue Politics and Integral Pluralism' [pdf] (accessed 20 April 2013), SSRN: ssrn.com/abstract=1918952 or dx.doi.org/10.2139/ssrn.1918952.

Cicero, M. T. (1999). *On the Commonwealth and On Laws* edited and introduced by J. G. Zetzel. New York: Cambridge University Press.

Dallmayr, F. (2004). 'Beyond Monologue: For a Comparative Political Theory'. *Perspectives on Politics* 2 (2), 249–57.

Delanty, G. and He, B. (2008). 'Cosmopolitan Perspectives on European and Asian Transnationalism'. *International Sociology* 23 (3), 323–44.

Freeden, M. V. and Vincent, A. (2013). *Comparative Political Thought*. Oxford: Routledge.

Held, D. (2003). 'Cosmopolitanism: globalization tamed?' *Review of International Studies* 29 (4), 465–80.

Inada, K. K. (1997). 'A Theory of Oriental Aesthetics: A Prolegomenon'. *Philosophy East and West* 47 (2), 117–31.

Ivanhoe, P. J. (2002). *Ethics in the Confucian Tradition* (2nd ed.). Indianapolis: Hackett Publishing Company.

Kant, I. (1956). *Critique of Practical Reason* translated by L. White Beck. Indianapolis: Bobbs-Merrill.

———. (1964). *Groundwork for the Metaphysics of Morals* translated by H. J. Paton. New York: Harper Torchbooks.

———. (2005). *Fundamental Principles of the Metaphysics of Morals* translated by T. Kingsmill Abbott. New York: Dover.

Klemme, H. (2010). 'The origin and aim of Kant's Critique of Practical Reason' in *Kant's Critique of Practical Reason* edited by A. Reath. and J. Timmermann. Cambridge: Cambridge University Press.

Kymlicka, W. (1995). *Multiple Citizenship: A Liberal Theory of Minority Rights*. Oxford: Oxford University Press.

March, A. (2009). 'What is Comparative Political Theory?' *The Review of Politics* 71 (4), 531–65.

Patrick, S. (2014). 'The Unruled World: The case for good enough global governance'. *Foreign Affairs*, 93(1).

Murray, A. (1997). *Reconstructing Realism*. Edinburgh: Keele University Press.

Needham, J. (1956). *Science and Civilization in Ancient China*. Cambridge: Cambridge University Press.

Nussbaum, Martha C. (2010) 'Kant and Cosmopolitanism' in *The Cosmopolitanism Reader*, edited by Brwon, W. G. and Held, D. Cambridge: Polity Press, 27–44.

O'Neill, O. (1989). *Constructions of Reason: Explorations of Kant's Practical Philosophy*. Cambridge: Cambridge University Press.

Reiss, H. (1970). *Kant's Political Writings*. Cambridge: Cambridge University Press.

Roetz, H. (2008). 'Confucianism between Tradition and Modernity, Religion, and Secularization: Questions to Tu Weiming'. *Dao* 7 (4), 367–80.

Singerland, E. (2003). *Confucius Analects: With Selections from Traditional Commentaries*. Indianapolis: Hackett Publishing Company.

Tu, W. (1996). 'Family, Nation, and the World: The Global Ethic as a Modern Confucian Quest' (3rd ed.). Reschauer Lecture, Fairbank Center for East Asian Research, Harvard University, April, tuweiming.com/lecture.3html.

———. (2008). 'Mutual Learning as an Agenda for Social Development' in *Asante*, edited by M. K., and Miike, Y. The Global Intercultural Reader. New York: Routledge, 329–33.

Wallace, R. Jay (2009). 'Practical Reason' in E. N. Zalta (ed.) *The Stanford Encyclopedia of Philosophy* (accessed 15 August 2013), plato.stanford.edu/archives/sum2009/entries/practical-reason/.

Wang, Y. (1916).*The Philosophy of Wang Yang-Ming* translated from Chinese by F. G. Henke. London: The Open Court Publishing Co.

———. (1963). *Instructions for Practical Living, and Other Neo-Confucian Writings* [e-book]. New York: Columbia University Press (accessed 5 June 2013), archive.org/details/instructionsforp00wang.

Wawrytko, S. A. (1982). 'Confucius and Kant: The ethics of respect'. *Philosophy East and West* 32 (3), 237–57.

FOUR

Back to the Future

Post-Multiculturalism; Immanent Cosmopolitanism

Sneja Gunew

As the binaries of West and non-West appear to be congealing once again, the debates in cosmopolitanism over the last decade are the latest attempt to imagine a new analytical framework that is more inclusive, to think in *planetary* rather than *globalized* terms. While cosmopolitan discussions have not engaged in a sustained way with literary and cultural studies, the paper argues that this field offers fertile possibilities for developing new forms of legibility for literatures of the world, including those multicultural writings traditionally marginalized in national and transnational formations. Post-multicultural writers need to be given critical recognition as mediating figures that facilitate new relations between national cultures and the global or, in the more felicitous terms suggested by Spivak and Gilroy, the 'planetary'. The very elements that have been traditionally associated with their constitutive oppression, the belief that they are at home nowhere or in more than one place, could be rethought to constitute their greatest attribute—that they can navigate the structures of belonging in multiple ways, not least by challenging the universalisms that undergird many forms of both nationalism and globalization. This chapter is part of a larger project analysing the possibilities for cosmopolitanism as a critical framework for cultural texts. What follows sketches a provisional cosmopolitan critical methodology specifically for literary texts. The project provides continuity with my earlier work of constructing rationales as to why multicultural texts and writers should be included in national literary studies as a matter of course (Gunew

1994, 2004). Taking into account the histories of migration over the last century, these speculations include diaspora studies and world literatures, all now provisionally assembled within frameworks of globalization.

NEGOTIATING A POLITICS OF PREPOSITIONS

The central argument is that these multicultural or ethnic artists (assigned marginalized minoritarian perspectives) provide a 'hinge'[1] between national cultures and globalization as well as put those concepts into crisis (in the way that the concept of a hinge does). To put it another way, if we think of national literatures as providing a basis for Ben Anderson's imagined communities, multicultural writers have always spoken *to* the nation but have often been heard (if heard at all) as speaking from outside the nation, and not necessarily on behalf of the global. The national anxieties provoked by the foreigner or the guest (captured by terms such as *Gastarbeiter*) have been represented in many ways. Those who are certified (part of the canon) as contributing to the imagined community speak *to* the nation *for* the nation, and do so *to* the global as well. The question here is how to make the case that these multicultural writers speak *for* the nation, to echo Homi Bhabha on Fanon, as a way of bringing about a nation without nationalism (Bhabha 1996: 192). The case for including their perspectives is the claim that they provide a more nuanced grammar for cultural legibility within globalization, a sensitivity and reflexivity towards what cannot be taken for granted in relation to nation-states, and their assertions of autonomy vis-à-vis the global.[2] A term that is often used to represent this other form of globalization in a more constructive way within these debates is *planetary* (more on this below). And here is where cosmopolitan critical approaches enter the picture.

SUMMARY OF COSMOPOLITANISM

In 1998, the late Ulrich Beck exhorted the readers of his 'Cosmopolitan Manifesto' in the following manner: 'Citizens of the world, unite!' (Beck 1998). Beck was, of course, referencing the Communist Manifesto, but his invocation of 'cosmos' and 'polis' also signalled that the internationalism that had characterized that project needed to be redefined in a globalized world. In 1998 as well, Pheng Cheah's and Bruce Robbins's collection, *Cosmpolitics: Thinking and Feeling Beyond the Nation*, was published.[3] There was also the 2002 collection, *Cosmopolitanism* (based on a special issue of *Public Culture*), in which Walter Mignolo spoke of critical cosmopolitanism in relation to border politics, and border studies have developed into their own field of inquiry. Clearly a new paradigm or model for relations of sociality was being sought. Emanating in the first instance from philosophy, sociology, legal studies, and anthropology, cosmopolitanism has only recently engaged with literary and cultural studies.[4] Pheng Cheah's more recent forays into reimagining world literatures is helping shape current attempts to situate literary studies more solidly in the field. Berthold Schoene's study of a new cosmopolitan novel exemplified by writers such as Hari Kunzru and David Mitchell (based on the theoretical categories of Jean-Luc Nancy) represent another contemporary direction. Robert Spencer analyses critical cosmopolitanism in relation to postcolonial studies in order to 'create and legitimize a global society that has left imperialism behind' (2011: 3).[5]

My own study (provisionally titled *Back to the Future: Post-Multiculturalism; Immanent Cosmopolitanism*) continues my work over three decades analysing the ways in which diasporic, immigrant, multicultural, and ethnic minority writers are situated in a kind of *cordon sanitaire* around national cultural formations: They function as an alibi for transnationalism while not being acknowledged as an intrinsic part of the national culture.[6] The neo-cosmopolitan debates provide ways of situating these writers in terms of new models of mediation. And as Gerard Delanty (2012) reminds us, the contemporary register carries an inherently '"post-western" orientation that is located neither on the national nor global level, but at the interface of the local and the global. . . . Taken together, these dimensions and characteristics of cosmopolitanism suggest a broad definition of cosmopolitanism as a condition of openness to the world and entailing self and societal transformation in light of the encounter with the Other' (Delanty 2012: 41).

The year 1998 was one watershed and 2001 another, the latter precipitating an increasing chorus that multiculturalism had failed, that tolerance for recognition of cultural differences needed to be scaled back, that nations were to be reimagined as newly coherent and unified in order to prevail authoritatively within globalization. In this model, globalization means the mobility of capital and the control of human mobility in terms of commodified movements between nations (e.g., in the form of tourism and, arguably, the social media conglomerates controlled by Google on the one hand and patrolled further by authoritarian states on the other). My argument that post-multicultural writers might be given critical recognition as mediating figures that facilitate new relations between national cultures and the global would prevail in the face of these anxieties. The very elements that have been traditionally deployed to illustrate their constitutive suffering and oppression (e.g., the migrant condition, or *migritude*),[7] the belief that their loyalty is suspect because they are at home nowhere and linked to more than one place, could be rethought to constitute their advantage—that they can navigate the structures of belonging (homeliness and unhomeliness) in numerous ways, not least by interrogating the complacent assumptions or self-evident universalisms that undergird many forms of both nationalism and globalization. Central questions in my study are: Who counts as human and what follows? Rights? Responsibilities? Central as well are the inherent problems with attempts to represent ethical relations towards alterity (including influential accounts of the ameliorating power of recognition). The current debates are often framed as cosmopolitanism from below to differentiate them from what were deemed to be earlier elitist forms of cosmopolitanism (even when these earlier forms often scapegoated the so-called rootless Jew). Now there is a growing recognition of the knowledge produced by those abjected by society (biopolitical waste, bare life), and critical cosmopolitanism is the framework for working with these different knowledge structures. Attempts to capture this are reflected in a proliferation of hyphenated terms such as vernacular, abject, vulgar, and demotic cosmopolitanism. Below is a brief summary of how these dynamics function.

INDIVIDUAL VERSUS COMMUNITY

Much tension exists in literary studies between the idea of the hyper-individualism of the author and the assumption that those who have been minoritized write on behalf of (both represent and are representative of) a group. That those awarded canonical status often write to and for the dominant group generally has not been entertained, although inroads have been made, for example, through feminist and postcolonial criticism. Within the constraints of transnational publishing, the privileging of the individualist author explains writers' dislike of being labeled *multicultural, ethnic,* and so on, terms that are correctly often perceived as signalling a patronizing stance. At the same time, critics within cosmopolitanism have alluded to the importance of rethinking the communal because the risk, as Ulrich Beck reiterated, is that there won't be a planet remaining if this is not done. The turbulence of climate change and so forth transcends the managerial capabilities of nations (much less individuals). Thus we have, for example, increasingly popular campaigns around the concept of the cultural commons. Kwame Anthony Appiah's version of the cosmopolitan includes the recognition that we are all part of permeable contaminated cultures; we are intertwined and interdependent in ways that make claims of originary purity (homogeneity rather than heterogeneity) sit rather oddly. While debates about citizenship, loyalty, and ethics focus on individuals, it is here that the planetary usefully challenges the debates.

PLANETARITY: CITIZENSHIP AND THE POSTHUMAN

Paul Gilroy's version of the planetary is associated with becoming more reflexively critical of one's own culture by cultivating an estrangement from it. He locates a blueprint for such a parallax view in Montesquieu's *Persian Letters* comprising the perspectives of 'Muslim' visitors to Paris in the eighteenth century. Gayatri Spivak's planetarity speaks of 'an impera-tive to reimagine the subject as planetary accident . . . rather than global agents' (Spivak 2012: 339).[8] In order to skirt the problems connected to imagining alterity, Spivak considers the planet from an outside vantage point as a way to emphasize that it is not up to the human subject to imagine the Other. The moment the Other is imagined into being, a hier-archy slides into place. This is repeatedly played out in studies that in-voke a form of the politics of recognition. Instead, Spivak refers to the Islamic concept of *haq* as a constitutive birthright that confers the respon-sibility to care for others. She differentiates this inherent responsibility from the concept of rights. Arguing for the rights of others is dubious because it constitutively reveals a gulf between those who have rights and those who do not. Such a process sets up an ethics inevitably haunted by an imperialist dynamic, whereas the concept of inherent re-sponsibility to and for others sets up a differentiated ethical dynamics.[9] How one relates this conceptual apparatus to literary interpretation is a challenge—Spivak conveys it through Mahasweta Devi's novella *Ptero-dactyl* via indigeneity and geological allocthonic demographic patterns—for which one meaning is 'rocks that migrate'. This reference brings us to the territory of the posthuman in relation to the new materialism, includ-ing, for example, Mel Chen's notion of animacy, where rocks also have agency. In other words, whereas much of the cosmopolitan debates are concerned with rethinking notions of individualism—as citizens, as hav-ing access to rights and to cultural franchise, there is another fruitful trajectory that links to debates concerning the posthuman, in which re-sponsibilities are extended beyond the traditional human to, for example, rocks and mountains.[10] Reaching for frameworks of spatiality and tem-porality may help organize these challenges of translating ethical and political concepts into cultural and literary ones.

SPATIALITY: MOBILITY

While cosmpolitanism is often represented as antinationalist, it is also recognized that institutions attached to nations remain the primary ways to counter capitalist forms of globalization.[11] It is therefore useful to be-gin with the nation as imagined community: What binds individuals to groups and what holds groups together? The print culture identified by Ben Anderson (1983 as fulfilling this role is taken to a further level by means of the new social media that create a plethora of micro-groups. As well there are the transnational links of ethno-cultural diasporas comprising religions (including, arguably, capitalism), languages, foods, histories, and so on. It also is noteworthy that, as with all 'imagined communities', we are dealing with fantasy structures. Just *how* these groups negotiate the spatial is very much part of the dynamic.

Included within considerations of spatiality are questions of mobility; the conflict between mobility and residentialism is at the heart of these debates. As Nikos Papastergiadis reminds us: 'If culture can only find sustenance when it is rooted in a specific place, what is the fate of those cultures that must co-exist in a common space and what is the cultural identity of people who are on the move?' (2012: 124). Furthermore, 'the residentialist view of culture not only poses a negative slant on the impact of mobility, it also makes the gloomy prognostication that moving beyond one's place is to risk cultural exclusion' (ibid: 125). There is a sense in which the unexamined assumptions concerning residentialism (rootedness, etc.) which one often finds within nationalism are inherently deleterious to the kinds of mobility (actual and symbolic) that contribute to a cosmopolitan arts practice.[12] Dimitris Vardoulakis (2008) casts an interesting light on these matters in his analysis of *nómos/nomós* (law) concerning who has the rights to impose the law. For example, some commentators identify the *nomos* (the law) with an etymological split that depends on whether one puts the accent on the first or second syllable. The first (*nómos*) relates to the sedentary and the propertied, and the second (*nomós*) to the pastoral and nomadic. This latter meaning has been taken up by Deleuze, for example, allowing him to develop it into his influential notion of nomadism.[13] Others, such as the political scientist Carl Schmitt, see the two terms as two aspects of the one phenomenon (Vardoulakis 2008: 148). As far as nationalisms are concerned, nomads and migrants remain suspect, including in their indigenous incarnations (e.g., in Canadian and Australian national cultures).

Consider texts such as Caryl Phillips's *A Distant Shore*, in which an African asylum seeker, after many perilous journeys, comes to rest in an English village and constructs a complex identity only to fall prey to local racism. Or consider Chinamanda Adichie's recent *Americanah*, which looks at the distinctions between African Americans and American Africans in identifying differing forms of racism. The novel includes the very different trajectories followed by a Ghanaian student who studies in the United States and the experiences of her boyfriend who enters the UK as an illegal immigrant and is deported back to the new Afropolitan Ghana.[14] The tensions between legitimate and illegitimate mobility are central to these debates and are addressed in more detail in my longer study, where the mobility of refugees and asylum seekers is captured in contradictory and concrete images of aborted communication. In Australian writer Maxine Beneba Clarke's (2014) astonishing story 'The Stilt

Fishermen of Kahaluwa', in her remarkable debut collection *Foreign Soil*, the protagonist, Tamil asylum seeker Asanka, deliberately and desperately sews up his lips after realizing that his pleas for sanctuary will never be heard. In David Malouf's *12 Edmonstone Street*, a series of linked autobiographical stories, there is one section, 'A Foot in the Stream', where the authorial persona writes of visiting a mosaic workshop in Agra, India:

> One of the boys (he might have been fifteen), using a pair of tweezers and a live coal, was engaged in setting the stones in a white paste. Suddenly, as the factory owner turned away a moment, he gave us a wild look and held up four fingers in some sort of appeal. Another demand for rupees? It looked like more than that. In a more melodramatic situation it would quite clearly have been a sign that he was being held against his will, a desperate cry for rescue.
>
> Nothing explained itself, we passed on. But I see that wordless gesture, four tense upthrust fingers and an open mouth as an image of what I have failed to understand here, a message I am deaf to and have not received, an uncomfortable reminder of the million tiny events I have been present at that escaped my attention and which added together would make a wall of darkness. (Malouf 1986: 122)

Malouf's 'wall of darkness' is a recurrent element in the noncommunication that stalks these texts. A decade ago I wrote an essay when, like many, I was haunted by the news reports of asylum seekers to Australia sewing up their lips and (perhaps) those of their children in an eloquent articulation of their despair (Refugees).[15] Here is how it ended:

> The postwar immigrants who entered Australia as displaced persons from all over the world harboured within their bodies the viruses and [metaphorically] noisy parasites (Attali 1977; Serres 1982) of languages other than English. They were feared as bearers of contamination whose linguistic pluralities registered the welts of their visible difference on the skin, even of those who looked 'white'. Their stammering apologies haunt the presence of those desperate contemporary refugees cast into desert camps in apparent perpetuity who have sewn up their own lips and those of their children. (Gunew 2003)

TEMPORALITY: MODERNITY/IES

Aspirational modernity is an element in all these debates: the advent of (tyranny of) modernity within which European subjectivity wanders. Modernity, as we know from postcolonial theory, is linked with concepts of universalism yoked to a proseltyzing, civilizing subject. Proliferating these moments of modernity constitutes strategies for showing precisely the localized manifestations of Europe (e.g., in Dipesh Chakrabarty's injunction to provincialize Europe). Terms such as *European* and the *West* require deconstruction to reveal their inner contradictions so that they can no longer be invoked as self-evidently heuristic categories in postcolonial debates, as in, for example, the oft-repeated phrase, 'West and the rest.' The new cosmopolitan debates provide avenues for recognizing the cultural heterogeneity of nation-states in which differing temporalities coexist. Recognizing the cosmopolitanism of subaltern groups facilitates this enterprise and helps construct a more inclusive perspective and differing modernities (Gaonkar 2001).

UNCANNY PSYCHIC TIME: THE ROLE OF LANGUAGE

Within these geopolitical national sovereignties, the question of multilingualism arises in an uncanny homology to the fate of the nomadic. Languages run riot in spectacularly unexpected ways, hence the many anxieties that spawn policies to discipline their manifestation. The role of English in this mix is complex. For example, within global English the meanings attached to linguistically enunciative positions differ (I speak; I am spoken), as do the geopolitical positions from which one speaks English. After Derrida, we have assimilated the fact that we are all strangers within language, any language. It certainly does not provide a stable foundation for identity: 'No, an identity is never given, received, or attained; only the interminable and indefinitely phantasmatic process of identification endures' (Derrida 1998: 28). So then what does it mean to be asked to reside precariously in another language, a language that always comes with historical (including ideological) baggage? Some of the answers depend on the 'monolingualism' of the culture:

> The monolingualism imposed by the other operates by relying upon that foundation, here, through a sovereignty whose presence is always colonial, which tends, repressively and irrepressibly, to reduce language to the One, that is, to the hegemony of the homogeneous. This can be verified everywhere, everywhere this homo-hegemony remains at work in the culture, effacing the folds and flattening the text. (Derrida 1998: 39–40)

World English is a quintessential example of 'homo-hegemony'. Thus it is more difficult to assert the legitimacy of other versions of English associated with multicultural writing within cultures that strenuously reiterate their monolingualism, such as Australia, than officially bilingual cultures such as Canada.[16] In terms of cultural texts, there is also increasingly the thematization of the English language as designating a passport to global mobility.[17]

WHAT DOES LITERARY COSMOPOLITANISM OFFER?

To some degree these debates are circulating within the framework of new ways of conceptualizing world literature. As Pheng Cheah points out: 'World literature is an important aspect of cosmopolitanism because it is a type of world-making activity that enables us to imagine a world' (2012: 138). Paul Gilroy suggests that 'imagining oneself as a stranger . . . might instructively be linked to actually becoming estranged from the cultural habits one was born into' (2006: 79) and cites the productive example of George Orwell within colonial England (ibid: 85). We can also think of texts that do comparable work, such as Toni Morrison's *Playing in the Dark* or Amitav Ghosh's *In an Antique Land*.[18] One important question to ask is whether cosmopolitanism resides in the literary work or in a method of reading. Like Robert Spencer (2011: 7), I am interested more in cosmopolitan readings than identifying cosmopolitan texts. Unlike Spencer, I am not so much concerned with identifying postcolonial texts as ideal candidates for cosmopolitan readings as offering a cosmopolitan reading of multicultural texts. Kwame Anthony Appiah (2006) suggests notions of infinitely intermingled cultures where 'contamination' and 'mongrelization' become terms of approval, and notions of cultural authenticity and purity are relinquished. Neil Lazarus advocates the kind of writing that allows readers to experience 'what it feels like to live on a given ground . . . a physical world, a mode of production, a specific set of social relationships, forms of belonging, custom and obligations' (2011: 133).[19] In a sense, what this produces is the writer as auto-ethnographer, something that resonates as well with Gilroy's vision of 'convivial' cosmopolitanism. A perfect example of this may be found in an early story by Amitav Ghosh, 'The Imam and the Indian' (2010), significantly set outside Europe in a plot where an Indian ethnographer encounters differing points of view in a village on the Nile delta.

GRAND NARRATIVES CHALLENGED BY THE EVERYDAY

Both cosmopolitanism and multiculturalism are currently often analysed in terms of the 'everyday'; for example, how people live together (or not) on the street in demotic ways. Such an approach underpins Paul Gilroy's concept of 'conviviality'. While there are many productive elements in this development, these manifestations of the 'glocal' may run the danger of reinforcing the old universalist parochialisms, particularly when they emanate from the former imperial urban centres. On the other hand, the invocation of the everyday does help change analytical perspectives, and is often a reminder of the ways in which relations of sociality are more benevolently entertained between individuals than nations. Ghosh's short story attempts to illustrate this.

Ghosh's story may be taken as a kind of parable for a cosmopolitan reading in ways that suggest the concept of *mise en abyme* popularized by the work of Lucien Dällenbach (1989), where an event within a story may reflexively suggest a framework for interpretation. The first-person narrator of Ghosh's story, named the 'Indian doctor' in the tale, juxtaposes two villagers as a way of producing a cautionary tale concerning 'false' and 'true' cosmopolitanism in ways that ultimately indict his own parochialism. One of these, Khamees the Rat, is an illiterate peasant hungry for news of the world; the other is the Imam who has read widely but had decided that the way ahead was to transform himself into a modern doctor through mastering the Western art of giving injections. The Imam is instantly offended when the Indian ethnographer questions him about his own medical traditions, since he was in the process of shedding this heritage and acquiring modernity: 'I knew that he would never talk to me about his craft . . . because his medicines were as discredited in his own eyes as they were in his clients' (Ghosh 2010: 4). Within the dynamics of the village, the narrator's ethnographic quest (linked to the dubious disciplinary project of acquiring knowledge about others) runs parallel with the villagers' curiosity concerning himself as emissary from another world. Their questioning instantly lands on perceptions of religious difference exacerbated by the non-translatability between English and Arabic. Interrogated concerning the Hindu practice of cremating the dead, the narrator is stymied by the fact that he does not know the Arabic term and 'I had to use the word "burn". That was unfortunate, for "burn" was the word for what happened to wood and straw and the eternally damned' (ibid: 7). In other words, the villagers assume that this cultural practice is due to lack of kindling. Coming to his rescue, Khamees the Rat suggests that it could actually be a cunning ploy to dispose of one's body so that one need not face the Day of Judgment. Meanwhile, the hostility of the Imam also precipitates the same direct accusation followed by a lecture on how the Indians needed to learn from the 'advanced' West who would never burn their dead. When the narrator suggests otherwise, the argument escalates in terms of which of their cultures is closer to the West, and this is measured by their capacity for warfare: 'So there we were, the Imam and I, delegates from two superseded civilizations vying with each other to lay claim to the violence of the West. . . . We were both travelling, he and I: we were travelling in the West . . . the West meant only this—science and tanks and guns and bombs' (ibid: 11). In the face of the realization that he envies the West, the narrator is given another lesson in ethics by Khameez the Rat, who leads him away from the conflict and comforts him by promising that he will visit but with a twinkle adds, 'But if I die, you must bury me' (ibid: 12).

VERNACULAR COSMOPOLITANISM

Another way of signaling a difference from earlier forms of elitist or *banal* cosmopolitanism (dedicated to consumption) is the term *vernacular cosmopolitanism*. But what does it attempt to capture? Vernacular cosmopolitanism encompasses everyday cosmopolitanism as well as a cosmopolitanism from below: a subaltern cosmopolitanism that makes claims for the recognition of the cosmopolitan nature (interactions with globalization) that are associated with groups that have been ruthlessly marginalized by nationalist enterprises—immigrants, refugees, asylum seekers, itinerant labour groups (*Gastarbeiter*) seeking work across the world within contexts of acute vulnerability (Nyers 2003; Tyler 2013). The oxymoronic dynamic of the phrase reflects the double movement within these debates. Sheldon Pollock points out that by including both the privileged world of the Greek *polis* and the Roman *verna*, or house-born slave, the phrase purposefully signals its inherent contradiction (Pollock 2002). And this is precisely its appeal.[20] In Homi Bhabha's (possible) coinage of the phrase, the concept attempts to capture the 'growing, global gulf between political citizenship, still largely negotiated in "national" and statist terms, and cultural citizenship which is often community-centred, transnational, diasporic, hybrid' (Bhabha 2002: 25). Bhabha also associates this concept with minorities who don't necessarily wish to claim majoritarianism and whose defining impetus is that of translating across cultures in an economy marked by iteration rather than teleology (Bhabha 1996). The way Bhabha structures these arguments pertains to his familiar dyad: the performative and pedagogical nation in which adding to does not mean adding up. Within cultural theory specifically, cosmopolitanism represents an impetus to use the literary and cultural productions of artists from those marginalized or subaltern groups as an entry point to question the supposed discreteness and homogeneity of dominant (rather than emergent) national cultures as well as the universality of globalization.[21] The claims are modest ones: to attempt to de-centre one's own vision of the world in order to see flaws that include an acute perception of unequal global power relations. Paul Gilroy names this approach '"vulgar" or "demotic" cosmopolitanism' (2006: 67).

Such a perspective is also captured in Stuart Hall's plea for what he terms an 'agnostic democratic process':

> We witness the situation of communities that are not simply isolated, atomistic individuals, nor are they well-bounded, singular, separated communities. We are in that open space that requires a kind of vernacular cosmopolitanism, that is to say a cosmopolitanism that is aware of the limitations of any one culture or any one identity and that is radically aware of its insufficiency in governing a wider society, but which nevertheless is not prepared to rescind its claims to the traces of difference, which makes its life important. (Hall 2002: 30)

Part of formulating a critical cosmopolitan pedagogy would be to point out that in fact all cosmopolitanisms are vernacular, and so the methodology would be to concentrate on the ways in which these supposedly vernacular texts (texts rooted in the vernacular) open up a different engagement with the world.[22] There is no question that this is an enterprise framed by utopianism, but this does not mean that it is blind to political hierarchies and global inequities. Peter Nyers's and Imogen Tyler's work on abject cosmopolitanism are cases in point.[23] Acknowledging these traces of difference, without their adding up to a master narrative or perspective, is at stake here.[24]

POST-MULTICULTURALISM

These kinds of perspectives also emerge from those diasporic figures who have been designated multicultural in some national contexts and leads to the question: What are the intersections of cosmopolitanism and multiculturalism? With their rhizomatic roots in diaspora, post-multicultural writers/artists connect the post–nation-state to the global in new ways: They redefine the nation as well as redefining and critiquing the global by helping to dislodge the sense of entitlement held by dominant groups. As Nicolas Bourriaud suggests in his concept of a radicant aesthetics:

> And yet the immigrant, the exile, the tourist, and the urban wanderer are the dominant figures of contemporary culture . . . one might say that the individual of those early years of the twenty-first century resembles those plants that do not depend on a single root but advance in all direction on whatever surfaces present themselves . . . It translates itself into the terms of the space in which it moves . . . caught between the need for a connection with its environment and the forces of uprooting, between globalization and singularity, between identity and opening to the other. It defines the subject as an object of negotiation. (Bourriaud 2009: 51)

However, as I suggested in 'Negotiating a Politics of Prepositions', how might one move from the old dynamics of state multiculturalism to new conceptualizations of this field as post-multicultural? One approach is to use the 'post' in Lyotard's manner of going back to ask what was left out in the various constructions of multiculturalism in its double usage: first, as a way for states to manage difference, and second, the attempts by various groups and individuals who felt excluded from national formations to argue for their own supplementary inclusions. Lyotard's logic was that the condition of postmodernism consists in part of going back to elements not taken up by modernism, so that the 'post' of postmodernism becomes not simply a future orientation so much as the future anterior (the future in the past or back to the future) structured by anamnesis, a recollection or going back that discovers other possibilities for alternatives to the period and movement we have come to call modernism.[25] In other words, in this precondition to modernism, we would not find the grand narratives of nationalism or internationalism, or even of West and non-West, but the *petits récits* of those differences within: ethnicity, indigeneity, and gender, all of which had, of course, always been lurking there. I am suggesting that inside these vernaculars we need to expose the cosmopolitan dimensions that connect us to a world that should not remain fully mediated by the nation-state or by globalization. My argument is that what was left out of the multiculturalism we know was the immanent cosmopolitan element, something that draws us into the world via the perspectives of those minority ethnics. Much of the longer study explores what I mean by finding the cosmopolitan in the vernacular that comes to us from the spaces we used to call multicultural.

CONCLUSION

All of these debates have at their core attempts to imagine fully the contradictory tensions that inhabit considerations of the one and the many: Bhabha's adding to does not mean adding up. Critical cosmopolitanism enables this tension to exist constructively by harnessing a logic of the oxymoron, and, not surprisingly, writers and artists have presented us with ways of imaging and imagining this dynamic. The new cosmopolitan cultural texts that elaborate and animate statistical data reach out to us from those cages[26] that too often comprise the ethnic and racialized dimensions of multiculturalism. A critical methodology on cosmopolitan literature would deal both with post-multicultural writers, who translate between very local and global sites, and those international writers who often write from metropolitan locations and offer a grammar to other cultures in terms of much-needed transnational cultural literacies that help undermine the current increasing polarization of belief systems across the world.

NOTES

1. In Derrida's (1976) sense of a link that is also a break.
2. A prime example of such a 'multicultural' writer is recent Nobel prize–winner Herta Müller. See Gunew 2013.
3. The collection was based on a special issue of the journal *Cultural Politics*, and a number of the names included have gone on to publish longer studies of neo-cosmopolitanism.
4. One exception, Tim Brennan, has been highly critical of the neo-cosmopolitan debates for some time and has identified them as largely synonymous with a globalized Americanization, including the fetishization of elite cosmo-celebratory figures such as Salman Rushdie or Amitav Ghosh, who, according to him, have become the iconic representatives of so-called Third World cultures.

5. I am struck by the thought that this approach is somewhat reminiscent of the Leavisite cultivation of a particular sensibility that was part of my own formative training in Australia. It may be that such competing forms of the civilizing mission are an inescapable part of any literary pedagogy, whether we like to admit it or not.

6. That image of a *cordon sanitaire* has gained horrific materialization recently in the Australian government's processing of refugees and asylum seekers in off-shore sites, thus creating unimaginable suffering to those who suffer already.

7. The term *migritude* is Shailja Patel's (2010) inspired coinage. My thanks to Susan Gingell for alerting me to her work.

8. Spivak invokes the 'planetary' in the final chapter of her *Death of a Discipline* as well as in 'Imperative to Re-imagine the Planet' in *An Aesthetic Education in the Era of Globalization*.

9. Spivak is at pains to point out that she is not speaking for Islam but merely trying to conceptualize a different ethical relationship from those associated with arguing for human rights. Such a dynamic is also at the centre of recent turns in critical race theory. Critical race theorists such as, for example, Denise Ferreira da Silva, have exposed within Western philosophy a logic in which racialized others such as slaves and the indigenous (we might add asylum seekers) are the constitutive elements of abjection upon which Western white subjectivity is founded. It is a trend in critical race theory that began perhaps with the 'necropolitics' of Achille Mbembe illustrating that the discourse of human rights, the desire for marginalized groups to be 'included' are misplaced enterprises because such groups *are* constitutively included in a conceptual system that owes its very ontological existence to their racialized abjection.

10. See, for example, Marisol de la Cadena's (2010) work here.

11. For example, Tim Brennan (2001).

12. Papastergiadis (2012) also tends to privilege collective arts practices over individual ones in *Cosmopolitanism and Culture*.

13. See, for example, the work of the Deleuzian feminist philosopher Rosi Braidotti (2011).

14. Adichie has distanced herself from the term 'Afropolitan' coined by Taye Selasie to counter the prevalent depictions of Africans as eternal victims.

15. The reference is to the following 2002 report: 'More than 200 people at the bleak desert centre began a hunger strike eight days ago. Immigration Minister Philip Ruddock ordered five children removed from the camp to protect them from having their lips sewn together like those of other children in the protest' (Refugees).

16. It is interesting here to consider the role of the oral/acoustic. Derrida spends a lot of time registering the 'accent' as a sign of 'impurity' within one's mother tongue.

17. For example, one of the chapters in the longer study analyses the thematization of 'English' in books written by Chinese authors both from the mainland and the diaspora.

18. There is also the work of Australian Aboriginal writer Kim Scott, whose latest novel, *That Deadman Dance*, puts indigenous world views (views of the world) at the centre in order to enable the indigenous inhabitants of global empires to assert their rights to have rights or to decolonize their own history. See Brewster interview (2012).

19. This resonates with Bishnupriya Ghosh's analysis of the contemporary Indian novel that identifies fourth-generation writers in English as 'cosmopolitical writers [who] render' India 'communicable' to a global audience' (2004: 50).

20. Pollock also points out the very different histories of vernacularization in Europe and South Asia as a way of warning against the reification of either 'vernacular' or 'cosmopolitan'.

21. One must remember that not all nationalisms are created equal, and an emergent nationalism striving for independence is a very different dynamic from an established nationalism (Calhoun 2007).

22. For example, towards more cellular modes of representation, something Schoene associates with the work of Hardt and Negri (Schoene 2009: 27).

23. But see Imogen Tyler's critique of abject cosmopolitanism as ignoring its material embodiments in ways that preclude agency (Tyler 2013). Tyler's notion of 'social abjection' is now a book-length study.

24. Elsewhere I have referred to the process of suggesting differences without producing comprehensive answers as a stammering pedagogy (Gunew 2004).

25. Tu comprends qu'ainsi compris, le 'post-' de 'postmoderne' ne signifie pas un mouvement de come back, de flash back, de feed back, c'est-à-dire de repetition, mais un process en 'ana-', un process d'analyse, d'anamnèse, d'anagogie, et d'anamorphose, qui élabore un 'oubli initial' (Lyotard 1986: 126). (My trans.: You understand that when understood like that, the 'post' of the postmodern does not mean a movement as in come-back, flash-back, feed-back, that is to say a repetition, but a process of 'ana', a process of analysis, anamnesis, anagogy, anamorphosis, which elaborates on an 'initial forgetting'.)

26. Ghassan Hage's (2003) productive image of 'ethnic caging' in Australian culture is pertinent here.

BIBLIOGRAPHY

Adichie, C. (2013). *Americanah*. Toronto: Knopf Canada.

Anderson, B. (1983). *Imagined Communities: Reflections on the Origins and Spread of Nationalisms*. London: Verso.

Appiah, K. A. (2006). *Cosmopolitanism: Ethics in a World of Strangers*. New York: Norton.

Attali, J. (1977). *Noise: The Political Economy of Music*. Minneapolis: University of Minnesota Press.

Beck, U. (1998.) 'The Cosmopolitan Manifesto'. *New Statesman* 127, 4377, 28–30.

Bhabha, H. K. (1996). 'Unsatisfied: Notes on Vernacular Cosmopolitanism' in L. Garcia-Moreno and P. C. Pfeiffer (eds.) *Text and Narration: Cross-Disciplinary Essays on Cultural and National Identities*. Columbia, SC: Camden, 191–207.

———, and Comaroff, J. (2002). 'Speaking of Postcoloniality, in the Continuous Present: A Conversation' in D. T. Goldberg and A. Quayson (eds.) *Relocating Postcolonialism*. Oxford: Blackwell, 15–46.

Bourriaud, N. (2009). *The Radicant* translated by J. Gussen and L. Portent. New York: Lukas & Sternberg.

Braidotti, R. (2011). *Nomadic Subjects: Embodiment and Sexual Difference in Contemporary Feminist Theory* (2nd ed.). New York: Columbia University Press.

Brennan, T. (2001). 'Cosmopolitanism and Internationalism'. *New Left Review* 7 (Jan/Feb): 75–84.

Brewster, A. (2012). 'Can You Anchor a Shimmering Nation State via Regional Indigenous Roots?' Kim Scott talks to Anne Brewster about *That Deadman Dance, Cultural Studies Review* 18.1 (March): 228–46.

Cadena, M. de la (2010). 'Indigenous Cosmopolitics in the Andes: Conceptual Reflections Beyond "Politics"' *Cultural Anthropology* 25.2, 334–70.

Calhoun, C. (2007). *Nations Matter: Culture, History, and the Cosmopolitan Dream*. London: Routledge.

Casanova, P. (2004). *The World Republic of Letters* translated by M. B. DeBevoise. Cambridge, MA: Harvard University Press.

Chakrabarty, D. (2000). *Provincializing Europe: Postcolonial Thought and Historical Difference*. New Jersey: Princeton University Press.

Cheah, P. (2012) 'What is a World? On World Literature as World-making Activity' in G. Delanty (ed.) *The Routledge Handbook of Cosmopolitan Studies*. London and New York: Routledge, 138–49.

———, and Robbins, B. (eds.) (1998). *Cosmopolitics: Thinking and Feeling Beyond the Nation*. Minneapolis: University of Minnesota Press.

Chen, M. Y. (2012) *Animacies: Biopolitics, Racial Mattering, and Queer Affect*. Durham and London: Duke University Press.

Clarke, M. B. (2014). *Foreign Soil*. Sydney: Hachette.

Dällenbach, L. (1989). *The Mirror in the Text* translated by J. Whiteley and E. Hughes. Chicago: University of Chicago Press.

Delanty, G. (2012). 'The Idea of Critical Cosmopolitanism' in G. Delanty (ed.) *The Routledge Handbook of Cosmopolitan Studies*. London and New York: Routledge, 38–46.

Derrida, J. (1976). 'The Hinge [La Brisure]' in *Of Grammatology* translated by G. C. Spivak. Baltimore: Johns Hopkins Press, 65–73.

———. (1998). *Monolingualism of the Other or The Prosthesis of Origin* translated by Patrick Mensah. Stanford, CA: Stanford University Press.

Gaonkar, D. P. (ed.) (2001). *Alternative Modernities*. Durham and London: Duke University Press.

Ghosh, A. (1992). *In an Antique Land*. London: Granta Books.

———. (2010). 'The Imam and the Indian' in *The Imam and the Indian: Prose Pieces*. London: Penguin, 1–12.

Ghosh, B. (2004). *When Borne Across: Literary Cosmopolitics in the Contemporary Indian Novel*. New Brunswick: Rutgers University Press.

Gilroy, P. (2006). *After Empire: Melancholia or Convivial Culture?* New York: Routledge.

Gunew, S. (1994). *Framing Marginality: Multicultural Literary Studies*. Interpretations Series. Melbourne: Melbourne University Press.

———. (2003). 'The Home of Language: A Pedagogy of the Stammer' in S. Ahmed, C. Castaneda, A-M Fortier, and M. Sheller (eds.) *Uprootings/Regroundings: Questions of Home and Migration*. Oxford: Berg, 41–58.

———. (2004). *Haunted Nations: The Colonial Dimensions of Multiculturalisms*. London: Routledge.

———. (2013). 'Estrangement as Pedagogy: The Cosmopolitan Vernacular' in R. Braidotti, P. Hanafin, and B. Blaagard (eds.) *After Cosmopolitanism*. London: Routledge/ GlassHouse Books, 132–48.

Hage, G. (2003). *Against Paranoid Nationalism: Searching for Hope in a Shrinking Society*. Annandale, NSW: Pluto.

Hall, S. (2002). 'Political Belonging in a World of Multiple Identities' in S. Vertovec and R. Cohen (eds.) *Conceiving Cosmopolitanism: Theory, Context, and Practice*. Oxford: Oxford University Press, 25–31.

Lazarus, N. (2011). 'Cosmopolitanism and the Specificity of the Local in World Literature'. *Journal of Commonwealth Literature*, 46.1, 119–37.

Lyotard, J-F. (1986). *Le Postmoderne éxpliqué aux enfants: Correspondance 1982-1985*. Paris: Galilée.

Malouf, D. (1986). 'A Foot in the Stream' in *12 Edmonstone Street*. London: Penguin, 103–22.

Morrison, T. (1992). *Playing in the Dark: Whiteness and the Literary Imagination*. Cambridge, MA: Harvard University Press.

Nyers, P. (2003). 'Abject Cosmopolitanism: The Politics of Protection in the Anti-deportation Movement'. *Third World Quarterly* 24, 6, 1069–93.

Papastergiadis, N. (2012). *Cosmopolitanism and Culture*. Cambridge: Polity Press.

Patel, S. (2010). *Migritude*. New York: Kaya Press.

Phillips, C. (2005). *A Distant Shore*. London: Vintage.

Pollock, S. (2000). 'Cosmopolitan and Vernacular in History'. *Public Culture* 12.3 Durham: Duke, 591–625.

———. 2002. 'Cosmopolitan and Vernacular in History' in C. A. Breckenridge, S. Pollock, H. K. Bhabha, and D. Chakrabarty (eds.) *Cosmopolitanism*. Durham and London: Duke University Press, 15–53.

'Refugees drink detergent as Australian protest grows' *Globe & Mail*, 24 January 2002, A, 14.

Schoene, B. (2009). *The Cosmopolitan Novel*. Edinburgh: Edinburgh University Press.

Serres, M. (1982). *The Parasite*. Baltimore: Johns Hopkins University Press.

Silva, D. F. da (2007). *Toward a Global Idea of Race*. Minneapolis: University of Minnesota Press.

Spencer, R. (2011). *Cosmopolitan Criticism and Postcolonial Literature*. London: Palgrave Macmillan.

Spivak, G. (2003). *Death of a Discipline*. New York: Columbia University Press.

———. (2012). 'Imperative to Re-imagine the Planet' in *An Aesthetic Education in the Era of Globalization*. Cambridge, MA: Harvard University Press, 335–50.

Tyler, I. (2013). 'Social Abjection' in *Revolting Subjects: Social Abjection and Resistance in Neoliberal Britain*. London: Zed Books, 19–47.

Vardoulakis, D. (2008). 'The "Poor Thing": The Cosmopolitan in Alasdair Gray's *Poor Things*'. *SubStance* 117, 37.3, 137–51.

FIVE

Writing—Through a Critical Cosmopolitan Lens

Anne Surma

In Kigali, the capital of Rwanda, a small group of women run their business out of a bus station, using manual typewriters to produce letters, reports, CVs, and fiction (Kwibuka 2013). The women are valued by their clients because they are knowledgeable and particularly proficient in producing administrative correspondence in 'crystal clear Kinyarwanda' (Kwibuka 2013). As part of its nation-building attempts following the genocide of the 1990s, English became the official language in Rwanda. However, while 90 percent of the population speaks Kinyarwanda, 8 percent speak French, and only 4 percent—principally the nation's ruling elite—speak English (Africa Portal 2012). However, the women's work is now under threat since a shop offering print and Internet services has opened behind their wooden bench 'office'; as well, street vending is banned, so the women risk being removed by the city's officials at any time.

This story provides a salutary reminder of how writing practices have been radically transformed by globalization processes. At the same time, it reminds us that writing, for all its potential for dissemination via myriad advanced technologies and media, is still a material, social practice, one motivated by specific purposes and having specific direct and indirect impacts. The Kigali typists and the writing they do represent a local and intimate social practice and a language (spoken by the majority of the population), which assert their interdependence, significance, and value alongside more technologically sophisticated, systematized communications processes, infrastructure, and exchange. However, there is no question that this local practice is dynamically tied to and modified by changes at a global level, and that it is becoming increasingly marginalized as an officially recognized means of communicating with others.

As a trope for the focus of this chapter, the context and activities of the Kigali typists can be interpreted from a critical cosmopolitan perspective, where writing in the local language is interpreted as a practice of the ethics of care. This is not intended to be a sentimental vision, however. Rather, it is one situated in a specific material and historical context in dialectical tension with competing interests and relationships, alternative languages, and modes of writing through local and global networks. In a context of globalization, involving the accelerated movements and flows of people, finance, trade, services, ideas, and communications across local, national, and international boundaries, the vernacular language of care, human interdependence, and responsibility may be subdued or even stymied. Thus the writing that the Kigali typists do in Kinyarwanda, the local language, is an expression of how care for others plays an integral part in supporting and enriching local and, even if indirectly, global interactions. That the practice and value of care struggles to survive and risks being subdued in a world where economic, corporate, or political expediencies have gained prominence does not lessen its centrality as a means of connecting us to and enriching our relationships with one another. In this chapter, I argue that writing (regardless of form or mode) calls up or signifies a relationship with and responsibility to the other, even when it explicitly denies it, and I aim to show that writing, as an encounter with the other, also has the potential to resist the dehumanizing and decontextualizing effects of a market economy-driven globalization.

I first outline my critical cosmopolitan approach to writing, one developed by drawing together threads from and reweaving the work of key theorists. I then turn to an analysis of recent writing on asylum seekers by the Australian Government. Here the intention is to demonstrate the part writing plays in articulating and shaping the nation's relationship with asylum seekers in a globalized environment. I explore how an increasingly strident, textual government voice, one that denies the humanity of the ('foreign', non-citizen) other, that elides an obligation to vulnerable subjects, and that insists on a parochial and restrictive notion of hospitality and home, is nonetheless insistently shadowed and disrupted by the responsibility to care and to forge caring, cosmopolitan relations with others far and near.

COSMOPOLITANISM AND WRITING

For professional writers, the proliferation of writing technologies (in tandem with other aspects of cultural change) has shifted the ways we can communicate with others—particularly in terms of the diverse modes, relative speeds, and the level of attention we might give to our writing activities.[1] Those writing technologies have also influenced the ways we might imagine, relate to, understand, or misunderstand both one another and the worlds we inhabit, through the texts we write and read. Thus, writing constitutes a form of human subjectivity, however disguised that may be, since it necessarily addresses the other, even when indirectly, unwittingly, or even unwillingly. This pivotal, relational dimension of language calls up its ethical aspect, and the question of a writer's obligations. In the global context of writing, the focus and extent of—and the pull between—several perhaps rival responsibilities to different (known and unknown) others becomes ever more a part of reflecting on communicative practices in general, and writing in particular.

Therefore, a key challenge today, in evaluating and in doing writing in professional and public contexts, is not merely to affirm or reaffirm the 'I' or the 'we' (in the face of the other)—which is increasingly the impulse and the prerogative of voices competing for attention in a consumerist and aggressively promotional Western culture. Paradoxically, given the fragility and indeterminacy (environmental, economic, political, and social) of the period in which we live, the ever-growing pressure facing writers, whether we are engaged in political, corporate, or community writing—in fact, most non-fiction writing—is the expectation that we will be unequivocal (or univocal), that we will eschew ambivalence and contingency in favour of bold, singular statements that declare 'truths' and assert 'how things really are'. We may, therefore, often feel compelled to write in abstractions and euphemisms, particularly if how things really are might cast us in a less than positive light or provoke reflection on the tensions and conflicts inherent in our claims. Situated, as this compulsion is, in a historical moment of accelerated speed, of present-ness, of the intensification and power of the image (and the word as image), it becomes important to interrogate the conceptions of, approaches to, and practices of writing that support, enable, and reinforce those impulses.

Kwame Appiah helps us understand that being a citizen of the world, a cosmopolitan, means being aware that we thereby have ties with and obligations to others beyond our own families, coworkers, compatriots. It also means appreciating the value of the specific lives and lifestyles of others (Appiah 2006: xv). This is not to suggest that cosmopolitanism attempts to reduce everything to the singular or the unified. On the contrary, and as Seyla Benhabib points out, it is 'a philosophical project of mediations, not of reductions or of totalizations' (Benhabib 2006: 20). By extension, Craig Calhoun remarks that cosmopolitanism 'is belonging to a social class able to identify itself with the universal' (2008: 440).

Language in general and writing in particular are means by which the individual and social relationships that constitute a cosmopolitan world can be enacted, imagined, realized, critiqued, and transformed. As much as anything, an exploration of cosmopolitanism as a philosophical and ethical commitment encourages us to reflect more deeply on what is important and valuable, exciting and potentially transformative and compelling about writing, as a critical, careful, and self-reflexive process (rather than merely an efficient skill or slick technique), and as a vital social practice in a global context. Most significantly, it highlights writing today, in a networked society, as a situated, dynamic, complex activity, involving the ongoing potential for mundane or vigorous, restricted or inclusive interactions—extrapolations, discussions, claims, refutations, responses, arguments, edits, rewrites, paraphrases, agreements, disagreements, affirmations—between writers and readers across various times and spaces. It involves interlocutors in obligations and responsibilities that they may not have actively sought and that they may wish or choose to ignore, but that are nonetheless real. The focus or concerns of writing may well be immediate, local, clear, and specific, but its impacts may well also be long-term or retrospective, global, uncertain, and wide-ranging. Cosmopolitanism underscores the idea that writers do writing in ethically ambivalent contexts, that they must confront and work within the constraints (whether economic, political, professional, institutional, legal, cultural, ethnic, or social) and conventions of their subjective or representative positions. It also highlights the way in which writing that merely rehearses and reiterates the same prejudices, or that entrenches the I/we while obscuring or objectifying the other/you, or that refuses to acknowledge the repercussions it may generate, is likely to be merely promotional, abstract, or both.

A critical cosmopolitan approach to doing and evaluating writing, as I conceive it, motivates reflexivity about the reach and value of writing and of writers (and, by extension, readers) as agents, actively responsible for and engaged in contact with (often unknown) others. It also provokes a means of imagining approaches to and practices of professional writing carried out in contexts in which local and global circumstances, events, and identities are imbricated. In this way, various discourses, rhetoric, and the narratives that animate them are mobilized in textual representations to serve particular interests and to marginalize others.

Writing responsibly in a cosmopolitan context demands the use of imagination: the capacity to think and feel and respond virtually, beyond one's own time and place and into another's. It involves reading between the lines; transgressing borders; inscribing and reading a world and set of relationships that may capture but must also exceed our immediate context and concerns, the taken-for-granted ways of our particular culture, the familiarity and predictability of our face-to-face encounters. Seen in this way, the act of imagining, one could argue, is thus inherently cosmopolitan. As professional writers, our imaginings of the other are at least partly constructed and then publicly articulated through the discursive and rhetorical choices we make. Discourses may work to expand or restrict the imaginative, cosmopolitan horizons we envision. As Norman Fairclough observes, 'Discourses include representations of how things are and have been, as well as imaginaries—representations of how things might or could or should be' (Fairclough 2003: 207). In turn, rhetoric brings us to the constituent persuasive elements of the text (produced by the writer and interpreted by the reader), and to a focus on the inscribed and interpretable impacts and effects (semiotic, practical, subjective, cultural, and global) of texts (constituted by discourses) produced, circulated, and read in specific contexts. However, both discourses, and the rhetorical devices that structure and organize them, remain abstract and ahistorical concepts until they are narrativized. If we consider narrative, at its simplest, as a situated account or story of the relationships and interactions between people, places, and events in time, then we can see the ways in which discourses become meaningful as they are integrated into and help to structure narrative. Thus, discourses are never neutral in their effects. They construct the world in particular ways. The manner and extent to which a given discourse or set of discourses are harnessed to represent the stories of particular individuals, places, and times will help determine what that narrative account might mean, how it may represent a persuasive version of reality. Depending on whose voice is telling the story, certain discourses are thereby likely to be privileged over others. In professional and public writing, our narratives help to frame and organize the relationships we have or wish to have with our interlocutors—they include or preclude the forging of contact across difference.

The critical turn in cosmopolitanism thus appreciates the political, economic, and cultural ambivalences and competing interests involved in the obligation to write responsibly in relation to locally and globally situated others, in public and professional contexts. On this view, a writer also must always be a different reader—in other words, a self-critical and reflexive reader of her own and others' writing practices, aware of the ways in which textual meanings and interpretations must be contested and contestable, transformative and transformable. Writing and the texts to which it gives rise are each inseparable from the material spaces and temporalities in which writing is developed and texts disseminated. Gerard Delanty uses the term *critical cosmopolitanism* to conceptualize the social world 'as an open horizon in which new cultural models take shape' (2006: 27). And Marianna Papastephanou claims that 'critical cosmopolitanism requires us to be at home with, and *respond* to, the hiss of history' (2011: 604; italics in original). Further, the reflective, critical, and dialogic disposition of this process is reinforced in reference to that dimension of cosmopolitanism involving 'the creation and articulation of communicative models of world openness in which societies undergo transformation' (Delanty 2006: 35; see also 2009: 251–52). The centrality of communicating to the process of inhabiting a critical cosmopolitan stance here suggests the significance of understanding and evaluating writing in relation to this ongoing project, particularly since the modes, purposes, and practices of writing, as means of forging contact and interacting with or representing or eliding one's own and the lives and worlds of others, have a potential reach and impact unimaginable just a couple of decades ago.

The shifting of local and global boundaries also influences and is influenced by the norms and conventions that guide, structure, and focus our writing practices, wherever we write: in local online or offline community contexts; within or on behalf of organizational, institutional, or corporate entities; or when representing government, private sector, or community interests. The boundaries that may delimit or expand writing approaches, practices, and effects are grammatical, syntactical, and semantic, as well as ethical and imaginative, discursive, and rhetorical. And just as cosmopolitanism can motivate our reflections on and critique of the functions and effects of globalization in terms of our relationships with others, so can it be harnessed to consider, question, and adapt our writing both alongside and in relation to other visual, oral, aural, and multimodal texts in a globalized world.

COSMOPOLITAN CARE

A feminist ethics of care, I argue, is pivotal to writing approaches and practices themselves, as well as to writing about issues related to responsibilities to care. In his discussion of critical cosmopolitanism, Delanty refers briefly to the importance of care to the cosmopolitan imagination (see, for example, 2009: 7). However, scholars such as Virginia Held and Fiona Robinson extend a feminist ethics of care into the global arena to represent what I read as a specifically imaginative and productive rendering of a contextualized cosmopolitanism. As Robinson says, a feminist ethics of care treats human beings 'not as autonomous subjects, but as being embedded in networks and relationships of care' (Robinson 2009). It determinedly situates discussions about relations between self and other at the centre of what we might imagine as valuable and important in both private and public life. Held puts it succinctly when she remarks that people are always and everywhere 'relational and . . . interdependent' (Held 2006: 156). The foundation for these relationships is grounded in an awareness of the fact that, as she points out, 'all persons need care for at least their early years. Prospects for human progress and flourishing hinge fundamentally on the care that those needing it receive, and the ethics of care stresses the moral force of the responsibility to respond to the needs of the dependent' (2006: 10). Held also argues that an ethics of care helps highlight the connections between people as emotionally rich and mutually sustaining relations of interdependence, not as exclusively rationally based or as centred on the lone individual (or self-contained person or private organization or single society). It is the emotions, Held argues, such as empathy, sensitivity, and responsiveness, that are better guides to what we should or shouldn't do, in moral terms (2006: 157). As practice and as a value, an ethics of care 'advocates attention to particulars, appreciation of context, narrative understanding, and communication and dialogue in moral deliberation, suspecting that the more general and abstract the recommendation, the less adequate for actual guidance' (2006: 157–58). The communicative dimension of care ethics is salient in these words. Held's discussion of an ethics of care in a global context as well reminds us how some of our responsibilities to care are not chosen but are nonetheless real and emerge from our social positioning and historical embeddedness (2006: 156). Thus caring relations 'are not limited to the personal contexts of family and friends. They can extend to fellow members of groups of various kinds, to fellow citizens, and beyond. We can, for instance, develop caring relations for persons who are suffering deprivation in distant parts of the globe' (2006: 157).

Just as Held draws a distinction as well as shows the overlap between caring as an attitude or disposition and caring as an activity (2006: 30–31), I do the same in my focus on care as integral to cosmopolitan approaches to, practices of, and reflections on writing in order to evoke the integral relation between care's ethical and substantive dimensions.

CARING ABOUT THE DISPLACED OTHER: AUSTRALIA'S ASYLUM SEEKERS

According to a recent report from the United Nations High Commissioner for Refugees (UNHCR), over fifty million people around the world are displaced—either taking refuge in camps or moving across borders—on the move because they are pushed by poverty, conflict, or fear of persecution (UNHCR 2014). The global movement of refugees and asylum seekers is inherently messy and chaotic, and largely impossible to 'manage' neatly (University of South Australia 2013: 5). Nonetheless, as the number of displaced people increases (UNHCR 2014: 6), powerful states are bolstering the legal, policy, military, discursive, and rhetorical barriers preventing asylum seekers from entering their territory.[2] The neoliberal push of globalization, fuelled by the corporate and governmental interests directing the market economy and the growth and protection of private interests, reconfigures and reinforces the concept of borders in general, and state borders in particular, as sites not of an encounter with the other but of economic competition and oppositional power struggle. In this process, dispossessed people are not only severely disadvantaged, but they are bound to lose.

In Australia in the twenty-first century, successive (Coalition, Labor, and again Coalition) governments, in an attempt to deter would-be asylum seekers arriving by boat, have mobilized increasingly punitive policies and laws, and run 'information' campaigns via print, electronic, and social media aiming to deter asylum seekers' passage. Between 2011 and 2013, the number of boat arrivals on Australian shores significantly increased. As a result, the fate of asylum seekers became a hotly contested election campaign issue between the major parties, each aiming to outdo the other by promising to introduce more punitive policies to deter boat arrivals (Parliament of Australia 2014). The Coalition party's electoral promise to 'stop the boats' arguably played a significant part in ensuring its victory at the polls in September 2013.[3]

Since that time, mainstream debate on the nation's treatment of asylum seekers has progressively shifted. Reshaping the discourse relating to the arrival by boat of asylum seekers to one of national security, the government has justified its restriction of information dissemination or engagement in open discussion about asylum seeker policy, attempted boat arrivals, and the status and welfare of asylum seekers being held in offshore detention. Prime Minister Tony Abbott and Immigration Minister Scott Morrison's remarks on the issue are largely confined to infrequent and guarded commentary in carefully managed press briefings or, much less frequently, in more spontaneous response to media questions. These discursive approaches heavily restrict the opportunities for asylum seekers to be represented or imagined as situated human subjects, to establish relationships with and to engage in interactions with the people of those states through which they pass and in which they seek refuge. Thus, the respective parts played by communicating in general, and writing in particular, in terms of inhibiting or precluding caring or relational connections between the Australian Government, the wider (national and international) community, and asylum seekers cannot be underestimated.

In the discussion that follows, I look at selected texts from three Australian Government-led campaigns to 'stop the boats' and to 'smash the business model' (ABC 2011) of people smugglers bringing asylum seekers to Australia by sea.[4] My comments and analysis are motivated and organized by the critical cosmopolitan framework outlined above. I highlight the ways in which writing, in addressing (would-be) asylum seekers, Australian citizens, and (albeit indirectly) the global community, has been deployed progressively to discipline and delimit the responsibility of individuals, government, and community to imagine and care for others beyond national borders. However, I also show how a critical cosmopolitan orientation enables us to reimagine the social practice of writing as folding in, however obliquely, our obligations to (care for) the other.

As a means of publicizing changes in policy aimed at restricting the rights of asylum seekers who arrive on Australian shores, the campaign launched by the Labor Government in 2012 used the banner of 'No Advantage' to communicate its key messages of deterrence, disseminated via YouTube, website, online, and hard copy posters and brochures, published in English but also in Arabic, Dari, Farsi, Pashto, Sinhalese, and Tamil.

The text from the 'No Advantage' brochure reads as follows:

> Legislation passed now enables Australia to transfer asylum seekers who arrive by boat to regional countries. People's claims will be processed no faster than those people waiting in refugee camps in other countries. Changes are being made to Australia's migration program which means people who come by boat will no longer be able to sponsor family members to Australia under the special humanitarian program. There is no guarantee people found to be refugees will be resettled in Australia.
>
> There is no advantage in taking a people smuggler's boat instead of applying for a refugee visa through regular channels.
>
> The key message to those seeking to use people smugglers to make the dangerous sea voyage to Australia is: do not get on that boat.
>
> Australians are hospitable people and believe in honouring their international protection obligations.
>
> However, Australia is committed to breaking the smugglers' business model and the trade in human misery on which the smugglers rely. Too many people seeking asylum have died on their way to Australia by boat—this has to stop.
>
> Anyone thinking about engaging people smugglers should think twice about spending significant amounts of money to be smuggled by sea to Australia in the knowledge they will gain no advantage over applying through normal channels.
>
> Irregular migration and people smuggling are global and regional problems that cannot be solved by one country alone, but must be tackled in partnership with other countries.
>
> Governments from countries in the region have agreed that irregular movement facilitated by people smugglers should be eliminated and that countries should support opportunities for orderly migration.
>
> The arrangements into which Australia has committed to entering with Nauru and Papua New Guinea are based on that principle.
>
> Australians have a legitimate expectation that those seeking access to this country will be subject to a fair and orderly process.
>
> The government believes that people who are seeking to join family should apply through the appropriate processes, not pay people smugglers to bring them to Australia and to risk a perilous journey.[5]

The discursive and rhetorical version of the world privileged by the Australian Government in this and other similar documents is one of bizarrely disembodied 'orderly migration', tidy queues, legitimate pathways, 'regular' or 'normal channels', 'appropriate processes', and visa documentation. To facilitate this commitment to so-called orderliness, in

May 2013 legislation was passed to excise the Australian mainland from the migration zone (Grewcock 2014). This was not to distinguish between the places of arrival in Australia, but between the modes of arrival. In other words, the legislation applies to asylum seekers arriving by boat but not by plane. Anyone arriving in Australia by boat cannot now apply for asylum from Australia, but will be sent to offshore processing centres. Thus a legal move endorsed an increasingly dominant discursive and rhetorical political move: As far as people seeking refuge on Australia's shores are concerned, there are no such people as asylum seekers and there is no such place of asylum as Australia.

In contrast to all the orderliness outlined above, the term *irregular migration* (which has been defined in legal discourse),[6] and its associations with disorder and inappropriateness, is used in the document to set up particular attitudes to the other, and to attempt to deny our responsibilities to care for them. In other words, the rhetoric serves to reinforce the principle of otherness. Here, what distinguishes 'us' from 'them' and, by implication, what opposes 'us' to 'them' is 'their' location in disorder, irregularity, inappropriate means of migration, or illegitimate passage.

The brochure exposes the discursive, rhetorical, and practical refusal to view the other from an imaginative, cosmopolitan perspective. The writing does not, for the most part, admit the persistence of inequity, the different degrees and kinds of vulnerability experienced by different people, or our and others' different needs (for care). Rather, and with a nod to a truism from the country of 'the fair go', as Australia is popularly self-described, the assumption is made that we all operate on a level playing field, and all share the view that 'no advantage' should be shown to one group over another.

As a consequence, and in the face of the approach taken in the campaign as a whole, the single sentence admitting a predisposition to care embedded in the text can most readily be read as disingenuous or hollow: 'Australians are hospitable people and believe in honouring their international protection obligations'. However, if we make ironic sense of that sentence, then it disrupts or opens a fissure in an overwhelmingly rationalist and abstract text. Even if only intending to preempt charges of Australia's callousness and lack of empathy in failing to imagine and accommodate the needs of asylum seekers, the words 'Australians are hospitable people' can be read as affirming the significance of a discourse of care, and it can therefore help mobilize a resistance to (or a rewriting of) the sidelining or silencing of care in the rest of the text. Most importantly, it brings the idea of care back to its ethical and, in this context, cosmopolitan home. As Jacques Derrida asserts, 'Hospitality is culture itself and not simply one ethic amongst others. Insofar as it has to do with the *ethos*, that is, the residence, one's home, the familiar place of dwelling, inasmuch as it is a manner of being there, the manner in which we relate to ourselves and to others, to others as our own or as foreigners, *ethics* is *hospitality*; ethics is so thoroughly coextensive with the experience of hospitality' (Derrida 2001: 16–17; italics in original). To bring Derrida's idea home to Australia, we see that the government text both reasserts Australia's hospitality and denies it, in much the same way that 'Australia' both exists in the national imagination and yet denies its existence to certain 'irregular' others.

The next text for analysis might be read as rehearsing or extending this notion of hospitality—or rather Australia's inhospitability to others—through an alternative approach. The text in question actually carries very little writing at all, since it is a cartoon strip. This text (and the final one discussed below) was released under the umbrella of the Operation Sovereign Borders initiative, launched by the Coalition (conservative) Government when it came to power in September 2013.[7] The military-style operation, overseen by the Minister of Immigration and led by Lieutenant General Angus Campbell, has concentrated on stopping and, where possible, turning back boats carrying would-be asylum seekers making for Australia (Australian Government 2014). Consisting of YouTube video, newspaper advertisements, online posters, and fact sheets (with slightly different copy aimed at readers in and outside Australia, respectively), the campaign outlines how 'the rules have changed'. Specifically, boats carrying asylum seekers entering Australian waters will now be intercepted and removed. For those asylum seekers who manage to reach Australia, they will be sent to Nauru or Manus Island for processing and detention, and, reinforcing the Labor Government's July 2013 decision, they will never be permanently settled in Australia. The rules apply to everyone, including unaccompanied children.

Published in November 2013, the comic strip text is aimed at would-be Afghani asylum seekers. The only written statement/text in the cartoon is on the first page and (repeated on) the last page, in Dari and Pashto. A translation of the text reads: 'If you go to Australia on a boat without a visa, you will not be settled there'.

The eighteen-page comic strip tells the story of a young man.[8] It begins by showing his home (in Afghanistan) and his work as a mechanic in the family business. As he carries out repairs on old cars (dilapidated signs of the hand-me-down trappings of the developed world) in a ramshackle shed, he dreams of moving to a western metropolis, with expansive leafy vistas and high-rise buildings. He discusses the move with his parents who, though sad to see him go, give him money they have saved and stored in a suitcase to pay for his trip. He leaves home and takes a long bus trip to Pakistan and the Jinnah international airport, where he meets men who hand him the travel documents he needs for the journey by plane to (what might be) Indonesia. Here, after a series of phone calls, he meets up with a man, apparently a people smuggler, who shows him a photo of the boat on which he can travel to Australia. He boards the boat (far more rickety than the one in the photo he was shown), and we see his anxiety as he boards with many others and hands over his mobile phone to one of the crew. The boat travels across rough seas and is tossed around by the waves, through several frames. Those on board then spot an army patrol boat and hold their arms out to the vessel for help. Men in armoured gear and helmets rescue them and bring them to shore. After carrying out a body search on each passenger, border control personnel usher them onto a bus and take them to a processing centre, where they are enclosed behind wire and stood over by guards, as they're ushered into a room to be addressed, as they sit on the floor, by an official. The asylum seekers are then seen onto another bus, taken to an airport, and flown to an island (which could be Manus or Nauru). By this stage, the young man is shown to be feeling unhappy and distressed. They arrive at the detention centre, which comprises a number of large tents, flanked by stern-looking guards (arms folded or hands on hips). Inside the tents are rows of camp beds, on which the young man and his fellow asylum seekers sit despondently, shoulders slumped or with head in hands. During the night the young man is attacked by mosquitoes, and he thinks longingly of home (and the festivities and dancing he has left behind!). Meanwhile, his parents, too, look depressed and despondent, the workshop closed up, no business because their son is not there to do the work. The penultimate page is a single frame showing the man in the foreground, sitting in his tent, head in hand; his fellow travellers sit or lie, similarly in limbo. The final page shows in one frame the distraught face of the young man. In the frame alongside is a red cloudy sky and beneath it the Australian Government logo. Across the top of each frame, the text from the first page is repeated: 'If you go to Australia on a boat without a visa, you will not be settled there'.

There is much to be said about this comic strip, but I want to draw attention to three key points here: first, the impoverished imaginative process through which it reinforces notions both of the otherness of the other, as well as the other's apparent indistinguishability from the (Western) self; second, the process through which it graphically personifies a jingoism aiming to legitimize a lack of care and inhumane treatment of vulnerable others; and finally, how the comic strip puts into images for non-citizen readers (and for other readers too) the notion of Australia as signifying no (potential) extension of hospitality to asylum seeker others, thus reinforcing ideas articulated in the writing in the 'No advantage brochure' discussed above. On one level, then, the government's comic strip may be interpreted as narrating a determinedly Western-centric, solipsistic story. However, its reinterpretation can make possible the construction of potential alternatives to the dominant stereotyped story about asylum seekers in national circulation.

The othering of the asylum seeker other, as figured in the strip's representation of the young man, operates by flip-flopping between an intensification of otherness and a diluting of the other into self (sameness). On the one hand, his otherness and objectification is emphasized through a very spare, tableau-like, visual rendering of his home situation, of his difficult journey as a naïve, disconnected dupe of ruthless people smugglers. On the other hand, there is an (arrogant) presumption that his life must also in some ways be 'like ours': that is, even if arduous, it is also relatively stable, peaceful, uneventful. And, in addition, it is suggested that his aspirations must inevitably be oriented towards the developed (Australian) world of high-rise capitalism and near-empty walkways, the sign of an affluent life 'like ours'.

There is a perverse logic at play here. Although the government (as the author of the strip) presumes, to a point, a shared way of life and shared values with the young man ('knowing' how he lives, 'knowing' that what he 'wants' are the same things as we Australians 'have'), the story shows how he will be met at the border as a trespasser, treated as a prisoner, and sent to a detention camp indefinitely—in other words, treated as an other, treated inhospitably. In this account, (his) difference is reductively conceived: either difference is distanced to the extent that the young man becomes the essentialized, objectified (and oppositional) other, unconnected to us so that we can treat him inhumanely with impunity; alternatively, difference is swallowed up by the same (we recognize him when he becomes like us), so that we cannot recognize and respond with caring responsibility to his unique story, his situated vulnerability.[9]

Although the cartoon was commissioned by the Labor Government, its publication, in November 2013, coincides with the Coalition Government's increasingly militaristic and aggressive stance towards asylum seekers.

Much is made in the comic strip of the border as a hostile place and its trespassing by the asylum seeker as inevitably doomed. The images depict, from the interception of the asylum seekers' boat at sea to the island detention centre, the regulation and control of asylum seeker movement by navy personnel, border control officials, and detention centre guards. The visual suggestion is that the management of asylum seekers is necessarily oppositional, tough, and uncompromising. This has been borne out in subsequent YouTube and print campaigns (Australian Government 2014), as we will see below. The images speak both (directly) to the harsh treatment asylum seekers can expect and (indirectly) to the security and protection consequently afforded to Australians (threatened by the invasion of alien others) as a result. A 'dichotomous logic' is at work here, as security and border control are set up in opposition to hospitality and humanitarianism (University of South Australia 2013: 8).

However, depending on how individual citizens and non-citizens read the images (or rewrite them), it is possible that the apparently hard and hostile protectors of the state are themselves othered, if the reader's sympathies do in fact linger with the young man whose story is being told (also see Fletcher 2014). Given the successive frames depicting his and his fellow asylum seekers' faces and bodies as forlorn, bent, and hopeless in contrast to those of the blank, stiffly upright (but equally bereft) demeanour of their guards, it might be that the reader's compassion is misplaced (in the comic strip author's terms). Nonetheless, while the oppositional stance between asylum seeker and guard is made stereotypically and reductively salient, their interdependence and the narrative complexity of their human and ethical interactions can only be rendered in richer, more textured accounts, which the government refuses to write, but that others have produced (for example, see Loewenstein 2013; *Guardian Australia* 2014). For the government's policy to succeed on its own terms, it must refuse a cosmopolitan orientation, a cosmopolitan commitment to care for the other.

I claimed above that the comic strip uses pictures to illustrate that, for asylum seekers arriving by boat, there is no hospitality and no home for them in Australia. I should be more precise: two concepts of an inhospitable home (a contradiction in terms) *are* shown. The first captures an aspect of the depopulated, reflective glass space of the neoliberal fantasy: city skyscrapers and the almost bare urbanscape of the young man's thought bubbles as he dreams of an apparently ideal life in Australia. The second is represented by the exclusionary, punitive forces of border control and the prison-like space of detention. Guarding the boundaries to the (invisible) real Australian home that only the privileged can enjoy, the defence and security personnel are the (unappealing) rhetorical face of the elusive home that the strip offers. It is this apparently blatant exposure of Australia as inhospitable (pictorial images do an effective job of essentializing the 'truth' of an object) that motivated a range of critical responses to and rewriting of the comic strip (for example, Ansari 2014; Fletcher 2014; George 2014).

Bringing us up to date, the final piece of government writing for brief consideration is selected from the materials comprising the 'No Way. You will not make Australia home' campaign, launched in February 2014. The focus here is on the poster aimed at would-be asylum seekers, though I also make brief reference to the fact sheet aimed at readers in Australia (family and friends of would-be asylum seekers), informing them about the changes. In this final example, we see how the rhetoric reflects the further hardening of government policy on asylum seekers, in a form of address that unashamedly taunts the asylum seeker with the promise that they 'will not make Australia home' if they try to seek refuge by boat.

The poster is dominated by the strap line 'NO WAY', in large red capitals centred on a blue-grey angry seascape on which a small boat is being tossed around. Above the text is a map of Australia with a red line diagonally crossed through it. Above that symbol is the Australian Government coat of arms. The text towards the foot of the poster reads as follows:

The Australian Government has introduced the toughest border protection measures ever. [10]

If you get on a boat without a visa, you will not end up in Australia.

Any vessel seeking to illegally enter Australia will be intercepted and safely removed beyond Australian waters.

The rules apply to everyone: families, children, unaccompanied children, educated and skilled.

No matter who you are or where you are from, you will not make Australia home.

THINK AGAIN BEFORE YOU WASTE YOUR MONEY. PEOPLE SMUGGLERS ARE LYING (Australian Government 2014a). [11]

The government voice, crafted as monological, declarative, and unwavering, has now implemented 'the toughest border protection measures ever'. This voice might be read as performing the 'orderly' approach to dealing with asylum seekers (who, if intercepted, are to be 'safely removed', rather like toxic waste), promoted in the 'No advantage' brochure discussed above. The use of the superlative ('toughest') and the adverb ('ever') reflects the rhetorical approach to border protection both as aggressive and competitive, in which the fending off or refusal of the other is unequivocally asserted. This voice is sustained throughout, and this is possible since the would-be asylum seeker is not recognized, not narrativized as a historical human subject, but as a generalized rather than a concrete other (Benhabib 1992). Refusing to write the story of *how* or *why* asylum seekers might come to board boats, and making immaterial their relational identities or origins, their extreme vulnerability and dependence on others for care, the government text can thus exercise a carefree style, concentrating on the harsh consequences for those who do: 'If you get on a boat without a visa, you will not end up in Australia'; 'No matter who you are or where you are from, you will not make Australia home'. As in the two previous samples, Australia is represented as a vacant, abstract 'home', while a material, lived-in world beyond its borders from which the asylum seekers come cannot or will not be imagined either, except, that is, in terms of the channels of organized migration. In one of the 'No way' campaign fact sheets, targeted readers in Australia are instructed to 'keep your family and friends safe—tell them to come the right way', through 'lawful migration' programs (Australian Government 2014a). This disingenuous advice ignores the tragic reality of the severely limited opportunities for making refugee applications, and of the disorderliness, the chaos of forced migration faced by millions of the world's vulnerable individuals.

CONCLUSION: WRITING (AS) COSMOPOLITAN CARE

The Kigali typists with whom I opened this chapter produce documents in the indigenous language of Rwanda, a language that flourishes in local communities but struggles to become visible in or adapt to the globalized public domain, as other languages and other modes of writing compete for prominence. Similarly, when we write in public, in a context of globalization, we risk obscuring the relations of care that motivate and make our lives and our daily activities, including writing, meaningful; we risk overlooking the ethical dimensions, scope, and impacts of all the different kinds of texts we produce in relation to others near and far. Given that we write in situations in which our interlocutors will have outlooks, experiences, and understandings other than our own, as far as our places of privilege, power, and voice allow, we can make sense in our communicating with them by imagining their differences, thinking ourselves otherwise, opening ourselves up to alternative conversations in other territories and different temporalities. This requires that we step back and reconsider our conventional rhetorical and discursive frameworks, patterns, and pace, checking to see how and whom they exclude, prioritize, or take for granted, and how we might therefore reconfigure our writing to accommodate others' interests and needs rather than just our own.

In terms of government writing about asylum seekers, it can of course be argued that a government's first obligation is to protect the nation and its own citizens, and that this should be reflected in its written as well as other communicative and discursive forms. However, why should this responsibility necessitate an oppositional, competitive, and militaristic stance in relation to non-Australians, particularly the most vulnerable? In a globalized world, are democratically elected governments exempted from modelling or directing ethical, caring relations within as well as beyond their borders?[12] Clearly, as the above discussion has shown, the Australian Government's writing practices confirm that it does not believe that it has such responsibility, with terrible and damaging consequences both for those asylum seekers held in indefinite detention, and also for the nation's opportunities for forging ties and acknowledging our human and ethical connections with others across the boundaries of difference. In such contexts, writing, rewriting, reflecting, and evaluating with a critical cosmopolitan sensibility serves to keep us aware of our interdependence with, rather than distinction from, others in a global world, looking beyond the oppositional to the relational, to what connects rather than separates us, and to where our respective responsibilities, as writers and as people, lie.

NOTES

1. This and the following section draw on, in modified form, material from Surma (2013).

2. Bryan S. Turner (2007) develops the notion of 'enclavement' to define and describe the way that processes of globalization result in the political production and regulation of forms of immobility for certain people and groups. He shows how, in its less benign manifestations, enclavement works to the detriment of the dispossessed and the underclass.

3. Polling during the election campaign indicated that 'asylum seekers' was the second most important election issue for voters. The most important was the economy (Parliament of Australia 2013, at www.aph.gov.au/About_Parliament/Parliamentary_Departments/Parliamentary_Library/pubs/rp/rp1314/FedElection2013.)

4. For a discussion of Australia's recent increasingly harsh approach to dealing with asylum seekers, in legal, humanitarian, and ethical terms, see Jane McAdam (2013).

5. This document has now been removed from the Australian Government website. However it is available on the Australian High Commission Malaysia's website, at www.malaysia.highcommission.gov.au/files/klpr/No%20Advantage%20flayer.pdf.

6. 'The term *irregular migration* typically refers to the cross-border flow of people who enter a country without that country's legal permission to do so. In contrast, the term *irregular migrants* typically refers to the stock of migrants in a country who are not entitled to reside there, either because they have never had a legal residence permit or because they have overstayed their time-limited permit' (Migration Observatory 2011).

7. While a screen shot from the cartoon strip is available on the Operation Sovereign Borders website (Australian Government 2014), only media professionals now have access to the full document. The cartoon strip can be located on non-government websites.

8. This is indeed a very rare concession on the part of the Australian Government: granting a narrative to a would-be asylum seeker. Typically, asylum seekers, if they are understood as people at all, are treated by government rhetoric as ahistorical, dehumanized objects. That said, the comic strip graphic refuses the identity of the asylum seeker as legitimate or authentic by depicting his home as a relatively secure and safe place and his assumed acquisitive aspirations to affluence as not only foolhardy but criminal. As Scott Morrison declared, in an interview about his discussions with Cambodia about possible settlement in that country of asylum seekers arriving in Australia: 'Now, remember, resettlement is freedom from persecution, it's not a ticket to a first-class economy (Morrison 2014). Here, Morrison appears to deny the view that privilege, power, and capacity mean that some may have greater responsibility than others to protect the vulnerable.

9. This is the basis of Roger Silverstone's critique of the contemporary mainstream media environment; see Silverstone (2007, 47).

10. This text is in larger font than that which follows, and is contained in a reversed-out white text box.

11. This text is in capitals and also is contained in a reversed-out white text box.

12. See Grewcock (2014) for a discussion of the deleterious impacts of the government's policies on asylum seekers as well as a discussion of alternative approaches to responding to their plight.

BIBLIOGRAPHY

ABC (2011). 'Lateline', Prime Minister Julia Gillard in an interview with Tony Jones, TV program transcript, at www.abc.net.au/lateline/content/2011/s3285862.htm.

Africal Portal (2012). 'The Costs and Consequences of Rwanda's Shift in Language Policy', at www.africaportal.org/articles/2012/05/31/costs-and-consequences-rwanda's-shift-language-policy.

Ansari, A. (2014). 'Operation Sovereign Borders (Australian Government Customs and Border Protection Service)' *Design and Violence* blog, at designandviolence.moma.org/operation-sovereign-borders-australian-government-customs-and-border-protection-service.

Appiah, K. A. (2006). *Cosmopolitanism: Ethics in a World of Strangers*. London: Penguin.

Australian Government (2014). 'Operation Sovereign Borders', at www.customs.gov.au/site/operation-sovereign-borders.asp.

———. (2014a). 'Counter People Smuggling Communication', at www.customs.gov.au/site/offshore-communication-campaign-people-smuggling.asp.

Benhabib, S. (1992). 'The Generalized and the Concrete Other: The Kohlberg–Gilligan Controversy and Moral Theory' in *Situating the Self: Gender, Community, and Postmodernism in Contemporary Ethics*, 148–77. New York: Routledge.

———. (2006) *Another Cosmopolitanism*. Oxford and New York: Oxford University Press.

Calhoun, C. (2008). 'Cosmopolitanism and Nationalism'. *Nations and Nationalism* 14, 3: 427–48.

Delanty, G. (2006). 'The Cosmopolitan Imagination: Critical Cosmopolitanism and Social Theory'. *The British Journal of Sociology* 57, 1: 25–47.

———. (2009). *The Cosmopolitan Imagination: The Renewal of Critical Social Theory*. Cambridge: Cambridge University Press.

Derrida, J. (2001). *On Cosmopolitanism and Forgiveness* translated by M. Dooley and M. Hughes. London and New York: Routledge.

Fairclough, N. (2003). *Analysing Discourse: Textual Analysis for Social Research*. London: Routledge.

Fletcher, M. (2014). 'I'm a Conservative, But This Asylum Seekers Comic Is Disgusting'. AusOpinion for *The Guardian*, 13 February, at www.theguardian.com/commentisfree/2014/feb/13/asylum-seekers-graphic-campaign.

George, P. (2014). 'Graphic Novel Versus Taliban: An Asylum Seeker Deterrent? *The Conversation* 13 February, at theconversation.com/graphic-novel-versus-taliban-an-asylum-seeker-deterrent-23122.

Grewcock, M. (2014). 'Back to the Future: Australian Border Policing Under Labor, 2007–2013'. *State Crime Journal* 3, 1, 102–25. Hawke Research Institute, University of South Australia, at www.unisa.edu.au/Global/EASS/HRI/National%20Asylum%20Summit%202013%20web.pdf.

The Guardian Australia online (2014). 'Manus Island Whistleblower Speaks Exclusively to *Guardian Australia*'. 28 April, at www.theguardian.com/world/video/2014/apr/28/manus-island-whistleblower-speaks-video.

Held, V. (2006). *The Ethics of Care: Personal, Political and Global*. Oxford and New York: Oxford University Press.

Kwibuka, E. (2013). 'Rwanda's Last Typewriter Users'. *The New Times Rwanda*, at www.newtimes.co.rw/news/index.php?a=13459&i=15292.

Loewenstein, A. (2013). *Profits of Doom: How Vulture Capitalism Is Swallowing the World*. Melbourne: Melbourne University Press.

McAdam, J. (2013). 'Australia and Asylum Seekers'. *International Journal of Refugee Law* 25, 3: 435–48.

Migration Observatory (2011). 'Irregular Migration in the UK: Definitions, Pathways and Scale', at www.migrationobservatory.ox.ac.uk/briefings/irregular-migration-uk-definitions-pathways-and-scale.

Morrison, S. (2014). 'Regional Resettlement Arrangement, Cambodia Visit, Children in Detention'. Interview ABC *7.30 Report*. 14 April, at www.minister.immi.gov.au/media/sm/2014/sm213407.htm.

Papastephanou, M. (2011). 'The "Cosmopolitan" Self Does Her Homework'. *Journal of Philosophy of Education* 45, 4, 597–612.

Parliament of Australia (2014). 'Federal Election 2013: Issues, Dynamics, Outcomes', at www.aph.gov.au/About_Parliament/Parliamentary_Departments/Parliamentary_Library/pubs/rp/rp1314/FedElection2013#_Toc378080113.

Robinson, F. (1999). *Globalizing Care: Ethics, Feminist Theory and International Relations.* Boulder, CO and Oxford: Westview Press.

———. (2009). 'EIA Interview: Fiona Robinson on the Ethics of Care'. Carnegie Council, at www.carnegiecouncil.org/resources/transcripts/0125.html.

———. (2011). *The Ethics of Care: A Feminist Approach to Human Security.* Philadelphia: Temple University Press.

Silverstone, R. (2007). *Media and Morality: On the Rise of the Mediapolis.* Cambridge and Malden, MA: Polity Press.

Surma, A. (2013). *Imagining the Cosmopolitan in Public and Professional Writing.* Basingstoke, Hants: Palgrave Macmillan.

Turner, B. S. (2007). 'The Enclave Society: Towards a Sociology of Immobility'. *European Journal of Social Theory* 10, 2: 287–304.

UNHCR (2014). *Global Trends 2013.* Geneva: United Nations High Commissioner for Refugees, at unhcr.org/trends2013/.

University of South Australia (2013). *National Asylum Summit 2013 Report*, at www.unisa.edu.au/Global/EASS/HRI/National%20Asylum%20Summit%202013%20web.pdf.

SIX

A New Cosmopolitan
World History?

Polycentrism and Beyond

Martin Hewson

The cosmopolitan ideal has as its main antithesis ethnocentrism. Classical cosmopolitanism sought to transcend ethnocentrisms of all kinds and so move towards a more universal, xenophilic world order. In recent years, *Eurocentrism* has become the target of a new and influential critique among world historians. A new model of history aims to undermine and transcend Eurocentrism. In place of the Eurocentric, this new model of history elevates the polycentric. Cosmopolitanism opposes ethnocentrism; the new polycentric account of world history opposes Eurocentrism. It seems there may be an affinity between the two. Is this so? Does the cosmopolitan ideal manifest the polycentric interpretation of world history? Is this a new cosmopolitan world history?

In what follows I describe the new polycentric, or anti-Eurocentric, model of world history, then assess its successes and failings. I argue that there is a notable difference between the cosmopolitan ideal and the polycentric model: Cosmopolitanism is contrary to all ethnocentrisms, while the new polycentric model of world history is contrary only to Eurocentrism and especially European exceptionalism.

The main aim of the polycentric model is to show that Europe was not exceptional, unique, or peculiar in world history. There are several possible labels one could use to describe this way of thinking. Besides polycentric, it has been called revisionist, multicultural, anti-Eurocentric, or anti-Western. It might also be called Asianist or anti-exceptionalist. But polycentric is both relatively neutral and indicates the content well.

AGAINST WESTERN EXCEPTIONALISM: OUTLINE OF THE POLYCENTRIC MODEL

The main exponents of polycentric history come from diverse disciplinary backgrounds. They include Andre Gunder Frank, an economist and one of the founders of dependency and world system analysis; Kenneth Pomeranz, an economic historian; John Hobson, a scholar of international relations; Jack Goldstone, an historical sociologist; Ian Morris, a classicist, archaeologist, and historian; and Jack Goody, an anthropologist. Several historians have sought to write general histories that bypass European exceptionalism. Felipe Fernandez-Armesto is one. Another is Christopher Bayly, whose history of the long nineteenth century, *The Birth of the Modern World: Global Connections and Comparisons, 1780–1914* (2004), partakes of the general spirit of anti-exceptionalism.

The polycentric model challenges several purported Western exceptions. In the following, I highlight the main ones.

Capitalism

A notable feature of polycentrism is the denial that Europe was exceptional in generating capitalism. This is shocking because several leading exponents of polycentrism have Marxist backgrounds. Andre Gunder Frank was an originator of dependency theory, which arose from Marxist theories of imperialism. Jack Goody was associated with the Cambridge Marxists of the late 1930s and 1940s, including Eric Hobsbawm. In the polycentric model, capitalism is posited to have existed for millennia. Goody recommends 'abandonment of the term "capitalism" altogether' (2006: 305). The idea of capitalism has gone from being the centrepiece of radical critique to an annoyance for its connotations of Western exceptionalism.

The rationale for abandoning the term *capitalism* is that mercantile activity, profit-making, long-distance trade, and capital accumulation have ancient roots that long predate the rise of the West. Frank (1998) argues that a 'world system' of capitalism has existed for five millennia, not (as he and others earlier thought) five centuries. Once these long continuities are foregrounded, Western exceptionalism fades from view. Yet, there is a weakness in this emphasis upon the very *longue durée*. Even if it agreed that some forms of capitalism are longstanding, that does not preclude the West having pioneered new forms of capitalism. Even if the West was not exceptional in originating capitalism, it was exceptional in originating new and especially, dynamic, forms of capitalism.

Modernity

Where capitalism goes, modernity follows. Proponents of the polycentric model are unconvinced with the notion that the West is exceptional by virtue of having pioneered modernity.

Beginning in the later 1990s, the noted anthropologist Jack Goody began publishing a series of books that took issue with previous theories of history as Eurocentric and began to outline an alternative. Goody's version of polycentrism emphasizes the long-run similarities and continuities of Eurasia since the Bronze Age. *Capitalism and Modernity* (2004) denies that capitalism or modernity were Western inventions. Markets and property-less labour, Goody argues, have existed since the Bronze Age. Such 'modern' phenomena as rationalism, pluralism, romantic love, secularism, and individualism have, Goody maintains, also appeared across Eurasia since the Bronze Age.

The Theft of History (Goody 2006) consists primarily of essays that take issue with Norbert Elias, Joseph Needham, and Fernand Braudel for being Eurocentric—that is, for regarding Europe as exceptional in one way or another. Other essays deny that such things as cities, humanism, or romantic love were peculiar to Europe. Goody tries to downplay the significance of the Renaissance, the scientific revolution, and the Industrial Revolution. There were, he counters, other renaissances, there was science before the scientific revolution, and there were factories before the Industrial Revolution.

In *The Eurasian Miracle* (2010a), Goody claims that instead of a 'European miracle', there was a Eurasian one. The crucial episode was the Bronze Age—only Eurasia had one; Africa and the Americas did not. Africa had the hoe only, no traction animals, no cities, and no writing. Since then, different parts of Eurasia alternated as first one then another region of Eurasia became central. In *Renaissances* (2010b), Goody argues that all the literate Eurasian civilizations have had efflorescences. Europe's was not unique, other than that it had lost so much with the fall of Rome and needed to recover so much.

Jack Goody has been remarkably prolific in his critique of European exceptionalism. Yet he has ended up affirming Eurasian exceptionalism. He has also ended up denying all discontinuity in history except one: the 'urban revolution' of five thousand years ago that brought the rise of cities, states, civilizations, and literacy. The rest of history is, in Goody's approach, flattened of all transformation and reduced to endless continuity. Once one denies that modernity is distinctive, in order to de-exceptionalize the West, then history becomes a flat, unchanging landscape.

Globalization

The polycentric model is against the idea that Europe was unusual in having instigated globalization. In *Re-Orient: Global Economy in the Asian Age* (1998), Frank denies that the world system was created by Europe, as standard world-system analysis had supposed. Instead, the world system had been created by Asia centuries or millennia before European expansion. Frank wants to convey the idea that Asia created it, and Europe only joined it. Hobson (2004: chaps. 2–4) follows suit. Globalization, he maintains, began with 'oriental globalisation' around 500 CE. The West was a mere latecomer.

Globalization theorist Jan Nederveen Pieterse (2006) has partially adopted the polycentric approach. For Pieterse, its essence is what he calls 'the Orient first thesis'. Asia was first with oriental globalization. Pieterse does, however, also raise some criticisms of the general polycentric approach. In centring the East and marginalizing the West, Pieterse points out that the revisionists simply reverse the binary. Revisionists tend towards Sinocentrism and Indocentrism, Pieterse complains, while Africa remains sketchy.

How plausible is this conception of oriental globalization? There is no doubt that linkages existed among the Old World civilizations in antiquity. But it would be more accurate to call this phenomenon 'Eurasianization'. It was extensive but it was not global in scope. The label 'globalization' should more legitimately be reserved for *worldwide* connections. If globalization refers specifically to global connections, then it begins no earlier than 1492 and is driven by Europeans. Even if the anti-exceptionalists are correct that globalization in some form predates Western expansion, we still are left needing to explain why Europeans were exceptional in forging a truly global globalization beyond the merely Eurasian globalization that came before.

Power

The polycentric model also challenges the notion that the West has, if nothing else, been exceptional in its power. Polycentrism portrays the West's global hegemony as late and temporary—a short interlude or aberration between a past of Chinese power and a future return of Chinese power.

The title of Ian Morris's book *Why the West Rules—For Now* (2011) indicates this idea. So does the book's content. Morris attempts to measure leadership in power or social development using an index featuring four traits: (1) energy capture, (2) size of largest city, (3) war-making power, and (4) literacy and communications technology (2011: 147–49). *Why the West Rules—For Now* is impressive for the estimates Morris generates on these factors over vast spans of time. According to Morris's estimates, China was slightly ahead from 500 CE to 1750. From 1750 to the present, the West was substantially ahead. Morris foresees China once again ruling in the near future.

There are several flaws in Morris's accounting of the long-run balance of power among regions. First, in the 500–1750 period, the differences were minor. After 1750, by Morris's estimates, a vast gulf opened up as the West surged ahead in every measure of social development. Second, Morris's focus upon energy, city-size, military power, and communications is open to the objection that he leaves out a great deal of what social development involves. He does not pay direct attention to income per capita, science, culture, or any measures of political development.

Andre Gunder Frank (1998) takes issue with the idea that Europe was exceptional as the core or hegemon of the early modern world system. Far from being a time of nascent European hegemony, prior to 1800 China was the core of the world system. It was still an Asian era. (And Frank anticipates it will soon revert to normality. A new Asian era is heralded.) Frank depicts the West as a peripheral and inferior part of the early modern world economy, its period of ascendancy brief and transient.

The claim that Western ascendancy is an intermission between the normal condition of Chinese rule also can be found in Martin Jacques book *When China Rules the World* (2012). Jacques anticipates that in the near future things will revert to what was the normal state of affairs before the intrusion of the West. One might object, however, that talk of 'ruling the world' is hyperbole. China did not rule the world, the West does not, and China will not.

Economic Development

A major focus of the polycentric model is to challenge the idea that Europe was exceptional in economic development and wealth in the early modern era, circa 1500–1800. According to polycentrism, Europe was no more advanced or wealthy than Asia in general, and China in particular, until after 1800. The great economic divergence, on this view, came late and sudden.

One immediate drawback of this line of argument is that it merely shifts the date of Europe's economic exceptionalism. The polycentric model does not and cannot deny that there was economic exceptionalism. Whether the exceptionalism appeared relatively early or relatively late is a secondary consideration. It does not matter all that much if Europe's economic divergence came gradually sometime after 1500 or suddenly around 1800. As usual with gradualist versus suddenist debates, the truth is probably a bit of both. Either way, the key point is that the West, whether gradually, suddenly, or a bit of both, ended up as economically exceptional.

Kenneth Pomeranz's *The Great Divergence* (2000), one of the most influential and respected works in the polycentric approach, is the main source to deny Europe was exceptional in economic development prior to about 1800. Pomeranz recognizes in the title of this work that there was a great economic divergence, but he claims it only happened after 1800. Before the Industrial Revolution, Europe was no different. Before the sudden and late great divergence, there was a great similarity. Pomeranz makes his case by comparing the two most advanced regions of Europe and China: England and the Yangzi Delta. According to Pomeranz, the two regions were similar in levels of commerce, urbanization, markets, private property, technology, and industry. But they were not similar in the most crucial way: per capita income. For all the economic parallels that Pomeranz marshals, he is not able to claim that incomes were similar. Even China's most advanced region was an area of low-income, high-population, labour-intensive subsistence agriculture. This is an enormous hole at the heart of the thesis of a great similarity.

Another challenge to the idea that Europe was exceptionally economically developed in early modernity comes from Jack A. Goldstone, an historical sociologist and well-known analyst of revolutions. Goldstone (2008) agrees with Pomeranz that Europe was no more advanced economically than China in the 1500–1800 era. But how, in that case, could it leap forward after 1800? Goldstone's answer is that early modern Britain was exceptional in one area: the science and technology of engineering. That is the initial variation from which came later divergence. Yet this only raises the question of why Britain generated an engineering culture of revolutionary consequence, but was otherwise no more economically advanced than Asia (or China).

There is an issue with conceptualizing change here. If there was parity of economic development before 1800, then it is hard to see how such enormous divergence could happen so quickly. Enormous variation cannot spring forth from initial uniformity. As the theory of evolution tells us, there has to be some early variation before there can be later divergence. A great similarity does not suddenly capsize into a great difference.

Navigation and Discovery

Were Europeans unusual in the realm of seafaring and exploration? It has become common to imply that they were not, by making reference to the Chinese fleets of Admiral Zheng He (Cheng Ho). In the period 1405–1433, Zheng led voyages from China to Southeast Asia and into the Indian Ocean. Now Zheng has become world famous. A Muslim and a eunuch, the admiral is lauded as an Asian hero, an equivalent to the European explorers and navigators of the age of reconnaissance. Statues of Zheng have begun to be erected in Asia, mirroring the older statues of

Columbus or Magellan. Zheng has become a symbol of Chinese exceptionalism: ships, fleets, and voyages supposedly far more advanced than
those of Europe.

But Zheng He was unknown until 1971 when he appeared in a volume of Joseph Needham's *Science and Civilisation in China* dealing with
civil engineering and nautics (1971: 487–535). Needham is clear: Zheng
He was not an explorer. His voyages went as far as Sri Lanka and possibly reached East Africa. But he did not discover these routes. The Chinese already had Arab and Persian guides for knowledge of the Indian
Ocean. Trade routes between East Asia, Southeast Asia, and South Asia
were long established. Merchant ships sailed these waters both before
and after Zheng's expeditions. Zheng's ships were on a 'show the flag'
tour, not a voyage of discovery.

The Modern State and the Nation-State

A further version of polycentrism wants to reject the notion that Europe was exceptional in giving rise to the modern state. Francis Fukuyama endorses this in his book *The Origins of Political Order*. Fukuyama hails
ancient China's state as a 'remarkable modernizing project' (2011: 110).
'Political modernization', Fukuyama argues, was initiated not by modern
Europeans, but by the First Emperor, the megalomaniac Shi Huangdi,
creator of the Terracotta Army, conqueror of the Warring States, and
founder of unified China. The positive feature of Fukuyama's attempt to
make Europe unexceptional is that it is a reminder that Europe did not
initiate states or political bureaucracies. The problem with it is that Fukuyama is defining 'political modernization' as the forging of a highly
effective bureaucratic despotism.

The standard scholarly view of nations and nationalism is known as
'modernism', and it holds that the nation and the nation-state are prod-
ucts of modern Europe. Nationality, in other words, is an instance of the
West's exceptionalism. This is one form of exceptionalism that goes un-
challenged in the main works of the polycentric approach. But there is
one outlier. Victor Lieberman, an historian of Southeast Asia, declines to
align himself with the main exponents of polycentrism. For one thing, he
advocates a 'less adversarial calculus of Eurasian difference' (2003: 73). In
addition, Lieberman's *Strange Parallels* (2003, 2009) is unusual in focusing
upon Southeast Asia—a notable contrast to the Sinocentrism of most anti-
exceptionalists. Instead of a contrast between the West and Asia, or Europe and China, Lieberman proposes a contrast between two zones of
Eurasia: the 'protected rimland' (Europe, Japan, and Southeast Asia) and
the 'exposed core' (the rest of Eurasia, including Russia) affected by prox-
imity to the military power of the horsemen of the arid zone.

Lieberman argues that processes of territorial consolidation, administrative centralization, and ethnic integration could be found in widely

dispersed areas. Europe was not unique in generating nation-states. Congruence between ethnicity and state could be found in Southeast Asia as well as Western Europe. Lieberman attributes this to their distance from the exposed zone. Both were in the protected rimland. Lieberman makes a strong case that the West was not unique in generating nations and nation-states, which poses a challenge to the prevailing account of nationalism.

Innovation and Dynamism

Is it plausible to challenge and reverse the idea that the West has been exceptional in its innovation and dynamism? Is the West no more inventive and creative than Asia? Several exponents of polycentrism have tried to make this case.

One strategy is to adopt a view of history that emphasizes continuity and constancy over change and discontinuity. Frank thinks a world system has existed for five millennia. Goody discerns no significant discontinuities since the Bronze Age Urban Revolution. Eurasian history has simply seen the elaboration of the city and mercantile life formed at that time. In their anxiety to deny Western exceptionalism, these radical writers have adopted a conservative conception of history. They insist that there is nothing new under the sun, that all the talk of revolutions, ruptures, discontinuities, or modernity is an illusion. This is one way to counter the idea that the West has been exceptional in creativity and dynamism.

Another strategy is adopted by John Hobson in his book *The Eastern Origins of Western Civilisation* (2004). Hobson argues that the West was not dynamic or innovative because it borrowed much during the Middle Ages. Most of the items he cites are well-known: financial and commercial instruments; gunpowder and the compass; Arabic, or rather, Indian numerals. But Hobson wants to claim that these borrowings created or made the West—thus the West has 'Eastern origins'.

There are several flaws in this argument. First, it is possible to borrow *and* to be innovative, to adopt some things *and* to invent others. So medieval Europe borrowed gunpowder but invented eyeglasses. That borrowing occurred does not demonstrate medieval Europe to have been stagnant or uncreative. Second, a sign of dynamism is the ability to further develop borrowed items. Though Europe originally borrowed gunpowder from China, it managed to develop the technology far beyond anything achieved elsewhere. Finally, it is hyperbole to claim that borrowing a few things means that one civilization has 'origins' in another. Hobson does not claim that Islam has Greek origins because of some borrowed Greek ideas, that China or Japan has Indian origins because it borrowed from Buddhism, or that modern Asia and Africa have Western origins because they borrowed many Western technologies and institutions.

In sum, the main aim of the polycentric model is to reject the idea that the West was special, distinctive, or unique. It was not the progenitor of a 'miracle'. The corollary aim is to propound the idea that the West was remarkably unexceptional. For some, the West has been similar, parallel, level, or equal. For others, the West is seen as inferior, backward, behind.

BASIC FEATURES OF THE POLYCENTRIC MODEL

I now consider the general characteristics of the polycentric model. I argue it has three bedrock features: (1) denial of Western exceptionalism, plus the corollaries, (2) acceptance of Eurasian exceptionalism, and (3) acceptance of North Eurasian exceptionalism.

The West Unexceptional

The main feature of the polycentric model of history is the critique of Western exceptionalism. Polycentrism challenges ideas that the West was exceptional in generating globalization, or in originating capitalism, or in early modern economic development, or in power, or in dynamism and innovation, or in originating nations and nation-states. But there are two exceptions to the rule: luck and predation. In the polycentric model, the West is portrayed as exceptionally lucky and exceptionally predatory or exploitative.

The polycentric model attributes an extraordinary role to luck in world history. According to numerous proponents of the polycentric model, the explanation for the West's unusual position is that it is lucky: fortunate to be close to the Americas, lucky to have a just-right geography, providentially blessed to have coal. Polycentrism needs to appeal to fortune. The single-minded effort to portray the West as unexceptional leaves the polycentric approach at a loss to explain the West's surge in power, wealth, and knowledge. For divergence cannot arise from uniformity. Evolution comes from variation. The fallback position is to attribute the West's position to luck. Frank (1998), Pomeranz (2000), and Hobson (2004) explicitly appeal to luck. But luck is an unsatisfying explanation. For one thing, it denies agency. For another, it merely raises the question of why the fortunate one was able to grasp the lucky circumstance that fate offered. If the West was exceptionally lucky, polycentrism still needs to consider why it was exceptionally adept at seizing its fortunate chances.

The other way that Europe was exceptional, according to the main polycentric view, was in predation, exploitation, and imperialism. Here is Frank denying European exceptionalism: 'Europe did not pull itself up by its own economic bootstraps, and certainly not thanks to any European exceptionalism of rationality, institutions, entrepreneurship, technology' (1998: 5). But on the next page Frank asserts a different, negative exceptionalism: 'Instead Europe used its American money to muscle in on and benefit from Asian production, markets, trade, in a word to profit from the predominant position of Asia in the world economy' (1998: 6). If Europe was exceptional in muscling in and profiting from others, to employ Frank's terms, then we need to ask whether the reason for that may have had some connection to the 'rationality, institutions, entrepreneurship, technology' that Frank had just dismissed.

Overall, there is a contradiction in the polycentric model. It denies Western exceptionalism, and thus it adopts a uniformitarianism. But then it violates this anti-exceptionalism in claiming that the West was unusually lucky and uniquely predatory. It looks like some kinds of exceptionalism are more equal than others.

Eurasia Exceptional

A second basic feature of the polycentric model is that while denying Western exceptionalism, it affirms Eurasian exceptionalism. Eurasia is held to be unique. Proponents of the polycentric model have underlined Eurasian globalization, Eurasian similarities, the ups and downs of Eurasian civilizations, Eurasian power, Eurasian dynamism and innovation, Eurasian borrowing, and numerous other peculiarities of Eurasia. Goody (2010a) is explicit in affirming that Eurasia is exceptional, perhaps because his early anthropological focus was Africa. But for other exponents of polycentrism, Eurasian uniqueness is assumed or implicit.

Why was Eurasia exceptional? Unfortunately, this is a question the polycentric approach has not addressed. Perhaps it cannot address it, owing to its exclusive focus on denying Western exceptionalism. The polycentric proponents silently assume Eurasian exceptionalism but make no effort to explain it. If analyses of Western exceptionalism are 'Eurocentric', then the polycentric model is 'Eurasia-centric'.

North Eurasia Exceptional

The third general feature of the polycentric approach is that it affirms what I shall call North Eurasian exceptionalism or Northern exceptionalism. In asserting the comparability of China and Europe, polycentrism also asserts their divergence from the rest of the world. A considerable proportion of the writings in the polycentric perspective are primarily about the West and China—which together form the northern tier of Eurasian civilizations.

The polycentric model is in many instances a bicentric model: It regards world history as centred upon two areas, China and the West, or Northeast Eurasia and Northwest Eurasia. Frank's *Re-Orient* (1998) is largely bicentric. It is mostly about China and the West. Pomeranz's

(2000) account of early modern economic development is entirely bicentric. It looks only at the Yangzi Delta and at England. Morris's (2011) account of social development begins in the Middle East, but then becomes bicentric in describing the two joint leaders in social development since the classical era, China and the West.

There is much to recommend in this line of thinking. It has gained significantly in plausibility with the recent rise of China. But there are also several flaws. One is that polycentrism does not explicitly recognize its bicentric approach. To do so would be to admit a 'North-Eurasia-centrism'. Another is that the polycentric model makes no attempt to explain why these two regions were so advanced and influential compared to all the other regions of the world. The polycentric model is tired of the discourse of 'the rise of the West'. But it needs instead to explain 'the rise of the North'. It needs to theorize why the northwestern and northeastern ends of Eurasia have been exceptional. No such theory has been forthcoming.

GAPS IN POLYCENTRISM

I now examine the gaps in the polycentric view of world history. The main problem is that its urge to de-exceptionalize the West goes too far. I shall argue that it fails to incorporate four great divergences that made the West peculiar. The polycentric model marginalizes (1) the great social divergence, (2) the first great economic divergence, (3) the great political divergence, and (4) the great intellectual divergence.

Anti-exceptionalism or polycentrism has not gone uncontested. An 'exceptionalist' or 'anti-polycentrist' counter-critique exists. There are works in this vein from Ricardo Duchesne (2011), Greg Melleuish (2012), and Martin Hewson (2012). Victor Lieberman has a foot in both camps. His monumental work *Strange Parallels* (2003, 2009) emphasizes similarities between Europe and parts of Asia (Southeast Asia especially) rather than Europe's peculiarities. But he has also condemned the single-minded effort to deny Europe's exceptionalism. These works are diverse, but they have in common an approach to world history that incorporates, rather than denies, the West's exceptionalism.

The Great Social Divergence

One major flaw of the polycentric model is that it fails to incorporate the great social divergence of the premodern West. In marriage and family systems, the West was exceptional from an early date.

The West was from antiquity unique among all the major agrarian civilizations in adopting legal monogamy rather than polygyny. Monogamy was the standard in the Greek, the Roman, and the Christian law codes. It is a common thread through the entire history of the West. By contrast, the law codes of complex agrarian societies in Asia, Africa, and the Americas all allowed polygamy. During the nineteenth and twentieth centuries, one of the first tasks of modernizing states, such as Siam, was to abolish polygamy. Because Hong Kong maintained the civil law of the Qing Legal Code even after China itself abolished it, polygamy remained legal there until 1971.

In addition, key parts of the West were exceptional from the early medieval period in transitioning away from familialism and clannism. Family organization took an unusual turn in the core of the West. Extended lineages or clans disappeared. Clannism decayed in the core areas of Europe. The transition was coeval with, and probably caused by, a strict ban on cousin-marriage by the Catholic Church. This ban was not enforced everywhere; it remained deeply entrenched in Ireland, the Scottish Highlands, and southern Italy, for example. In those places, clannism and familialism remained the organizing principle of society. By contrast to the West, clans prevailed, often reinforced with cousin-marriage, in the Islamic world and in China. Goody recognizes this peculiarity of the West. He writes that there was a unique 'lateral attenuation of kinship in that wider networks and layer groups of kin . . . have become less significant' (2010a: 21).

Where there are clans and clannism, solidarity and identification with the extended lineage prevails. In such societies, there is less opportunity for civil society to develop. Civil society means a social order of voluntary, non-kin associations. It would include everything from colleges to clubs to non-family firms. Clans are the opposite: involuntary or ascriptive, rather than voluntary. An individual can belong to only one exclusive kin-community, but an individual may belong to many overlapping civil society associations. Clannism and civil society are antithetical (Wiener 2013).

The First Great Economic Divergence

A second flaw in polycentrism is its failure to incorporate the first great economic divergence. Long before Pomeranz's 'great divergence' of the Industrial Revolution, income levels in parts of premodern Europe were already diverging from Asia. Recent estimates of historical income levels are pointing to a late medieval and early modern European economic exceptionalism.

Broadberry (2013) has assembled the latest income estimates for Europe and Asia. China had a high point of $1,328 per capita during the Northern Song period at AD 980. But thereafter it steadily slid, to $600 in 1850. India was at $682 during the Mughal period in 1600, but also slid to $556 by 1850. Japan was at $554 in 1450, but in contrast steadily grew thereafter, signalling an early start to its divergence from the rest of Asia.

The North Sea region was the most exceptional. England and Holland had in 1400 $1,090 and $1,245, respectively. Both increased thereafter. England grew to $1,123 in 1600 and $2,080 in 1800. Holland increased to $2,372 in 1600, but dropped back to $1,752 in 1800. The techniques of historical national accounting are steadily improving. If these data are reliable, then it is a major empirical blow against the polycentric mode.

What explains this great income divergence? Broadberry (2013) regards several factors as potentially decisive. Family may be one. In Europe and Japan, women married at a later age than in China or India. Method of agriculture may be another. Pastoral farming was more important in northwest Europe than elsewhere. Among other possible explanations are varying institutions and differing levels of work ethic or industriousness.

The import of these estimates is that the polycentric model is flawed in supposing that before the industrial revolution economic parallelism was paramount and economic divergence was nugatory. There was significant variation among preindustrial economies. Asian economies supported large populations with labour-intensive agricultural methods but low per capita incomes. At least parts of Western Europe were already taking a different path from the late Middle Ages towards higher-productivity, higher-income economies. There was, in short, a premodern great economic divergence before the great industrial divergence.

The Great Political Divergence

A third flaw in polycentrism is its blind eye towards the West's great political divergence. The West was, from the Middle Ages on, politically exceptional.

Francis Fukuyama's world history of political structures, *The Origins of Political Order*, is a useful guide. Fukuyama (2011) focuses upon three kinds of political institution: effective bureaucratic states, the rule of law, and accountability. The first was found through many parts of premodern Eurasia. The Chinese Mandarinate was the most developed. I noted earlier that Fukuyama wants to downplay Western exceptionalism. He calls ancient China the model for political modernization. Fukuyama's second key political institution is the rule of law. It was partially developed in premodern India and Islam. But it was most effectively institutionalized in medieval Europe. The third—accountability—was a peculiarity of the West. Only there were rulers made accountable to representative assemblies. More precisely, it was only in the North Sea area (Britain and the Netherlands) where parliaments won effective power. There was a little political divergence within Europe as well as a great political divergence. The West, points out Fukuyama, was the only region able to assemble all three political institutions together, so as to have states that were at once effective, constrained by law, and accountable. This constitutes a great political divergence.

The Great Intellectual Divergence

Fourth, the polycentric model is flawed by its failure to incorporate the great intellectual divergence. The West was peculiar in that it generated a sustained advance of reliable knowledge.

The growth of knowledge involved a range of activities, each of which was peculiar to the West. One was the scientific revolution. Another was the upsurge in exploration. A further one was the challenge to traditional orthodoxies during the Enlightenment. Yet another was the unprecedented growth of literacy, mainly in the Protestant countries. There was nothing comparable to the systematic, institutionalized curiosity and search for knowledge that arose around 1600, or earlier, on some accounts, in Europe. This was no temporary efflorescence, but the early stages of a transformation that kept accelerating and expanding.

It is noteworthy that some proponents of the polycentric model have recognized this as a form of Western exceptionalism. Patrick K. O'Brien (2013), a leading exponent of global economic history, acknowledges the peculiarity of the West in generating the scientific revolution. Jack Goldstone, one of the early advocates of polycentrism, has recently acknowledged (2012) that there was a great intellectual divergence—the West took a unique intellectual path long before the industrial revolution. Only in the West, writes Goldstone, were the reigning intellectual orthodoxies of the classical epoch successfully challenged.

CONCLUSION

The cosmopolitan ideal, which is opposed to Eurocentrism and indeed all kinds of ethnocentrism, appears at first sight to fit well with the new polycentric model of world history. But a verdict on the polycentric model would need to be mixed. On the positive side, its overall ethos—to level the landscape of world history and to bring the West down a notch by denying its exceptionalism—has inspired much new writing. The goal of moving from the Eurocentric to the polycentric is an attractive one.

But the polycentric model is not especially animated by the cosmopolitan ideal. The polycentric approach is comfortable enough with Eurasia-centrism, Asia-centrism and Sinocentrism. It does not advance the cosmopolitan ideal to attack European exceptionalism alone and to label it 'Eurocentrism'. Moreover, the polycentric approach is deeply flawed in failing to pay attention to several great divergences.

I conclude that a new post-polycentric or neo-polycentric model is needed. It would have to be a hybrid. It would aim to comprehend and explain both the parallels and the divergences in history. It would seek to incorporate a mix of the polycentric, the bicentric, and the unicentric. It would pay attention to both the West's unexceptional and its exceptional features. It would advance the cosmopolitan ideal by rigorously questioning the value of all exceptionalisms.

BIBLIOGRAPHY

Bayly, C. (2004). *The Birth of the Modern World: Global Connections and Comparisons, 1780–1914*. Oxford: Blackwell.

Broadberry, S. (2013). 'Accounting for the Great Divergence' University of Warwick: Dept. of Economics. www2.warwick.ac.uk/fac/soc/economics/research/centres/cage/events/conferences/longrungrowth/broadberry.pdf.

Delanty, G. (ed.) (2006). *Europe and Asia: Beyond East and West*. London: Routledge.

Duchesne, R. (2011). *The Uniqueness of Western Civilization*. Leiden: Brill.

Frank, A. G. (1998.) *Re-Orient: Global Economy in the Asian Age*. Berkeley: University of California Press.

Fukuyama, F. (2011). *The Origins of Political Order: From Prehuman Times to the French Revolution*. New York: Farrar, Straus and Giroux.

Goldstone, J. A. (2008). *Why Europe? The Rise of the West in Global History, 1500–1850*. New York: McGraw-Hill.

———. (2012) 'Divergence in Cultural Trajectories: The Power of the Traditional within the Early Modern' in D. Porter (ed.) *Comparative Early Modernities, 1100–1800*. New York: Palgrave-Macmillan.

Goody, J. (2004). *Capitalism and Modernity: The Great Debate*. Cambridge: Polity Press.

———. (2006) *The Theft of History*. Cambridge: Cambridge University Press.

———. (2010a) *The Eurasian Miracle*. Cambridge: Polity Press.

———. (2010b) *Renaissances: The One or the Many?* Cambridge: Cambridge University Press.

Hewson, M. (2012). 'Multicultural and Post-Multicultural World History'. *Cliodynamics: Journal of Theoretical and Mathematical History* 3.2, 306–24.

Hobson, J. M. (2004). *The Eastern Origins of Western Civilisation*. Cambridge: Cambridge University Press.

Jacques, M. (2012). *When China Rules the World: The End of the Western World and the Birth of a New Global Order*. London: Penguin.

Lieberman, V. B. (2003). *Strange Parallels: Vol. 1 Southeast Asia in Global Context c. 800–1830*. Cambridge: Cambridge University Press.

———. (2009). *Strange Parallels: Vol. 2 Mainland Mirrors: Europe, Japan, China, South Asia, and the Islands*. Cambridge: Cambridge University Press.

Melleuish, G. (2012). *Is the West Special? World History and Western Civilisation*. Melbourne: Institute of Public Affairs.

Morris, I. (2011). *Why the West Rules—For Now: The Patterns of History and What They Reveal About the Future*. New York: Farrar, Straus and Giroux.

Needham, J. (1971). *Science and Civilisation in China, Vol. IV Part 3: Civil Engineering and Nautics*. Cambridge: Cambridge University Press.

O'Brien, P. K. (2013). 'Historical foundations for a global perspective on the emergence of a Western European regime for the discovery, development and diffusion of useful and reliable knowledge'. *Journal of Global History* 8.1, 1–24.

Pieterse, J. N. (2006). 'Oriental Globalization: Past and Present' in G. Delanty (ed.) *Europe and Asia: Beyond East and West*. London: Routledge.

Pomeranz, K. (2000). *The Great Divergence: China, Europe, and the Making of the Modern World Economy*. Princeton: Princeton University Press.

Wiener, M. S. (2013). *The Rule of the Clan*. New York: Macmillan.

III

The Challenges of Pluralism and Difference

SEVEN

The Cosmopolitan Ideal and the Civilizing Process

Expanding Citizenship for Peace

Geneviève Souillac

This chapter critically explores the civilizing process for a cosmopolitan ethics of peace and the reduction of harm. As I argue, it is possible to target the democratic potential of cosmopolitan modernity for a renewed civilizing process to be defined. A top-down approach to international norms can be complemented by a bottom-up, people-oriented model of peace ethics. The civilizing process can be reappropriated to indicate a community's violence reduction goals and to signify a relational model grounded in citizenship, civic life, and civility. I use the terms *deep citizenship* and *expanded identity* to evoke an expansion of the civic experience to structure a new kind of civilizing process as a vehicle of political hope for an era of nonviolence and peace. Cosmopolitanism favorably explores the increased interconnectedness and interdependence between states, groups, and individuals brought forth by globalization. It positively evokes the awakening to collective responsibility and to the stewardship of the planet and humanity. But it also echoes the Enlightenment and its modern, linear conception of human progress. One source of disillusionment with modernity is the debt of violence that has accompanied a civilizing process understood as the legacy of Western imperialism and colonialism.

A revised civilizing process will be appropriate on two conditions. First, the dilemmas of a civilizing process promoted by a Western-centric model of development must be identified and addressed. Second, as suggested in the second part of the chapter, the new social and political realities of a globalized world must be investigated and analysed ethnographically, theoretically, and philosophically. This includes a survey of the gains and limits of a global model inspired by democratic achievements. I argue that the unique characteristics and opportunities of contemporary life support new conceptual strategies, outlined in the third and final part of the chapter. An appropriate and sustainable civilizing process will be expressed where actors choose to inhabit expanded forms of identities and deepen their approach to citizenship. Expanded identity and deep citizenship are vehicles of necessary hermeneutic practices in a complex world. Civilizational dialogue, narrative exchange, historical reflexivity, and conflict transformation prioritize alternative goals such as nonviolence and cooperation.

Overall, as I suggest in this chapter, reappropriating the civilizing process as a historically conscious concern with the reduction of harm stimulates political hope and forges an ethical legacy for future generations. This renewal depends on a transparent and accountable approach to the shadowy aspects of all civilizational narratives, and of all local histories. To address a pervasive geopolitical legacy of violence and harm, all civilizations must strengthen forces of civility such as self-restraint and historical reflexivity. Restraint and rules of civility are traditionally associated with the civilizing process, but their ethical reach can be widened as nonviolent and inclusive practices and processes are explored. In addition, layers of experience require a hospitable approach to our contemporary universe to sustain a new civilizing spirit. The reality of multiple encounters suggests the need for a horizontal and immanent model which highlights antidotes to the forces of social fragmentation and exclusion. Recognizing the tragic as much as the progressive aspects of any civilizational heritage, including modernity, blurs rigid boundaries between communities. It loosens established narratives and conflicts of representation, and common existential concerns can then orient dialogic exchange towards superordinate goals such as peace.

THE CIVILIZING PROCESS AND THE PROBLEM OF HARM

In *Critical Theory and World Politics* and *The Problem of Harm in World Politics*, Andrew Linklater (2007, 2011) investigates the problem of harm in international relations. Following his lifelong inquiry into the moral development of the international community (Linklater 1998; c.f. Linklater and Suganami 2006), he explores the progression of instruments for the global reduction of harm and the legal, moral, and political controversies surrounding it. An exploding demography, limited resources, and new global risks make the dependence of human beings on each other and on their natural environment clearer than ever. Managing harm appears not only as a worthy goal, but also as a necessary one for ultimate survival. But, as Linklater notes, the connection between the development of nations and the moral obligation not to harm either others or the planet has been tenuous (Linklater 2007). No doubt an ethical turn emphasizing the obligation not to harm can be sourced in Christian and Stoic influences. Yet a consensus on the undesirability of inflicting unnecessary suffering did not emerge from the universally intelligible observation of a shared biological inheritance of physical vulnerability. Nor has it shaped the way sovereign power has exerted itself. Why then has the international society pursued, if only to a degree, efforts to curb unnecessary harm and senseless violence, notably through what Linklater (ibid: 9) calls cosmopolitan harm conventions? And why does the model of citizenship and civility that accompanies modern nation-states continue to inspire cosmopolitan arguments?

Civic life is at the heart of the republican project on which the cosmopolitan proposal relies to make the case for belonging to a shared world. The classical republican model of civic life does not, however, in a world system of nation-states, succeed in making a successful case for the reduction of harm as a matter of global concern, or even as a democratic goal. The republican practice of citizenship is traditionally associated with concern for the common good and participation in a modern democratic state. At the same time, the abstraction of cosmopolitan values is opposed to an easier allegiance to local customs reinforced through the centuries and through the nation. Where the local and the global are opposed both spatially and temporally, global norms are distant and new, whereas local values are near, but old. These dichotomies are difficult to sustain in an interdependent world. Local values and global norms intersect whether they converge or clash. Many cultures include abstract considerations about human life and dignity, and condemn harm and destruction, while views differ on what constitutes harm, or human dignity, or the right reason to wage war. Rather than being mutually exclusive, norms expressing universal moral concern coexist with local values, both locally and globally. Here the exposure of values and practices to each other raises conflicts and dilemmas which demand to be resolved. The Kantian insight about the moral development of humanity in the context of an emerging community of states reflected the understanding that forces giving rise to world society also rendered political, social, and cultural life more complex. Not only orderly, but also disorderly forces influence the interface of local and cosmopolitan configurations of competition and cooperation. As Linklater summarizes, the problem of community evolves into the problem of citizenship and then into the problem of harm (ibid: 8).

For Linklater (2011: 250–57), however, there are limits to explaining a collective learning process with reference to political modernity and to Kantian cognitive rationalism alone. The concern with regulating and

containing the potential disorder of modernity culminated in the twentieth century and its first and second world wars. But the wide variety of
forms of organized violence in the late nineteenth and twentieth century,
from the exploitation of labour in modern industrial society to genocide
and intra-state conflicts, contribute to the disillusionment with modern
conceptions of moral progress. Linklater (2007: 160–77) turns here to the
historical and sociological scrutiny of international relations, and specifically to the civilizing process. For Norbert Elias (2000), the term refers to
changing attitudes to gratuitous violence through various codes of be-
havioural constraint over five centuries of European history (Linklater
2007: 10). While the rise of stable states allowed for a degree of pacification expressed in growing social interdependence, Elias also maintained
that the specifically modern civilizing process 'had little influence on
interstate relations' (ibid: 165). He critically distinguished between the
invocation of a civilized condition to justify claims of superiority, and the
notion of a civilizing process revisited as specifically concerned with violence and harm (ibid). This approach was constructivist even as it described responses to the changing contours of social, political, and economic life, combining the growth of social networks with the centralization of power. In this sense, Elias reflected the concerns of the Frankfurt
School to analyse the rise of Nazi Germany. The rise of urbanism and
cities encouraged the related notions of sociability, civility, and civilization, which were contrasted with hypothetical states of nature seen as
perpetually violent. Yet rupture was always possible.

The comparative sociological approach as defended by Linklater
stands out in three ways, or three Cs: Capacity, Concern, Cosmopolitan.
First, it focuses foremost on *capacity*, implying that empirical description
and explanatory inquiry yield insights into potential. The civilizing process stresses the potential of a society to harness its full capacity with
regard to building ties of civility. A historical and sociological approach
which highlights 'the nature and potentiality of modernity organized as a
system of states' (Linklater 2007: 131) shines, as it were, the light on
possible roads ahead. This predictive method gathers empirical and theoretical evidence yet also invites further normative discussion about sustaining an (implicitly just) international political order (ibid: 159). Second,
it is a *cosmopolitan* sociology of state systems because its central question
is the extent to which the notion of a world community motivated the
progress towards the restraint of harm as a matter of universal obligation. Third, it emphasizes the *concern* with senseless harm. Elias associated the civilizing process not with rational modernity but with the concern
with violence, introducing new categories to evoke the psychodynamic
forces of empathetic connection and recognition as criteria for civility. For
Linklater, Elias's main objective was to:

understand long-term patterns of change in Europe which affected not only the organization of political and economic life but also the emotional lives of individual persons. Analysing the relationship between social and political structures (the sociogenetic) and the emotional lives of individuals, including their perceptions of guilt, shame, and so forth (the psychogenetic) is a strikingly original feature of Elias's standpoint with immense significance for the study of international relations. On those foundations, Elias developed the argument that the inhabitants of modern societies have come to enjoy levels of physical security that are rare when viewed in the broadest historical context. (Linklater 2007: 167)

Linklater argues persuasively, following Elias, that the civilizing process remains a viable indicator if it is identified with the rejection of violence. Connections exist between the modern conceptions of political community, collective normative goals, and moral learning. The hypothesis that the modern integration of economic, social, political, and even cultural life has necessitated a new outlook on harm and violence explains at least some increase in cooperative ventures to bring ethics into world politics. Moreover, the human security project builds on the insights of the civilizing process as it intersects with transborder solidarity. The expansion of the United Nations (UN) as a forum of international cooperation on matters of common interest, the growth of international treaty law, especially in human rights, humanitarian, and environmental law, are evidence that the voice of morality is heard—even if it is fragile. Despite the originality of Elias's interdisciplinary methodology, however, the notion of a civilizing process is challenged in the current geopolitical context. The double standards historically evidenced by the various forms taken by the European and Western *mission civilisatrice*, combined with the postcolonial critique of the historiography of European politics, show that a European vantage point dominates in our global normative universe.

A cosmopolitan sphere is slowly developing through an active civil society, which targets the exchange of knowledge on matters of transnational interests in the field of the delegitimization of violence. Addressing the legacy of violence, attenuating violence, and preventing violence, both direct and structural, are goals that have been emerging as matters of common concern. But cosmopolitan harm conventions (CHCs) and the normative debates surrounding them emerged under conditions of reflexive modernity (Linklater 2007: 133). Linklater distinguishes between three forms of understandings 'relevant for the emancipatory project', namely 'anthropological understanding', 'because it requires the empathetic skill of appreciating what is unique or different about the other', 'Socratic understanding', because it enables doubt and reciprocal critique, and 'moral-political understanding', because it includes discussion about rules of inclusion, exclusion, and coexistence (ibid: 56). These terms cover a wide area of application, including dialogue with past or potential victims, and compensation for actual or future suffering (ibid: 133). It remains that the language of Western philosophical tradition can circumscribe the moral desirability of these processes as a Western issue. As Oliver Richmond advocates in the case of post-conflict peacebuilding, the reconstruction of political communities under the auspices of the international community is limited by the legitimacy deficit of liberal peace projects imposed by external institutions to local communities (Richmond 2007; Geis and Wagner 2011).

Putting the insights mentioned above into practice will necessitate a wider range of actors than state representatives, and alternative views on the nature of dialogue itself will need to be heard, even if not agreed with. Conceptual tools that address the imperfect and complex nature of communication can sustain Elias's insights about the civilizing process as the increasing restraint of harm. The methodological objection that a state-centred world historical approach risks confining the investigation to an international society which finds its originality (both in the sense of its origin, and its exceptionality) in Western culture raises two fundamental questions. The first concerns the feasibility of a multiphonic dialogue about the civilizing process and its varied interpretations. Rigid and self-centred accounts of civilization need to be challenged, and genuinely egalitarian foundations for a dialogue about civilizing process(es) further explored. Loyalty to particular civilizational perspectives can be accommodated while dialogic cooperation across divides and borders is encouraged. One received idea about civilizations is the narrative that their preservation necessitates conflict and exclusion. Conversely, conflicts are routinely approached in civilizational and religious terms. Broader comparative work necessitates both reflexive *and* interpretive dimensions as a matter of methodological priority. Richard Shapcott (2001) studies the application of philosophical hermeneutics to issues of solidarity and justice in international society, testing the viability of the term *conversation* in a global context. This in turn raises the second question: that of the democratization of the civilizing process. Linklater (2007: 142–43) focuses on nation-states but recognizes the historically complementary role of civil society actors which has culminated in the twenty-first century. For Richard Falk (2000, 2013), Mary Kaldor (2003, 2007, 2012), and others in the field of critical security studies, analyses of violence and harm which give a central place to civilians have been an important part of grassroots emancipatory projects.

The rest of this chapter examines how democratic ethics supplements the civilizing process. The distinction between territorial and normative allegiance is challenged by the consensus slowly emerging on the need for checks on power monopolies and gratuitous violence. As I argue, additional conceptual tools are needed to continue to democratically anchor a civilizing process defined as the collective project to reduce and ultimately eliminate unnecessary harm. Linklater's project takes as its point of departure a historical sociology of states that, he claims, we are only beginning to document and explain. Indeed, the world is not merely plural, but complex. Globalization induces ambiguities and ambivalence regarding community and borders. Sovereign and economic interests limit collective action on behalf of a shared but fragile environment. Increased exposure creates new knowledge about the world, and in turn more ethical questions, but also poses new questions on the *how* of relating, the nature of boundaries, and legitimate forms of communication. Yet gaps clearly remain in our understanding of what role peace values and conflict transformation processes might play in the management of complex pluralism. Intercultural dialogue and an inclusive approach to the management of difference remain elusive in the midst of entrenched power imbalances and imperviousness to the pernicious aspects of conflict (Souillac 2012). To forge a newly defined civilizing process for peace and nonviolence from multiple and overlapping identities requires the engagement with complex diversity. Here, extending the democratic model of citizenship further develops the hypothesis that a collective learning process in the area of normative identity exists.

DEMOCRATIC ETHICS, COSMOPOLITANISM, AND CIVIC LIFE IN A COMPLEX WORLD

Can a democratic identity grounded in the commitment to human rights include allegiance to the goals of human security, environmental concerns, and further, peace and nonviolence? The model of deep citizenship I defend below arises from a political and social anthropology of contemporary life, including its difficulties and yearnings. Complex realities constitute the fertile ground for deep citizenship and expanded identities to become working tools for an ethical future. The dilemmas of pluralism reflect disenchantment with the legitimacy deficit of democracy in the Western world. This in turn has made the shift from the description of citizenship, to normative claims about the obligations contained therein, problematic in the history of political thought and, as Linklater (2007: 34) points out, difficult, if not impossible to achieve. The bounded nature of legal and civic belonging in modern states, combined with the growth of nationalism, has made the case for limiting moral obligation to the nation particularly strong. But the tension between universalist and particularist approaches has long troubled claims for a cosmopolitan extension of the civic experience to include concern with global harm, such as the poverty burden. At one end, the agonistic reading of democracy, as Chantal Mouffe (2009, 2013) argues, makes it incompatible with cosmopolitanism since any form of consensus runs the risk of diluting the democratic energies of dissent. But Jürgen Habermas (2001), too, has been circumspect about the quest for democratic consensus and the emergence of a public sphere on a global level.

This also explains why a revised civilizing process will not be able to circumvent the democratic dilemmas of cosmopolitanism. The alleged incompatibility between allegiance to country and local community, versus motivation on behalf of distant strangers, is mirrored in the perceived incompatibility between civic action motivated by interest-based and local alliances, and a civic life arising from concern with abstract or universal causes such as the suffering of humanity. Yet a survey of democratic resources at theoretical and empirical levels can begin to unravel the debate between particularism and universalism. The tight distinction between particularist and universalist values and norms is increasingly unsustainable. In the agonist model of democracy, active citizenship including mobilization, defiance, and what Pierre Rosanvallon (2008) even calls 'counter-democracy' challenge the moral and political legitimacy of governments and policies. Such democratic forces of dissent are an effective tool to question the concentration and collusion of power on a global scale, and are not limited by local forms of identity. Further, the specificities of a democratic public sphere accommodating diverse views are already visible, if to a lesser degree, with the advent of global media and increased connectivity. The sociology of economic and migratory flows in contemporary cities reveals the degree of networking that exists globally, whether for good or for bad.[1] Informal and formal voices now participate as the variety of communicative opportunities widens.

The work of Habermas (1996, 1998) on communicative ethics has opened multiple avenues from which to further explore how citizenship is appropriated. Debates on pluralist justice inspired by communicative ethics show to what extent the public sphere can accommodate multiple interpretations of a diverse world. This includes forms of dissent but also of normative consensus crucial to democratic procedures. As James Bohman (2007) argues, to fully address pluralism in a contemporary era means to reframe the *demos* as composed of as many *demoi* participating in, reinterpreting, and enriching the public sphere. In Bohman's account, cosmopolitan and democratic values are interdependent insofar as both support non-elitist and inclusive processes. Here, dissent does not preclude the goals of consensus. Pluralist conceptions of democratic justice shift the debate by showing how the confrontation between particularist perspectives and universal norms prevent democratic stagnation and promote democratic renewal from the grassroots. Iris Marion Young's work on difference, exclusion, and inclusion has stretched the limits of legitimate forms of deliberation and its goals (Young 2002). Seyla Benhabib (2008, 2011) in turn envisages a model of democratic iteration to deepen legal and ethical debate. Both Young and Benhabib argue that breakthroughs in the reconfiguration of social meaning through democratic means are necessary, though they disagree on the possibility of global democracy (Benhabib 2008; Young 2006, 2013). Nevertheless, these pluralist models of democratic justice reconfigure the limits of what constitutes a democratic process, and situate democracy within a broader, contested cosmopolitan framework.

Interest in complex pluralism either explicitly supports, or implicitly requires, a model of expanded identity and deep citizenship. Pluralist conceptions of democratic justice in a diverse world facilitate the expansion of political and social identities through processes of recognition and moral learning, though Benhabib expands less on this issue than Young (2006) or Gerard Delanty (2009). The transformation of views is not a classical goal of participatory citizenship, though it is conceivably one of its byproducts. Nor does active or virtuous citizenship include the goals of conflict management. Yet, as most acknowledge, the cultural divides and normative codes pose challenges. A preliminary distinction between the literal, administrative definition of national citizenship and the symbolic appropriation of the *experience* of citizenship can help clarify the ambiguities and ambivalences discussed here. Legal citizenship, in particular democratic forms of citizenship, offers a wide range of features. These include substantive aspects of local belonging within national histories, but also principled, normative claims that have universal reach and situate us within a broader, comparative historical narrative about the emancipation of all peoples as well as of our own. When a distinction is drawn between a particular and a universal claim, the possibility of intersections between these claims across cultural or civilizational borders is often overlooked, and the bridging potential of constitutional forms of patriotism is misrecognized (see the work of Laborde on civic patriotism and critical republicanism, e.g., Laborde 2008). Indeed the problem is not geographical. It lies instead in the arbitrary opposition between the local and the universal, and in the assumption that particularist views by definition cannot resonate with those of others, or be affected by them. A highly particular situation, as literature demonstrates, can evoke universal qualities and resonate with many.[2] For Kwame Appiah (2007), conversation is the defining characteristic of the cosmopolitan attitude, regardless of one's geographical or, indeed, socioeconomic and cultural situation. The cosmopolitan citizen need not be associated with limited elites. The dialogue between particular configurations of meaning, with universality, lies at the beginning of the conversation.

Expanded identity and deep citizenship can be defined here as embracing the whole spatial and temporal span of the political *and* sociological experience of inhabiting citizenship. A social and political anthropology of contemporary forms of democracy clarifies the conceptual relationship between the particular and the universal, and the configurations of citizenship across belonging and difference. A political anthropology of democracy combined with sociological approaches to global modernization offer additional tools from which to realistically evoke both the limits and the potential of contemporary life.[3] As an unfinished project of modernity, a cosmopolitan civilizing process must critically address the reasons for disenchantment with the democratic project and the discouragement with regard to normative globalization. Increased mobility, information flows, and the exchange of knowledge and perspectives can strengthen the deterritorialization and expansion of already layered and fluid identities. Yet our ambivalent implication in a globalized world featuring intersection of local histories, and our sometimes strenuous encounters with difference both within and across borders, can also limit the positive experience of globalization. Democratic discouragement converges with forces of dynamic polarization, exclusion, and fragmentation worldwide that illuminate in turn the dilemmas and tensions induced by social complexity within national borders. While pluralism draws attention to divides across culture, religion, language, ethnicity, and civilization, complexity draws attention to how diverse configurations across divisions of social and political opportunities are embodied. We experience confrontations within ourselves and with others, and dynamics of polarization, resentment, humiliation, and dehumanization accompany the constitution of bounded identities. Psychosocial needs are fulfilled across complex patterns of belonging, affiliation, loyalty, and emancipatory projects. The lack of a social emotive or corporeal dimension in Habermas's work, despite its lineage with Frankfurt School Critical Theory, is, as mentioned earlier, noted by Linklater (2007: 187). The rationalist defense of discourse ethics has attracted the attention of commentators who emphasize the psychosocial elements of complex diversity, from gender and racial difference to the geopolitical asymmetries of a postcolonial order and indigenous forms of knowledge (Young 1990, 2002; Kapoor 2002; Thomassen 2006; Souillac and Fry 2014).

Contemporary experience is characterized by complexity, both temporally and spatially: encounter with difference; encounter with the past and memory, and with potential future(s); and encounter with the vulnerability that accompanies all these mutations. Contemporary actors sometimes navigate these global waters with difficulty, as exemplified by responses that range from indifference to extremism. The cognitive fatigue of the contemporary self was first observed by Christopher Lasch (1984) with his notion of the minimal self, interestingly translated into French as the 'besieged' self. Axel Honneth (1996) has tackled the new normative challenges posed by the contours of social conflict today, which take the classical approach to patterns of domination and submission, mastery, and resentment to the new emotional depths of humiliation across generations. He convincingly argues for the psychopolitical role of recognition for justice goals in a contemporary society (ibid). Dominique Moïsi's (2010) unique exploration into the geopolitics of humiliation echoes this concern. Indeed, complexity also arises where conflicts are mediated not only through discourse but also through image(s) and across an often virtual grid of perceptions and representations circulating in the information economy (Möller 2013). As this 'thickening' of virtual spaces occurs, material borders such as the construction of walls, sophisticated surveillance, and other means of securitization, become denser. As I have suggested elsewhere (Souillac 2012), examining the work of Etienne Balibar (2001) on European citizenship, borders have become an internal experience as much as an external one. Borders of all kinds, literal but also symbolic, have mushroomed and become the signifiers of uninvestigated forms of malaise. The tension between the forces of dissimulation and obfuscation, and the insistence on transparency, in turn deflects our attention from the real causes and effects of conflict.

The uncertainties of contemporary life affect not only political trust, but also political hope after the end of the grand narratives of modern emancipation, and a dubious pacification of society. To undermine dualist narratives that set us up against others, we must remain vigilant and persist in our cognitive and affective resistance. Spanish political philosopher Daniel Innerarity (2006, 2009, 2012) discusses effects of distortion and confusion in our mixed experience of social reality. He argues for the cultivation of surprise and innovation as tools to deal with a reality that we also critically monitor—what he calls 'spying on the real'. As he suggests, forces of irruption and disruption in consensual but sometimes oppressive representations of reality can help restore political hope amid pervasive deception with regard to the ruins of ideologies of progress and control. Innerarity makes the observation that different conceptions of political time can overlap, meet, and confront each other. While our perception of the world is shrinking spatially, we are not following suit in our perception of time(s). With an accelerated exchange of information, and as global world politics swing between order and crisis, boundaries are crossed temporally and no longer only spatially. Yet the diversity of human life is matched by a plurality of conceptions of time, and difference is also contained in how the other experiences time. The media and the public sphere mask these complex realities and impose a political rhythm as well as a narrative about this rhythm. As a result, exclusion from the public sphere, or disagreement, indicates gaps or disconnects with regard to the perception of political time. For Innerarity, the cynicism, fatigue, or discouragement caused by modern disillusionment can be replaced by what he calls an optimistic skepticism. Harnessing curiosity and welcoming the destabilizing element of surprise in the confrontation with difference replaces mere tolerance and re-enchants coexistence.

While these insights are important, the antidote for a disillusionment arising from the ruins of grand narratives and the saturation with social conflict further lies in a political anthropology which retains the gains of democracy but challenges its limits to embrace and address social complexity. Innerarity is correct to seek new conceptual tools for a multidimensional problem including an intricate mix of political, social, cultural, and psychological issues. As I continue to argue, deep citizenship dynamically builds on this framework, inclusively managing various levels of experience of belonging and allegiance. Clearly, overlapping worlds and the emergence of new public concerns require our cognitive attention, as well as historical and ethical reflection. But culturally specific values and universal principles affirmed through global normative institutions are often mutually enriching. The scrutiny of inherited forms of violence and of bio-sustainable goals further anchors this dialogue.

MANAGING COMPLEXITY IN A POST-HEROIC WORLD

As I have been arguing, the conceptual resources of the civilizing process can be reassessed. Revisiting democratic participation supports the reappropriation of the civilizing process, understood as the exploration of restorative social ties. The tensions, dilemmas, and even discomfort introduced by a complex, fragmented, and conflicted world signal to new forms of civility. Actors require new skills in the communication and exchange of contested conceptions of life, ethics, and civilization itself. Skills to manage difference and conflict have their place in an agora that is complex and plural. They support the democratic spirit of participation, emancipation, and justice. Disagreement and conflicts structure our contemporary universe, but are just the tip of the iceberg of long-standing histories of direct and structural violence. The mutations of the contemporary world also reveal the less triumphant, disturbing experience of our contemporary lives. These defy promises of false peace encouraged by residual emancipatory and unifying ideologies. Daniel Innerarity has called for a post-heroic society to dismantle democratic hubris while affirming emancipatory values classically associated with democratic ethics. As I argue below, a post-heroic conception of the tasks of deep citizenship also arises from the recognition that alternative social and political rhythms require skills, practices, and spaces which explore existential questions from the point of view of historical *longue durée*.

In two essays, 'On the Public Use of History' and 'Learning from Catastrophe?', Jürgen Habermas (2001) discusses how public reflection provides the distance needed to address the legacies of sovereignty and empire. Political communities take shape within communities of meaning. The profound psychosocial upheavals through which Germany came to terms with its past is indeed an exemplary case where a 'civilizing process', in Elias's definition, occurred *after* a crisis in civilization. If this term expresses the political and psychosocial move forward towards less violence and more restraint, this shift may be said to have successfully and democratically occurred in post-war Germany through public communicative practices. Habermas offers a similar analysis of European unification after two world conflicts. Denser forms of solidarity, or what he calls the solidarization around democratic and human rights values, established a normative community centred on the future avoidance of war. Again, historical scrutiny of the civilizational milieus which led to conflict and violence in Europe supported this new community. These two examples show that political sustainability is achieved where the containment of violence is seen as a necessary condition. Local struggles for democratic ownership reflect the difficulties inherent in the negotiation of meanings from different perspectives. However, violent conflict is avoided if dialogic spaces that embrace complexity and understand the historical origins of both local values and universal norms are supported.

The retelling of stories across emancipatory struggles and strenuous encounters more adequately reflects the communicative processes across *demoi* advocated by James Bohman. As cherished values and norms are examined historically and contextually reinterpreted, received ideas of democratic ownership are challenged. Conversely, reflecting on the historical nature of norms as they are discussed and challenged makes us aware of their fragility. Further, such processes institute nonviolence and conflict transformation for the recovery of community. The disclosure of emancipatory narratives shows that while we may experience democracy in its immediacy, there is no final point to democracy. Democracy is forged sometimes at the cost of rupture with the past, and always through discussion and compromise between groups. There is always a before and an after of democracy. Democracy is elaborated from the mix and match of collective representations, memories, and identities. The public sphere of debate and deliberation highlights the complexity of overlapping narratives, but also strengthens and normalizes reflexive, inclusive, and cooperative responses. The emergence of superordinate spaces such as the European Union, and processes of reconciliation and reconstruction which work through war guilt as occurred in post-Apartheid South Africa,[4] reveal the degree to which conflict transformation is important to sustain political recovery and the delegitimization of violence. By addressing the historical legacies of violence, we create the epistemic conditions for the transformation of conflict. Constructively addressing conflict in turn unveils hidden forms of violence.

The historical territorialization of civilization can be supplemented by the deterritorialization of the experience of the civilizing process on the scene of cosmopolitanism. Identity assembles with citizenship, where skills and capacities are invoked, so that contested accounts of reality can be debated and converge. Public spaces which highlight the mediation of conflict spawn the awareness of how violence and nonviolence, encounter and exclusion, history and responsibility also constitute the field of civic life classically associated with rights, freedom, and equality. Further, they delegitimize violence and constructively address conflict, further constellating identities around ethical norms of civility and conflict transformation. If mechanisms are encouraged for all voices to be heard and all experiences recognized, civic participants remain empowered despite difficulties. But the confrontation of diverse views, to move beyond adversarial models, requires platforms which reenact the interface between identities, and invests in the resources contained in communities of interpretation. Open, hermeneutic practices encourage cognitive capacities with regard to social complexity and social skills such as empathy. For example, the encounters with the past just discussed stimulate historical reflexivity about patterns of conquest and domination. Knowledge of our enmeshment in processes of which the consequences are harmful is facilitated in turn by psychosocial approaches to the recognition of suffering. We can then move through the confrontation of narratives and continue targeting both conflict transformation and the identification of shared concerns across longitudinal dimensions.

We have reached the point where the deepening of ties of civility will reflect the inclusion of complex time as expressed in contested narratives of historical suffering and recovery. The asynchrony of civilizational times implies a shift in the perception of uniform historical progress, and a new form of existential political will. When we engage with our own histories, we recognize that alternative perceptions of political time exist and must be negotiated within the public sphere. Indeed, to operate 'historically' requires a critical reconfiguration of our relationship to historical time and space, to broaden our subjective experience and constructively consider the histories of others as they overlap with ours. But our experience as historical beings also encourages the anthropological function of the shaping of shared meaning around the recovery and survival of community. Resourcing shared knowledge and political will across civilizational divides for the sake of survival depends on the exchange of historical narratives about survival, even where memories are contested. Innerarity's call to vigilance and Habermas's public function of history suggest that wariness not only of uniformity but also of polarized narratives cultivates the accommodation of pluralist histories *and* the nonviolent search for common ground. The scrutiny of historical narratives pioneers a hermeneutic, open-ended deconstruction and reconstruction. It does not seek closure but rather values the process itself, and makes space for mutual recognition. This recalibrates the value of equilibrium in a world of extremes and of exclusion as the default response to intractable conflict or historical violence.

Hospitality is a useful metaphor here. Our contemporary condition particularly calls for its cultivation. The communities of meaning from which spring the moral power of values and norms carry historical vulnerability. Dialogue is born from mechanisms of recognition which remain to be identified. With a hospitable disposition comes the will to compassionately and open-endedly listen to the narratives of others. For Innerarity, hospitality crystallizes those demands placed upon us by so-

cial complexity but provides a counter response. It displaces the immediacy which permeates our contemporary social and political existence. It
also offers a momentary suspension to halt the perpetual acceleration of
time and prevent too hasty closures on meaning. Inducing the political
will to elaborate shared spaces does not always succeed from a discursive
platform which limits itself to the exchange of justifications. Hospitality
assists in producing a space conducive to recognition. A hospitable exchange of interpretations in turn highlights the fossilizations which take
place across borders of identity, and across time. Finally, hospitality carries with it the experience of encounter and humility—even of shared
vulnerability, as hospitality is conducive to existential reflection on the
experience of possession and dispossession that are elements of life.
Complex time reframes the present to reveal how past and future are
interdependent, and how we share interdependent historical destinies of
which the ultimate concern is sustainable life.

Both democratic and cosmopolitan lives are built on the conscious
involvement with historical destinies, and with others whom we inevitably meet on our journey. Grassroots communities of meaning are about
the creation of collective life and identity. They possess resources for the
exploration of values and practices which enhance a burgeoning experience of responsibility as a positive form of participation. As historical and
hospitable beings, we share in common our vulnerability and are commonly empowered: We are both acted upon, and acting on, the world
historical stage. Shared vulnerability, whether the encounter feels comfortable or confrontational, can be channelled into opportunities for innovation in how we think of social linkages not only spatially but also
temporally. The shared human value placed on survival is in turn reinforced by democratic and inclusive processes, generating a virtuous cy-
cle. Intersubjective and critical memory practices, hospitality, and the
encounter with difference all enhance the dialogic dimension of a civic
world articulated through borders of space and time, and of a shared
world where our existential vulnerability calls us to greater cooperation.
Uncertainty is built into these realities. Welcoming uncertainty restruc-
tures our thinking away from linear and causal models, towards the creative imagination of better futures. Collective responsibility with regard to
a sustainable future can then emerge.

A public stewardship of humanity will be grounded in historical vulnerability. Both memory and legacy feature in transgenerational transmission for the sake of wise policy formation. Jeffrey Sachs, in his defense
of the UN Millenium Goals, spoke in 2007 about 'survival in the anthroposcene' to refer to a shared world struck by disease, the devastation of
poverty, and violent conflict.[5] For Habermas, past catastrophes must be
discussed publicly. Echoing Jacques Derrida and other thinkers of the
apocalyptic dimension of modernity, Richard Falk (2008: 65) also pro-
phetically once spoke in Japan of the need to collectively address 'catas-

trophes to come'. The nuclear catastrophe at Fukushima in Japan in 2011 highlighted the need for a generational conception of legitimacy and justice which is careful of how policies might affect future generations. The intensity of this disaster echoes the great melancholia that came with the devastation wrought by the use of the atomic bomb in Hiroshima and persists to this day. But our melancholy and frustrations need neither echo the modernist theme of the implosion of civilization nor make us clutch at outdated narratives of linear, ethnocentric progress. Richard Falk (1995) has also called for a law of humanity composed of norms of universal relevance to human life and well-being. Superordinate goals such as peace and bio-sustainability are useful points of focus towards which to continue yoking classical democratic forces and recast these in cooperative terms for survival across time.

CONCLUSION

Recognizing human suffering and vulnerability to violence in all its forms calls for a renewed understanding of the civilizing process where human survival and flourishing meet classical emancipatory projects and redefine democratic goals. For Andrew Linklater, the intuitive intelligibility of our shared vulnerability as biological beings was not sufficient, in the past, to inspire states to greater cooperation and restraint. Today, the experience of our own limits as imposed by environmental concerns and enduring violence allows us to reflect on the cooperative management of human diversity and complexity in the future. Our future will be intersubjective and interdependent. Our contemporary experience is unique in a cosmopolitical sense: demographically, technologically, politically, and culturally. One of the challenges of cosmopolitanism has been to integrate the demands of pluralist democratic justice on a transnational level, and retain its progressive implications with discernment about cherished traditions. But democracy must continue to support the civilizing process as the reduction of harm in a cosmopolitan context. The move towards a cosmopolitical vision of peace and sustainability will be a democratic process in that it concerns people and a civilizing process in that it concerns relationships. New ways of inhabiting citizenship and expanded identities point to a post-heroic world which critically and cooperatively revisits the civilizing process and harnesses democratic and cosmopolitan ethics.

When mobilized across borders, the democratic spirit can further serve to disentangle the world historical process of the civilizing process from state and empire building. Cosmopolitan ethics are democratically and nonviolently shaped in an open, dialogic, and reflexive practice of encounter and learning through deep citizenship and an expanded approach to identity. Deep citizenship works from the complexity of levels of identity, from local affiliations to universal allegiances. It extends the cosmopolitan and democratic purposes of human rights, ethics, norms, and justice in an irreversibly pluralist landscape, reappropriating diversity and complexity in a spirit of active recognition as well as mutual respect. Citizenship can now be approached as a three-tiered framework. The first level of citizenship, in a world structured around the nation-state, reflects national belonging. The second level of citizenship involves participation in civil society where private concerns and the public sphere converge. At a third level of civic life, however, common belonging to shared world(s) occurs. This is experienced in the recognition of the common goal of survival in an increasingly complex and interdependent context in which the effects of biopolitics, neoimperial economics, and sovereign power remain active.

Deep citizenship expands from multiple sites of social, civic, and civil experience, forming a community of which the agenda arises from the shared historical experiences of vulnerability and suffering. Superordinate existential goals are affirmed in a decentralized, borderless space, recognizable nonetheless by its emphasis on nonviolence, conflict resolution, and peace-making. Complex patterns of belonging cover intricate and often painful relationships which include not only the achievements of humanity, but also the various forms of dehumanization that shape our history. As the importance of peace and cooperation are prioritized, so do these values in turn become key elements in both cosmopolitan and democratic landscapes. Both constructive critique, and a realistic but positive anticipation of the future can be yoked in renewed political hope. This finds its source neither in a limited historical materialism, nor in an appeal to transcendental idealism. Instead, it takes seriously the shared vulnerability that lurks behind the heightened perception of the legacies of history.

NOTES

1. See the work of Ulrich Beck (1992, 2006) on reflexive modernization and globalization. For a more critical perspective, see the work of sociologist of globalization Saskia Sassen (1991, 1996, 2007).
2. Martha Nussbaum (1995, 2013) combines the defense of cognitive universalism with an Aristotelian concern with political virtue, exploring concepts such as capability and vulnerability, aesthetic expression, and emotion in the humanities.
3. Marcel Gauchet (2005) most distinctly advocates a political anthropology of democracy. See also Honneth (1996).
4. There is extensive literature in this field. See, for example, E. M. Cousins, C. Kumar, and K. Wermester (2000). A reference point on transitional justice is N. Roht-Arriaza and J. Mariezcurrena (2006), and in the field of conflict transformation, the many works of John Paul Lederach, including Lederach (2005).
5. See Jeffrey Sachs's 2007 BBC Reith lectures, Lecture 3, 'Survival in the Anthropocene', given at the China Centre for Economic Research at Beijing University on 25 April 2007.

BIBLIOGRAPHY

Appiah, K. A. (2007). *Cosmopolitanism: Ethics in a World of Strangers*. New York: W. W. Norton.

Balibar, E. (2001). *We, the People of Europe? Reflections on Transnational Citizenship* translated by J. Swenson. Princeton, NJ: Princeton University Press.

Beck, U. (1992). *Risk Society: Towards a New Modernity*. London: Sage.

———. (2006). *The Cosmopolitan Vision*. Cambridge: Polity Press.

Benhabib, S. (2002). *The Claims of Cultures: Equality and Diversity in the Global Era*. Princeton, NJ: Princeton University Press.

———. (2004). *The Rights of Others: Aliens, Residents and Citizens*. Cambridge: Cambridge University Press.

———. (2008). *Another Cosmopolitanism* with J. Waldron, B. Honig, and W. Kymlicka. Oxford: Oxford University Press.

———. (2011). *Dignity in Adversity: Human Rights in Troubled Times*. Cambridge: Polity Press.

Bohman, J. (2000). *Public Deliberation: Pluralism, Complexity and Democracy*. Cambridge, MA: MIT Press.

———. (2007). *Democracy across Borders: From Dêmos to Dêmoi*. Cambridge, MA: MIT Press.

Cousins, E. M., Kumar, C., and Wermester, K. (eds.) (2000). *Peacebuilding in Politics: Cultivating Peace in Fragile Societies*. Boulder, CO: Lynne Riener.

Delanty, G. (2009). *The Cosmopolitan Imagination: The Renewal of Critical Social Theory*. Cambridge: Cambridge University Press.

Elias, N. (2000). *The Civilizing Process: Sociogenetic and Psychogenetic Investigation*. Oxford: Blackwell.

Falk, R. (1995). 'The World Order between inter-state law and the law of humanity: The role of civil society institutions' in D. Archibugi and D. Held (eds.) *Cosmopolitan Democracy*. Cambridge: Polity Press.

———. (2000). *Human Rights Horizons: The Pursuit of Justice in a Globalizing World*. New York: Routledge.

———. (2008). 'War and peace in an age of terror and state terrorism' in Y. Murakami and T. Schoenbaum (eds.) *A Grand Design for Peace and Reconciliation: Achieving Kyôsei in East Asia*. Northampton, MA: Edward Elgar.

———. (2013). *(Re)Imagining Humane Global Governance*. New York: Routledge.

Gauchet, M. (2005). *La condition politique*. Paris: Gallimard.

Geis, A. and Wagner, W. (2011). 'How far is it from Königsberg to Kandahar? Democratic peace and democratic violence in international relations' in *Review of International Studies* 37, 1555–77.

Habermas, J. (1996). *Between Facts and Norms: Contributions to a Discourse Theory of Law and Democracy* translated by W. Rehg. Cambridge: Polity Press.

———. (1998). *The Inclusion of the Other: Studies in Political Theory*. Cambridge, MA: MIT Press.

———. (2001). *The Postnational Constellation: Political Essays* translated by M. Pensky. Cambridge, MA: MIT Press.

Honneth, A. (1996). *The Struggle for Recognition: The Moral Grammar of Social Conflicts* translated by J. Anderson. Cambridge, MA: MIT Press.

Innerarity, D. (2006). *La sociedad invisible*. Madrid: Espasa.

———. (2009). *Ethique de l'hospitalité*. Quebec: Presses de l'Université Laval.

———. (2012). *The Future and Its Enemies: In Defense of Political Hope*. Stanford, CA: Stanford University Press.

Kaldor, M. (2003). *Global Civil Society. An Answer to War*. Cambridge: Polity Press.

———. (2007). *Human Security*. Cambridge: Polity Press.

———. (2012). *New and Old Wars: Organized Violence in a Global Era* (3rd ed.). Stanford, CA: Stanford University Press.

Kapoor, I. (2002). 'Deliberative democracy or agonistic pluralism? The relevance of the Habermas-Mouffe debate for Third World politics' in *Alternatives* 27, 459–87.

Laborde, C. (2008). *Critical Republicanism: The Hijab Controversy and Political Philosophy.* Oxford: Oxford University Press.

Lasch, C. (1984). *The Minimal Self: Psychic Survival in Troubled Times.* New York: W. W. Norton.

Lederach, J. P. (2005). *The Moral Imagination: The Art and Soul of Building Peace.* Oxford: Oxford University Press.

Linklater, A. (1998). *The Transformation of Political Community: Ethical Foundations of the Post-Westphalian Era.* Cambridge: Polity Press.

———. (2007). *Critical Theory and World Politics: Citizenship, Sovereignty and Humanity.* New York: Routledge.

———. (2011). *The Problem of Harm in World Politics: Theoretical Investigation.* Cambridge: Cambridge University Press.

——— and Suganami, H. (eds.) (2006). *The English School of International Relations: A Contemporary Reassessment.* Cambridge: Cambridge University Press.

Moïsi, D. (2010). *The Geopolitics of Emotion: How Cultures of Fear, Humiliation and Hope Are Reshaping the World.* New York: Anchor Books.

Möller, F. (2013). *Visual Peace: Images, Spectatorship and the Politics of Violence.* Basingstoke: Palgrave.

Mouffe, C. (2009). *The Democratic Paradox.* London: Verso.

———. (2013). *Agonistics: Thinking the World Politically.* London: Verso.

Nussbaum, M. (1995). *Poetic Justice: The Literary Imagination and Public Life.* Boston: Beacon Press.

———. (2013). *Political Emotions: Why Love Matters for Justice.* Cambridge, MA: Harvard University Press.

Richmond, O. (2007). 'Critical research agendas for peace: The missing link in the study of international relations' in *Alternatives* 32, 247–74.

Roht-Arriaza, N. and Mariezcurrena, J. (eds.) (2006). *Transitional Justice in the 21st Century: Beyond Truth Versus Justice.* Cambridge: Cambridge University Press.

Rosanvallon, P. (2008). *Counter-Democracy: Politics in an Age of Distrust* translated by A. Goldhammer. Cambridge: Cambridge University Press.

Sachs, J. (2007). 'Survival in the anthroposcene'. 3rd Reith Lecture delivered at the China Centre for Economic Research, Beijing University, 25 April.

Sassen, S. (1991). *The Global City: New York, London, Tokyo.* Princeton, NJ: Princeton University Press.

———. (1996). *Losing Control? Sovereignty in an Age of Globalization.* New York: Columbia University Press.

———. (2007). *Elements for a Sociology of Globalization.* New York: W. W. Norton.

Shapcott, R. (2001). *Justice, Community and Dialogue in International Relations.* Cambridge: Cambridge University Press.

Souillac, G. (2011). *The Burden of Democracy: The Claims of Cultures, Public Culture and Democratic Memory.* London: Lexington Books.

———. (2012). *A Study in Transborder Ethics: Justice, Citizenship, Civility.* Brussels: Peter Lang.

——— and Fry, D. P. (2014). 'Indigenous Lessons for Conflict Resolution' in P. Coleman, M. Deutsch, and E. Marcus (eds.) *The Handbook of Conflict Resolution: Theory and Practice* (3rd ed.). San Francisco, CA: Jossey-Bass.

Thomassen, L. (2006). 'The inclusion of the Other? Habermas and the Paradox of Tolerance' in *Political Theory* 34, 4, 439–62.

Young, I. M. (1990). *Justice and the Politics of Difference.* Princeton, NJ: Princeton University Press.

———. (2002). *Inclusion and Democracy.* Oxford: Oxford University Press.

———. (2006). *Global Challenges: War, Self-determination, and Responsibility for Justice.* Cambridge: Polity Press.

———. (2013). *Responsibility for Justice.* Oxford: Oxford University Press.

EIGHT

Critical Cosmopolitan Democracy and Representation

Sybille De La Rosa

Daniele Archibugi and other theorists of global democracy pay little attention to problems that are connected with the terms *representation* in general and *intercultural representation* in particular. But as I will argue, democratic institutions' legitimacy on a global level will depend heavily on the ability to answer questions about who and what will be represented, and how intercultural representation is possible. Therefore, I propose to conceive of the development of a cosmopolitan public sphere as a cornerstone for the development of real cosmopolitan practices and institutions.

According to Habermas, a global civil solidarity has not yet emerged, making a global civil society impossible. Hence, the question arises of how to legitimate post-national democratic decisions, unless there is a change in self-determination or citizenship (Habermas 2001: 107–10). Daniele Archibugi proposes to go beyond this in order to represent citizens in a world parliament, to reform the United Nations Security Council, and to institute an international criminal court. For Archibugi, 'the expansion of the geo-social space (global civil and economic society) calls for the construction of an expanded geo-political space' (Urbinati 2003: 4). Archibugi and Held expect that the creation of a global political space is beneficial in order to overcome the post-democratic tendencies of national democracies, because it might help to strengthen the political primacy over the economic sphere (Held 1995: 236–37).

Archibugi therefore argues for a concept of global democracy that puts some constraints on governments' exercise of sovereignty, but he believes that these constraints should not be exercised by other states. He rather proposes that this can be done by intergovernmental action or the global civil society: 'The attainment of democracy at the international level requires us to steer between the Scylla of a mass of independent autonomous states and the Charybdis of a planetary Leviathan' (Archibugi 1995: 133 f).[1] Global democracy attempts to design such a model. Archibugi argues that this is necessary because social and cultural globalization create a situation in which many aspects of citizens' everyday lives are beyond the scope of their political participation, and therefore 'the inhabitants of the planet should be given political representation beyond their borders and independently from their national governments' (Archibugi 1995: 134). While I agree with Archibugi on the point that the economic and political global order calls for a more just and respectful treatment of the world's inhabitants, and political representation beyond nation-state borders, I think that the model Archibugi proposes is at its core based upon a very traditional imaginary of citizenship and representation.

He proposes a reform of the United Nations (1995: 135) that would implement a world parliament 'that serves as the expression of individuals and not of their governments' and that 'would allow direct representation of national minorities and of the opposition' (Archibugi 1995: 141). Archibugi transfers traditional concepts of representation and sovereignty to the global level, but, as Urbinati argues, thereby also transfers 'all the "vices" that have plagued modern parliamentary democracy' (Urbinati 2003: 6). Therefore, I first want to question this copy-and-paste process, and then propose to revise the traditional models in order to ask if they adequately respond to the challenges that democracy on a global level poses. Second, I want to question the implicit assumption that instituting a world parliament will automatically lead to the emergence of a global civil solidarity. Instead I will argue that the emergence of a global civil solidarity will depend heavily on shared vocabularies and new democratic practices and institutions that cope not only with the challenges of a democratic order but also with the challenges of intercultural communication. Therefore, it is crucial to advance a critical and real *cosmopolitan* cosmopolitism and not just a *global* cosmopolitism.[2] While global cosmopolitism accounts for the challenges of globalization, a real cosmopolitan cosmopolitism affirms the plurality of human identities and experiences and is sensitive to the voices of excluded groups (see Nascimento in this volume).

WHAT CAN BE ARTICULATED WITH A
GLOBAL SECOND LANGUAGE?

In his reasoning, Archibugi draws on a rather liberal understanding, namely, the representation of *interests* (1995: 131). Based on this understanding of representation, he then proposes to solve communicative problems, in the world parliament in particular and the global community in general, by arguing that a global second or third language is required in order to facilitate representation (Archibugi 2005). I will argue that Archibugi's proposal addresses intercultural challenges only in reference to problems related to language. And even though he addresses this problem, his articulation of the problem includes various depoliticizing aspects that negate power implications related to language. But languages and questions of representation are strongly connected to power aspects, because they are linked to the questions of what can be articulated and who and what is represented.

The claim that a global second language is required and that this language should be English has to be reflected upon more thoroughly. Languages are not independent from a society and its historical experiences; they are rather the reflection of the specific perspective on the world of every society. But at the same time, languages are the medium through which human actors understand and appropriate the world; therefore, languages can be changed. As 'self interpreting animals' (Taylor 1985), we depend heavily on the ability to find narratives that help us to structure and understand the world we live in. The use of a language always favours specific perspectives on a problem, because it offers a special set of words, meanings, and metaphors to describe a problem and a special range of grammatical structures. Many traditional narrations have become quasi natural, but through processes of decolonization and globalization, they are more and more contested. So, in order to think about an inclusive global democracy, a language which is open for its appropriation is required, or a use of the English language that is open to new meanings, which gives way to new and more inclusive narrations.

Esperanto has been discussed as such a language for the European context (Christiansen 2006), but it seems—at least at this moment—that there is little hope for Esperanto to become a global or even a European language, although it offers much space for creative articulations, and, probably most importantly, it is an artificial language and could therefore be appropriated without causing any conflicts with native speakers and their language tradition. But there is no infrastructure to teach it, and so far, there is no economic or political necessity to learn it.

But there seems to be an alternative: the appropriation of English. As research on language changes has shown, English has become a global language insofar as it was multiplied when British imperialism gained force (Crystal 2003: 74; Bolton and Kachru 2006). It became the language that promised access to knowledge, and in many places of the world, it became useful to master it (Crystal 2003: 77 ff). But the spread of the English language came with a consequence: It has been appropriated and changed in a totally unpredictable way (Crystal 2003: 142). These changes gave rise to a number of 'new Englishes', beginning with American English. Crystal identifies at least four new Englishes in Asia, Africa, and the Caribbean, not counting Australia, Canada, and New Zealand. Those new Englishes are characterized by borrowings from indigenous languages and the extension of the vocabulary, few grammatical changes, and changes in discourses, meaning, and phonology (Crystal 2003: 147). This trend of new Englishes could be extended to make the English language not just a global but also an inclusive and cosmopolitan second language. But for this it would be indispensable to maintain the plurality of first languages, which could stay the main loci for the political and social appropriation of the world. The new Englishes as a second language then could draw from the first languages. They could be used to translate meaning from the first into the second language by creatively hybridizing English and the first language. In this way, the imperial effort to enforce English as a dominant language could be turned into an appropriation of English which allows the integration of vernacular meaning.

Hybridizing English in this way opens up the possibility to translate perspectives and meanings from other languages into the English language. But more efforts are necessary in order to make the English language not just a global but also a cosmopolitan second language. Besides its meaning aspects, language also has relational and therefore power aspects, as has been shown, especially by the postcolonial studies.

Gayatri Spivak was one of the first to raise attention to the fact that dominant discourses can silence actors with other perspectives of the world. This is not because they lack the ability to express their wishes and positions, but because dominant discourses tend to distort the meaning of formulations and expressions, and therefore also complicate the appropriate representation of the perspectives of others (Spivak 2008). This occurs because of the excluding and including rules of discourse, but also because of the modes of communicative interaction. Power relations become even more visible in Mignolo's and Schiwy's concept of translation, which is based on the idea of two different modes of communicative appropriation.[3] Their concept makes power relations between speakers become even more apparent than Spivak does with the discursive concept.

Translation for Mignolo and Schiwy is unidirectional and hierarchical, and therefore has been a pillar for the foundation and reproduction of the colonial difference. It was practiced from the beginning of the conquest. Exemplary for unidirectional translation were the efforts of Christian missionaries who translated for assimilation: 'The approximately fifty years (from 1528 to 1578) that the Franciscan Bernardino de Sahagun devoted to translate Nahuatl into Latin and Spanish and the time that many religious orders devoted to translate Spanish and Latin into Nahuatl for the purpose of conversion are dramatic and exemplary cases of translation for assimilation. They are dramatic and exemplary because these became models that later were reconverted and adapted by subsequent religious orders in Africa and Asia' (Mignolo and Schiwy 2003: 5).

Double translation in turn starts with a clash, which is caused when two different realities encounter each other. 'This clash produces a space of contact and conflict wherein translation takes place' (Mignolo and Schiwy 2003: 13). After the clash, a process of remodelling and reeducation starts, which 'rearticulated the colonial difference from a subaltern position and that makes the new kind of translation/transculturation possible. It creates experiences that open up new ways of thinking, not as inescapable or necessarily so, but as a possibility' (Mignolo and Schiwy 2003: 15). Mignolo and Schiwy describe the process of double translation from the position of the subaltern as a clash with hegemony that causes new thinking, new perspectives.

On the other side, the nonindigenous members of the EZLN went through a process of reeducation and remodelling because they realized that they needed to listen to the native members (Mignolo and Schiwy 2003: 13). What is striking about their description of the double translation process is that the nonindigenous members were reeducated by the indigenous people. So it could seem like they just changed positions in a still-hierarchical communication process. In order to overcome a hierarchical model of communication, I propose to instead describe this creative communication process that Mignolo and Schiwy grapple with in hermeneutical terms.

In my opinion,[4] Gadamer has shown that language has—besides the traditional aspects, which cannot be neglected—a creative side that is based on the necessity to appropriate the world through language (De La Rosa 2012). This necessity can be explained by Charles Taylor's understanding of human beings as self-interpreting animals who depend heavily on their ability to make sense of their lives and surroundings (Taylor 1985). Like Taylor, Gadamer also draws on the idea that we have to constantly reappropriate and therefore retell the narrative of the world that surrounds us, and our identity in relation to this world. If we don't do so, or cannot do so, we experience alienation. Therefore, written texts are alienated texts for Gadamer that need to be appropriated in order to make them meaningful for contemporary speakers. Appropriation of texts that have been produced in the past is, according to Gadamer, only possible because there are commonalities between the language of the past and the contemporary language. At the same time, language is vivid and changing; therefore, the language of the past and the contemporary language are different. This difference generates a deep abyss between the past and the present. We can only cope with it by narrating stories that hide it and build a kind of narrative bridge that helps us to make sense of history and to tell meaningful stories about the past. And this is exactly the creative side of language that emerges from our need as self-interpreting animals to reappropriate the world through language.

Language is the medium through which we take possession of the world and open up the possibility to say new things. It offers a variety of instruments to articulate new meaning or new perspectives as metaphors, analogies, or the invention of new words or new grammar structures (Gadamer 1999: 436). The community of speakers has to decide if they utilize the traditional rules, words, and practices, or if they are not adequate anymore because of changes in the world—the social or political context. When they are considered inadequate, they can be changed, although certainly not all at once, because too many changes at a time will distort the processes of understanding, which are always fragile. But they can be changed gradually. Therefore, Gadamer argues that traditions always have to be reappropriated; they are not just there, but they have to be reaffirmed in order to persist. But this means also that they can be questioned and changed (Gadamer 1999: 448).

But as Gadamer shows, there can be an obstacle for change, which is not caused by language but by a type of relation which determines the understanding process. It is characterized by the recognition of the other as a person, but at the same time ignoring his or her claim by asserting to know what his or her claim should be. This relation, says Gadamer, is linked to Nietzsche's *Willen zur Macht* (will for mastery), because it ignores the other's communicative intervention in order to maintain its point of view without any irritation. Gadamer supposes that this is not the only possible relation between a speaker and his or her addressee. There is also a relation which starts from the question about the claims of the other. It is determined by an openness that asks. This openness is fundamental for dialogic processes of communication (Gadamer 1999: 366).

In my book *Aneignung und interkulturelle Repräsentation*, I have tried to show in detail how Gadamer's differentiation of communicative relations fit with Bhabha's and Arendt's considerations of power; therefore, I only want to mention that the necessity to appropriate the world can lead either to a more imitating appropriation or a creative appropriation (De La Rosa 2012). While imitating appropriation tends to reproduce traditional perspectives through the reproduction of traditional meaning and imaginaries in present contexts, creative appropriation offers the possibility to create new perspectives by creating new words, new grammar structures, new languages, new meaning. This creative type of appropriation always takes place when a speaker is confronted with what Mignolo calls a clash of realities. It means an epistemic disruption, which we strive to heal by the reconstruction or the new invention of sense (De La Rosa 2012: 196 ff).

But this creative type has to be, as Gadamer has shown, again split up into two further types in order to distinguish between an objectifying-instrumental appropriation that tends to ignore the claim of the other, build hierarchies, and therefore cause exclusion, and a voluntary-dialogical appropriation. Mignolo would call the former unidirectional translation because it appropriates the perspective of the other into one's own perspective without the other's opinion. The voluntary-dialogical appropriation starts from an openness for the claims of the others and leads to new perspectives on the world by identifying shared ideas without neglecting differences. This is possible in a hermeneutical process that seeks to understand the other by listening and understanding his or her perspective as a first step, without judging its implications. If this is practiced by those involved in the conversation, it is possible to identify shared meaning, ideas, or perspectives and, perhaps even more important, similar historical or present experiences in order to build a common ground of understanding in a second step (De La Rosa 2012).

Referring to spoken utterances, Gadamer has also argued that communication has the task to exchange opinions and experiences, which cannot be demonstrated like mathematical rules. Therefore, a persuasive kind of power needs to unfold, which depends, according to Gadamer, on the openness of the addressee of claims (Gadamer 1999: 368). Ethics depend on rhetoric because there are no mathematical rules that force us to act ethically. So the strength of ethics is located in words, which can only try to show the evidence of an utterance and ask for an openness of the addressee towards the claim. Arendt also states that rhetoric is crucial for the emergence and reproduction of a public opinion and emphasizes the fundamental role of a common sense that arises out of communicative forms that recognize the other's claims (Arendt 1978).

Postcolonial and decolonizing studies demand a shift in power structures because they have realized how, for example, the subaltern, the 'orientals', or the indigenous claims are ignored, and how their narratives, beliefs, and languages are excluded (Said 2003; Bhabha 1994; Mignolo 2009; Spivak 2004, 2008). An adequate cosmopolitan concept of representation for this reason depends heavily on its ability to show how these voices and claims can be heard, and how an open communicative process can be secured.

Hence I will argue that the traditional concept of representation as representation of interests has to be changed in a global context, because even in a national context, as the critics of Young and other theorists have shown, the concept of representation as the representation of interests does not cope adequately with the challenges of multicultural societies, which often still have to fight with historical inequalities and misrepresentation. The challenges on a global level are even more complex, because more languages have to be included and even more claims have to be integrated.

THE PROBLEMS OF POLITICAL REPRESENTATION IN A
MULTICULTURAL BUT STILL NATIONAL CONTEXT

In her book *The Concept of Representation*, from 1967, Hanna Pitkin has argued that the term *representation* is highly contested and has been used in a variety of ways, even in concepts that focus on a national level (Pitkin 1967). Since Pitkin's book has been published, the number of concepts of representation has increased rapidly. However, I want to discuss here only two concepts that grapple explicitly with the exclusion of groups, difference, and power aspects at a national level, because they are informative for a discussion of global institutions insofar as they deliver (a) a changed understanding of representation and (b) a sensibility to the challenges of difference and experiences of exclusion. The first is Nadia Urbinati's approach of representation as advocacy, and the second is Iris Marion Young's approach of an asymmetrical reciprocity. Both form part of a new understanding of representation as participation (Thaa 2008), but mainly addressed to a national level.[5]

Nadia Urbinati argues that representation and participation are not opposites, but representation in modern democracies has to be understood 'as to be on a continuum with participation' (Urbinati 2000: 766). This is possible when representatives become advocates of the ones who voted for them and mediators between voters and the political system. They have the task to make citizens feel 'as if they are standing, deliberating, and deciding simultaneously in the assembly' (Urbinati 2000: 766).

The mission of representatives, therefore, is not neutral or principle-oriented decision-making or the *aggregation* of interests, but rather the temporal *mediation* between wishes and interests and at the same time the preservation of disagreements. The representatives have the task to pick up the wishes and interests from society in order to discuss them publicly, and to constantly produce solutions for problems that are infinite in character because of the democratic processes and pluralism. So the function of representation as advocacy for the political system is twofold: It permanently includes wishes and interests into the political debate, solves some of them temporarily, and helps to maintain the legitimacy of the political system because it promises that the next time a problem is discussed, some other group might win. This concept emphasizes how dependent the legitimacy of a political system is in its capacity to permanently include new wishes and interests into the political debate.

But at the same time, Urbinati does not argue for a consensus model of deliberation as Habermas has done. Instead she argues for an agonistic model of deliberative democracy: 'Deliberation enriches knowledge, disposes the individual mind to make public use of reason, refines citizens power of intelligence and combination and encourages citizens to pursue their claims through friendly rivalry' (2000: 774). She argues that democratic deliberations consist of self-revision and self-learning that leads democracies perpetually towards mistakes, but they are perpetually correcting them too. So the acknowledgement of fallibility and plurality, which leads to dissent . . . makes democracy the most reasonable regime' (Urbinati 2000: 774). In order to function adequately, it needs representation as a 'comprehensive filtering, refining and mediating process of political will formation and expression. . . . It shapes the object, style and procedures of political competition. Finally, it helps to depersonalize claims and opinions, and in this way makes them a vehicle for the mingling and associating of citizens' (Urbinati 2000: 760).

Urbinati's argument on representation as advocacy and mediation can be interpreted in two ways: The first starts from a traditional setting of representation within a representative democracy in the sense that there are representatives as part of political parties that advocate interests of citizens in the assembly. The second starts from Urbinati's understanding of exclusion. She describes exclusion as 'the form of silence, of not being heard or represented' (Urbinati 2000: 773) in the political arena. This can also be the case if there is no representative or no other citizen who articulates a person's interests in public debates. Choosing the second interpretation, the political debate is not limited to the debates in parliament, and therefore the claim would be that only those are excluded whose claims are not represented or articulated in public debates. This also widens the scope of representatives because then they are not limited to formally elected representatives anymore. Greenpeace, for example, would also be a representative of citizens' interests and political parties; it would be only one kind of representative among others. Urbinati does not draw on this kind of informal representation, but it might be beneficial to do so, especially in a global context, as Young has shown. I will get back to this later; for now I want to again draw attention to Urbinati's understanding of representation.

There is a traditionally liberal moment in Urbinati's understanding of representation that limits representation to the representation of interests and that should be called into question. This is because it is a conceptual move that is not self-evident, especially not with Mill as reference. For Mill, individual expressiveness and liberty are intimately connected. The free expression of opinions forms part of his concept of freedom. Therefore, he claims that every prevention of free expression of an opinion— and not just interests—means to assume infallibility and erases the possibility to adjust a mistaken opinion (Mill 2001: 20–22).[6] And in his book *Considerations on Representative Government*, he argues that 'we need not suppose that when power resides in an exclusive class, that class will knowingly and deliberately sacrifice the other classes to themselves: it suffices that, in the absence of its natural defenders, the interest of the excluded is always in danger of being overlooked; and, when looked at, is seen with very different eyes from those of the persons whom it directly concerns' (Mill 2004: 40). This is because the representatives of privileged groups do not look at any question with the eyes of a working man (Mill 2004: 41).

So limiting representation to the representation of interests excludes the other aspects of Mill's idea of individual expressiveness, which are opinion and taking perspective. Being excluded then can be specified as opinions, interests, or perspectives not being heard or represented in the assembly or the political debates.

Therefore, I now want to discuss Young's concept of representation as representation of interests, opinions, and perspectives and argue that Young provides a model of agonistic but still deliberative democracy that differentiates between those three aspects of representation, and therefore is more sensible to the intercultural challenges of cosmopolitan forms of representation.

For Young, too, democracy should be about public deliberation, as Habermas claimed, in which problems, conflicts, interests, and needs can be articulated, and where actors strive to convince the others but at the same time also are open to their claims. In contrast to Habermas, Young does not believe that inclusion and justice can be secured by formal procedures such as the ones Habermas argues for (Young 2000: 34). Because 'where there are structural inequalities of wealth and power, formally democratic procedures are likely to reinforce them, because privileged people are able to marginalize the voices and issues of those less privileged' (Young 2000: 34), and this is not always but sometimes due to the fact that they are not sensitive to differences, and therefore misrepresent and misunderstand the others' claims and perspectives.

In *Inclusion and Democracy*, Iris Marion Young has argued that suppression of difference is a problem for all representation (2000: 351). It starts at the moment one person is supposed to represent many. Therefore, Young argues that representation should not be characterized by a relationship of identity, but rather be understood as a differentiated relationship which recognizes the diversity of those being represented (Young 2000: 123).

Stressing the diversity of those being represented could lead to a claim for more representatives, but Young warns that the inclusion of more voices into a political arena can suppress other voices, as in the case of Latino representatives who might inadvertently represent only straight Latinos and not lesbian and gay Latinos (2000: 350). Therefore, Young asks us to rethink the relationship between the representative and the represented. She argues that to understand the interests of a person, knowledge about this person's worldview is required to at least some extent—historical or social background, opinions about how the political institutions should be and which goals they should pursue. In other words, Young distinguishes between interests, opinions, and perspectives. She defines *interests* 'as what is important to the life prospects of individuals, or the goals of organizations' (Young 2000: 134). *Opinions*, in contrast, refer to 'the principles, values, and priorities held by a person as these bear on and condition his or her judgment about what policies should be pursued and ends sought' (Young 2000: 135). They are based in worldviews or the history of social practices. *Perspectives*, finally, do not contain a specific content. The term *social perspectives* is meant to capture group-specific experiences without suggesting that shared experiences lead automatically to shared opinions or interests. The core idea behind this is that representatives have to represent the diversity of those being represented, and this is only possible when they are informed about the variety of interests, opinions, and perspectives of those being represented. Therefore, representatives have to learn about the historical and contemporary embedding in society of the groups they represent. But for this, they have to listen to the represented, and Young is very sceptical about the understanding processes because she fears that understanding will lead to misrepresentation.

> The images of symmetry and reversibility suggest that people are able to understand one another's perspectives because, while not identical, they are similarly shaped, and for that reason replaceable with one another. The mirroring evoked by the ideas of symmetry and reversibility suggests that we are able to understand one another because we are able to see ourselves reflected in the other people and find that they see themselves reflected in us. But such images of reflexion and substitutability, I suggest, support a conceptual projection of sameness among people and perspectives, at the expense of their differences. (Young 1997: 44)

The risk of misrepresentation is especially high when privileged people try to take the perspective of those who are less privileged, because they tend to take the other's position but do so with their own experiences and privileges.

The only correction to such a misrepresentation that supposes sameness—although there is difference too—is the other's ability to tell me that I am wrong about them (Young 1997: 45). But to make this work, I have to listen to them, and I have to recognize them as 'others that have irreducible points of view, and active interests that respectful interaction must consider' (Young 1997: 47 f).

Because Young shows the barriers of understanding and representation, she could be understood as negating that we can understand each other. But she refuses this: 'Understanding across differences is both possible and necessary', but she admits, 'Recognizing the asymmetry of subjects, however, does imply giving a different account at what understanding is and what makes it possible' (Young 1997: 52). Therefore, she proposes to interpret understanding as 'sometimes getting out of ourselves and learning something new' (Young 1997: 53) by 'suspending my assumptions in order to listen'. But Young cannot interpret understanding as suspension without contradicting herself; some pages earlier she argues that 'it is hard to see how any of us could suspend our perspectives mediated by our relations to others, in order to adopt their perspectives mediated by their relation to us. The infinity of the dialectical process of selves in relation to others both makes it impossible to suspend our own positioning and leaves an excess of experiences when I try to put myself in the others person's place' (Young 1997: 47).

As Gadamer has shown, understanding always draws from previous knowledge on language and the world; therefore, we cannot suspend all our assumptions at the same time. But we can question some of our assumptions, and that means we can open up the system of assumptions and prejudices in order to question and modify them. The function of questioning becomes crucial because 'it is not possible to make a new experience without actively questioning' (Gadamer 1999: 368, translated by De La Rosa). So openness becomes crucial.

In addition to misrepresentation, Young addresses forms of external and internal exclusion as reason for deficient forms of representation. External exclusion refers to the ways individuals and groups that ought to be included are left out of fora for discussion and decision-making. 'Back-door brokering, for example, is a typical form of political exclusion. The easiest way for powerful people to get what they want out of the political process is to set up exclusive self-appointed committees that deliberate privately to set the agenda and arrive at policies which they then introduce to public debate as accomplished facts' (Young 2000: 54). Young argues that this form of exclusion can best be treated by special representation of marginalized groups. Therefore, she claims assistance and financial support of marginalized groups in order to (a) help them to develop a sense of identity and shared experiences (collective empowerment), (b) secure the distribution of their proposals and analysis as well as to foster their considerations into decision-making processes, and (c) institutionalize veto rights for marginalized groups in areas which affect them directly (Young 1995: 188).

Internal exclusion, in contrast, refers to the inability to 'influence the thinking of others even when they have access to fora and procedures of decision-making because the dominant may find their ideas or modes of expression silly or simple, and not worthy of consideration' (Young 2000: 55). Young argues that this form of exclusion should be treated by practices of public acknowledgement and greeting in order to demonstrate respect and attention to these people.

In a hermeneutical perspective, the external and internal practices of exclusion described by Young seem to be more like the symptoms than the origins of exclusion, because they result from a cognitive seclusion of other perspectives. Therefore, I doubt that imposing respectful practices may change this habitus, because it is *meant* to exclude or include. Imposed practices might lead to a change of some practices, but they will not change the habitus. Changing the habitus requires an openness that allows others to question our actions, and the will to change them when we are convinced that criticism is justified. Criticism as Gadamer (1999: 104) and Arendt (1978) have shown cannot work with mathematical reasons. But it can refer to analogies (Gadamer 1999: 436), and it can reveal when actors refer to normative principles in their narration of themselves and the world they live in, but at the same time contradict themselves with their actions (Butler 1997: 227). The principle of democracy, for example, has been referred to in order to include more and more people with equal rights. While democracy in its beginnings was meant to protect the equality of white men, there were no good normative reasons that could defend the permanent exclusion of women and people of colour (Butler 1997: 227). This is because the idea of the supremacy of white men is not compatible with the idea of equality. And the discussion here asks on what grounds we do not open up mental and physical borders and consider a global citizenship, again referring to the idea of equality. So it can be said that the idea of democracy tends to have an inner logic which justifies inclusion and questions exclusion.

There is another element that Young does not develop systematically but that seems more promising as a method to open up established ways of thinking and acting: Forms of public protest that 'make us wonder about what we are doing, to rupture a stream of thought, rather than to weave an argument' (Young 2000: 687). Young argues for creative forms of public protest in order to question established ways of thinking and acting. Questioning and interrupting the flow of established thinking might be a more powerful instrument to create openness, because it can be used to direct attention to the aforementioned contradictions.

In addition to creative forms of public protest, Young argues for a variety of informal procedures and fora, because she is more sceptical about formal representatives' ability to include the claims of all citizens into the assembly and political fora as Urbinati. Therefore, she is also concerned about tendencies of alienation. To counter these tendencies, Young argues for the formation of additional institutions of political will: 'All existing representative democracies could be improved by additional procedures and fora through which citizens discuss with one another and with representatives their evaluation of policies representatives have supported' (Young 2000: 132).

Young has been criticized for claiming special rights for marginalized groups, first because it remains unclear how a group is determined (Barry 2001: 302). In the following, I will therefore not share Young's arguments on special rights for marginalized groups. Instead, I will emphasize the need to secure additional institutions that give varying forms of articulation a forum. Young has been also criticized because she creates a tension between her deliberative and her agonistic arguments, fencing the agonistic game by the argument of historical injustices (Thaa 2013: 203–4). Therefore, I will not draw on Young's argument of historical injustices, but instead I will argue for agonistic debates in friendly rivalry, which will be accompanied by dialogic practices that address practices of dominance and which are sensible to power aspects and differences.

For a cosmopolitan and not just a global democracy, a concept is required that explains how representation can help to create new inclusive perspectives, ideas, and imaginaries in order to create a cosmopolitan second language, and institutions and practices that fit with this goal, in a way that it turns representation into a dialogic catalyst of new ways of thinking and speaking.

WHO, HOW, AND WHAT SHOULD BE REPRESENTED IN A COSMOPOLITAN PUBLIC SPHERE AND A COSMOPOLITAN DEMOCRACY?

In her deliberations on a transnational public sphere, Nancy Fraser has shown that for a concept of a truly transnational public sphere it is crucial to overcome the Westphalian Frame, which is connected to the supposition of a nation-state as addressee of public opinion, participants as fellow members of bounded political communities drawing mainly on a national language and the use of media such as national press and national broadcasting (Fraser 2014: 12). A transnational public, in contrast, Fraser argues, gains its legitimacy 'from a communicative process in which all potentially affected can participate as peers, regardless of political citizenship' (Fraser 2014: 33). Analysing the transnational public sphere and measuring its legitimacy as Fraser does is very illuminating, but it should be also asked how the creation of a transnational or cosmopolitan public sphere can be strengthened. Because, as Fraser argues, 'the current constitution of public opinion burst open the Westphalian frame' (Fraser 2014: 20–23). But at the same time, it is still connected to practices and power relations that are the heritage of a Westphalian division of political space and therefore also of colonial practices (Keck and Sikkink 1998). Hence it needs to be clarified which are the challenges for the emergence of a cosmopolitan public sphere and how to face them.

Institutions arise out of communicative processes, and their legitimacy is always linked with imaginaries, ideas, words, meanings, and values (Taylor 1993). Therefore, global institutions of representation should be the result of a wide range of inclusive communicative processes that broach the issue of power relations, language, and representation, instead of being implemented in a copy-and-paste process. I want to propose starting and strengthening practices and institutions that help advance a global public sphere in order to establish loci for cosmopolitan communication, where global institutions can be discussed and then institutionalized (for example, a global parliament). Transnational social movements and institutions like the world social forum might be a good example for this kind of loci, especially when they reflect on the power asymmetries and varying perspectives and cultures of the participating actors.

With Young and Urbinati, I have tried to show some of the challenges of cosmopolitan representative relations. To sum up, it can be said that there are three crucial points: (1) The problem that representing interests does not reflect all politically relevant aspects of a person and therefore has to be enlarged to the representation of opinion and perspective. (2) Representatives' task has to be described as advocacy *and* mediation because the action of advocacy alone leads to the articulation of interests, perspectives, and opinions, but does not lead to integration. Therefore, the second task of representatives is the task of mediation, which integrates creatively varying and sometimes even opposing opinions, perspectives, and interests. (3) The action of advocacy easily leads to misrepresentations because privileged groups tend to judge opinions, perspectives, and interests from their perspective. Therefore, the following is required: (a) guidelines for good practice of representation which is sensitive to (intercultural) differences and (b) practices of protest which question traditional ways of thinking and acting.

Hence, representatives in a cosmopolitan public sphere could be informal representatives whose task is to pick up wishes, interests, opinions, and perspectives with global relevance and to discuss them publicly. It would be also the place for discussions on a global second language, on further global institutions, and so on. But in order to include all voices, a public sphere would have to be open to informal procedures, like councils or open debates and creative forms of protest, including street art performances or theatre. Only the variety of practices can guarantee that all groups can find a medium to articulate their claims in the way they feel comfortable with. So instead of enforcing state-like global institutions, the focus should be on the enforcement of a cosmopolitan public sphere and the institutions and practices that could foster and stabilize its emergence.

Urbinati's understanding of representation as a communicative relation that includes advocacy and mediation can build the basic assumption for an adequate imaginary of cosmopolitan representation processes when it is connected with Young's assumptions on difference and a concept of intercultural communication that sheds light on power aspects. This is because Urbinati brings to the debate the claim to describe the task of representatives as advocacy and mediation. As advocates they pick up the claims from global society, and as mediators they have the task to creatively combine claims or to preserve disagreement. But as Young has shown, in multicultural debates it is not enough to do this in respect to interests; it also has to be done in respect to opinions and perspectives, because opinions refer to values and principles, and perspectives to group-specific experiences of injustice and/or exclusion. Interests are only one aspect of what gives us a political presence. Adequate representation includes not just interests but also perspectives and opinions about the world we live in, because they are of political relevance as much as interests are. Hence, the task of a cosmopolitan representative would be the advocacy of interests, opinions, and perspectives which can be challenging to understand, such as, for example, the opinion of a conservative bank manager or a member of the Zapatistas movement. In a second step, it becomes even more challenging, because the task now is not only to understand and to speak for these opinions or perspectives but to mediate them. This means to propose ways in which these perspectives or opinions can be put in relation to each other, combined, and/or differentiated. A global second language can be dangerous for this process, but it can also be of use. It can be dangerous because, as I argued earlier, a language always transports a certain perspective on the world. Choosing English as a global second language could lead to a dominating 'English' perspective of the world, not only commanding global discourses but also penetrating other languages and determining what can be said in the first languages. But choosing English as a cosmopolitan second language could be of use as long as speakers succeed in appropriating English to express issues that can be articulated in their first language or issues that are cosmopolitan in character. The latter would be the task of cosmopolitan representatives. In mediating between varying perspectives and opinions, their challenge consists of finding new metaphors, vocabularies, and expressions to create cosmopolitan narratives and vocabularies to frame and describe problems as well as solutions to problems.

Yet, as I argued before, exclusion starts with the communicative relationship that is based on a narration of superiority and inferiority or a narration of inclusion and exclusion. Therefore, power aspects have to be mentioned and discussed extensively in order to keep them transparent and open to contestation and transformation.

The public debate can be thought of as loci of 'friendly rivalry', as Urbinati called it,[7] but the agon has to be tamed by dialogical practices and institutions that are sensible to power aspects. Intercultural representation, instead of being thought of as identical with national representation, should therefore be thought of as a communicative relation that challenges the creative mediation abilities of the representative. Informal representatives understood as advocates and mediators can help to create new inclusive perspectives, ideas, and imaginaries that can build a common ground for state-like democratic cosmopolitan institutions. The global public sphere would have to become the place for re-democratizing practices that are strong enough to fence economic imperatives and post-democratic tendencies.

Informal representatives' mission then would consist of the task of debating wishes, interests, and, with Young, we can add opinions and perspectives. In order to strengthen their position as representatives, although informal, the democratization of movements—social actors like Amnesty International, Greenpeace, or institutions like the world social forum—would be crucial. Although not elected, NGOs, transnational advocacy networks, and transnational social movements[8] could strengthen their political role as representatives by following democratic practices that are innovative in articulating practices of dominance and difference sensibility.

Once there is a vivid cosmopolitan public space with informal representatives that are sensible to cultural differences and power aspects related to language and social practices, it would be their task to call for a constituent assembly to specify the character of the global institutions.

Young has been criticized by Jörke (2013) for drawing on institutions like the world social forum. He argues that political actors with an emancipatory impulse who could fill informal institutions with political life are missing, and that the depolitization of political questions by international organizations such as the European Commission or the WTO Council, through expert decision-making, impose a barrier to the kind of representation Young calls for. But there is a range of actors, such as indigenous movements, human rights movements, environmental movements, antiglobalization movements,[9] and so on, so instead what is missing are shared imaginaries and 'chains of equivalences', and an idea of cosmopolitan solidarity that would stabilize their cooperation.

Coming back to the leading question of who, how, and what should be represented in a cosmopolitan public sphere behind the background of a deliberative understanding of democracy, the answer can be that all affected should be given the possibility to participate, regardless of political citizenship, through direct participation or representation. If they are represented, it will be the task of representatives to advocate opinions, interests, and perspectives in a different and power-sensible way before they mediate them with other opinions and perspectives in order to create new cosmopolitan narrations and a cosmopolitan second language, which helps to articulate the varying claims.

To create a vivid cosmopolitan public space will be a challenging test for not just global but also cosmopolitan institutions. If it is not possible to support the emergence of a cosmopolitan public sphere where the diversity of world citizens will be respected, perhaps it would be better to distance oneself from the idea of global democracy. A global democracy without cosmopolitan citizens and a vivid public sphere will indicate that we might be on the way to a planetary post-democratic Leviathan instead of a cosmopolitan democracy.

NOTES

1. But Urbinati argues that what he proposes 'seems to be a quasi state but with a low democratic standard because its parliament is supposed to hold only a consultative function and no checking power over the Council' (Urbinati 2003: 3).

2. For more on this distinction, see Amos Nascimento in this volume.

3. Mignolo and Schiwy draw on the experiences of the EZLN (Ejército Zapatista de Liberación Nacional), a revolutionary leftist group based in Chiapas. Since 1994, the group has been in a declared war 'against the Mexican state,' though this war has been primarily nonviolent and defensive against paramilitary and corporate incursions into Chiapas. Their members are indigenous people and former leftist guerrilla fighters.

4. Which differs from Habermas's view on Gadamer (Habermas 1973) and which I develop in *Aneignung und interkulturelle Repräsentation* (De La Rosa 2012).

5. In *Global Challenges: War, Self-Determination and Responsibility for Justice*, Young (2007) argues for a reform of the United Nations, including the establishment of a people's parliament, but she does not develop a concept of global representation. Urbinati, in turn, is rather sceptical about global democracy (Urbinati 2003: 6).

6. If all mankind minus one, were of one opinion, and only one person were of the contrary opinion, mankind would be no more justified in silencing that one person, than he, if he had the power, would be justified in silencing mankind. Were an opinion a personal possession of no value except to the owner; if to be obstructed in the enjoyment of it were simply a private injury, it would make some difference whether the injury was inflicted only on a few persons or on many. But the peculiar evil of silencing the expression of an opinion is, that it is robbing the human race; posterity as well as the existing generation; those who dissent from the opinion, still more than those who hold it. If the opinion is right, they are deprived of the opportunity of exchanging error for truth: if wrong, they lose, what is almost as great a benefit, the clearer perception and livelier impression of truth, produced by its collision with error (Mill 1869) (www.bartleby.com/130/2.html).

7. Urbinati (2000: 774).

8. As described by Keck and Sikkink (1998) and also Nash (2014).

9. The term antiglobalization is somewhat misleading, because many of those actors are against neoliberal tendencies of globalization, not against globalization itself (Pleyers 2010: 16).

BIBLIOGRAPHY

Archibugi, D. (1995). 'From the United Nations to Cosmopolitan Democracy' in D. Archibugi and D. Held (eds.) (1995). *Cosmopolitan Democracy: An Agenda for a New World Order*. Cambridge: Polity Press.

———. (2005) 'The Language of Democracy: Vernacular or Esperanto? A Comparison between the Multiculturalist and Cosmopolitan Perspectives'. *Political Studies* 53: 537–55.

Arendt, H. (1978). *The Life of the Mind*. New York: Harcourt Brace Javanovich.

Barry, B. (2001). *Culture and Equality: An Egalitarian Critique of Multiculturalism*. Cambridge, MA: Harvard University Press.

Bhabha, H. K. (1994). *The Location of Culture*. London, New York: Routledge.

Bolton, K. and Kachru, B. B. (2006). *Asian Englishes: The History and Development of World Englishes*. London: Routledge.

Butler, J. (1997). *Excitable Speech. A Politics of the Performative*. New York: Routledge.

Christiansen, P. V. (2006). 'Language Policy in the European Union: Eurpean/English/ Elite/Equal/Esperanto Union!' *Language Problems & Language Planing* 3 (1): 21–44.

Crystal, D. (2003). *English as a Global Language* (2nd ed.). Cambridge: Cambridge University Press.

De La Rosa, S. (2012). *Aneignung und interkulturelle Repräsentation: Grundlagen einer kritischen Theorie politischer Kommunikation.* Wiesbaden: Springer VS.

Fraser, N. (2014). 'Transnationalizing the Public Sphere: On the Legitimacy and Efficacy of Public Opinion in a Post-Westphalian World' in Kate Nash (ed.) *Transnationalizing the Public Sphere.* Cambridge: Polity Press, 8–42.

Gadamer, H-G. (1999). 'Hermeneutik I: Wahrheit und Methode' in Hans-Georg Gadamer (ed.) *Gesammelte Werke.* Tübingen: UTB.

Habermas, J. (1973). 'Zu Gadamers "Wahrheit und Methode"' in J. Habermas, D. Henrich, and J. Taubes (eds.) *Hermeneutik und Ideologiekritik.* Frankfurt/Main: Suhrkamp, 45–46.

——. (2001) *The Postnational Constellation and the Future of Democracy.* Cambridge MA: The MIT Press.

Held, D. (1995). *Democracy and the Global Order: From the Modern State to Cosmopolitan Governance.* Cambridge: Polity Press.

Jörke, D. (2013). 'Motive und Probleme in Iris Marion Youngs Demokratietheorie' in P. Nielsen (eds.) *Zwischen Demokratie und globaler Verantwortung: Iris Marion Youngs Theorie politischer Normativität.* Baden-Baden: Nomos, 151–65.

Keck, M. E. and Sikkink, K. (1998). *Activists Beyond Borders: Advocacy Networks in International Politics.* Ithaca, N.Y.: Cornell University Press.

Mignolo, W. D. (2009). 'Epistemic Disobedience, Independent Thought and Decolonial Freedom'. *Theory, Culture & Society* 26 (7–8): 159–81.

—— and Schiwy, F. (2003). 'Transculturation and the Colonial Difference: Double Translation' in T. Maranhão and B. Streck (eds.) *Translation and Ethnography: The Anthropological Challenge of Intercultural Understanding.* Tucson: University of Arizona Press, 12–34.

Mill, J. S. (2001). *On Liberty.* Kitchener, Ontario: Batoche Books.

——. (2004). *Considerations on Representative Government.* Accessed 9 July 2014, www2.hn.psu.edu/faculty/jmanis/jsmill/considerations.pdf.

Nash, K. (2014). 'Towards Transnational Democratization?' in N. Fraser and K. Nash (eds.) *Transnationalizing the Public Sphere.* Cambridge: Polity Press, 60–78.

Pitkin, H. F. (1967). *The Concept of Representation.* Berkeley: University of California Press.

Pleyers, G. (2010). *Alter-Globalization: Becoming Actors in the Global Age.* Cambridge: Polity Press.

Said, E. W. (2003). *Orientalism.* London: Penguin Books.

Spivak, G. C. (2004). 'Righting Wrongs'. *The South Atlantic Quarterly* 103 (2/3): 523–81.

——. (2008). *Can the Subaltern Speak? Postkolonialität und subalterne Artikulation.* Wien: Turia + Kant.

Taylor, C. (1985). 'Self-interpreting animals' in C. Taylor (ed.) *Human Agency and Language: Philosophical Papers 1.* Cambridge: Cambridge University Press, 45–76.

—— (ed.) (1993). *Reconciling the Solitudes: Essays on Canadian Federalism and Nationalism.* Montréal, Buffalo: McGill-Queen's University Press.

Thaa, W. (2008). 'Kritik und Neubewertung politischer Repräsentation: Vom Hindernis zur Möglichkeitsbedingung politischer Freiheit'. *Politische Vierteljahresschrift* 49 (4): 618–40.

——. (2013). 'Gruppenrepräsentation und demokratischer Prozess bei Iris Marion Young' in P. Niesen (ed.) *Zwischen Demokratie und Globaler Verantwortung: Iris Marion Youngs Theorie Politischer Normativität.* Baden-Baden: Nomos, 187–206.

Urbinati, N. (2000). 'Representation as Advocacy: A Study of Democratic Deliberation'. *Political Theory* 28 (6): 758–86.

——. (2003). 'Can Cosmopolitical Democracy Be Democratic?' Accessed 9 July 2014, www.politicaltheory.info/essays/urbinati.htm.

Young, I. M. (1997). *Intersecting Voices: Dilemmas of Gender, Political Philosophy, and Policy*. Princeton. Princeton University Press.
———. (2000). *Inclusion and Democracy*. Oxford Scholarship Online: November 2003.
———. (2007). *Global Challenges: War, Self-Determination and Responsibility for Justice*. Cambridge: Polity Press.

NINE

Jacques Derrida and the Case of Cosmopolitanism

'Cities of Refuge' in the Twenty-First Century

Spiros Makris

DERRIDA'S FAMILIAR MONSTROSITY; OR TOWARDS A NEW COSMOPOLITAN HOSPITALITY

It's needless to say that *'cities of refuge'* is not an ordinary theoretical proposal or just an ethical categorical imperative for the renewal of international law. As Jacques Derrida rightly points out from the start of his seminal essay 'On Cosmopolitanism', cities of refuge are 'something more and other than merely banal articles in the literature of international law' (Derrida 2001: 4). And he concludes as follows: These must be conceived as 'an audacious call for a genuine innovation in the history of the right to asylum or the duty to hospitality' (Derrida 2001: 4). In this regard, cities of refuge is a par excellence Derridean poststructuralist and above all postmodern philosophical project towards a new radical political ontology in favor of the city (*demos*) and against the state sovereignty and the modern state-centric international system. As Jacques Derrida says emphatically in his famous last interview:

> One has to 'raise' (sublation/*Aufheben*) the cosmopolitical. When one says 'political', one uses a Greek word, a European concept that has always pressuposed the state, the concept of *polis* (emphasis added) that is linked to the concept of national territory and autochthony. Notwithstanding the interruptions in the flow of this history, this remains the dominant concept of the political, even as numerous forces

177

attempt to dislodge it: the concept of state sovereignty is no longer tied
to the land . . . this dislocation throws old European ideas of the political into crisis . . . But I don't think that we need to set ourselves against
the concept of the political. That goes also for the concept of sovereignty, which I think retains its validity in certain circumstances, for example in resisting certain forces of a global market. Here again it is a
matter of a European heritage being both safeguarded and reformed.
(Derrida 2004: 14–15)

From this specific point of view, we could argue substantially that the
Derridean project of a refuge or a free city in the twenty-first century is an
argument in favor of a new culture of hospitality or, in terms of Jacques
Derrida, of a new ethic, a new cosmopolitics of the cities of refuge (Derrida 2004: 5). Is this ambitious project achievable in our globalized world?
In this chapter we shall try to show how Jacques Derrida, by deconstruct-
ing the Kantian state-centric laws of hospitality, seeks through a new
reading of the political modernity to establish a new right to human
dignity which has much in common with Hannah Arendt's concept of
the 'right to have rights' (Benhabib 2004: 49–70). Therefore, the contemporary radical and postmodern political and ethical philosophy on cosmopolitanism, particularly the so-called cosmopolitan examinations and
critiques on Immanuel Kant's cosmopolitanism, should necessarily consider the thorny question of the cities of refuge (Brown and Held 2012:
373–443). Summarizing thus far, it could be argued that this critical question raises two partial issues regarding hospitality: on one hand, the ontological status of cities of refuge, and on the other, the ethical and political
or institutional implications of this new, explicitly unconditional cosmopolitan right. Especially when the crisis of the political takes place in a
dark and gloomy era, when millions of people all around the world either have been violently impoverished by the new cyclical global capitalist deregulation or forcibly deported from their homes due to the contemporary wars of fundamentalism, the fate of the foreigner (the immigrant,
the exiled, the stateless, the homeless, etc.) arises de facto and de jure at
the heart of the new cosmopolitanism, by making Jacques Derrida's radical and postmodern approach on hospitality a strong request for a new
human condition that has to come (*à venir*) in the future in the form of a
democracy to come, which is not simply the given model of modern
liberal democracy, but rather a democratic form that 'appeals to classical
understandings of the *demos*, as that which seeks to observe a double law
of unconditional freedom and absolute equality' (Wortham 2010: 34).

Having in mind all that has been mentioned above, it is worth noting
that speaking about Jacques Derrida's new cosmopolitanism means first
and foremost speaking about the 'ethical and political turn in Derrida's
thinking from the 1990s on' (Glendinning 2011: 79). Although prima facie
this seems to be a totally minor question on Jacques Derrida's intellectual
development from the 1960s up to 2000s compared with the very mean-

ing of his thought and specifically of his ethical and political philosophy (Glendinning 2011: 82), it gives us the academic and theoretical opportunity to consider primarily Derrida himself as a Shakespearean specter; as the absolute Other; or as the Socratic 'foreigner', 'a mythic creature', as James K. A. Smith supports, 'that either inspires rapture or provokes terror' (Smith 2005: 2). By framing the question of hospitality as the metonymy of the question of the foreigner, Derrida clarifies that 'sometimes the foreigner is Socrates himself, Socrates the disturbing man of question and irony (which is to say, of question, another meaning of the word "irony"), the man of the midwifery question. Socrates himself has the characteristics of the foreigner, he represents, he figures the foreigner, he *plays* the foreigner he is not' (Derrida and Dufourmantelle 2000: 13). In that sense, let me paraphrase Jacques Derrida by saying the following: 'Specters of Derrida'. The title of this chapter would commit one to speak first of all about Derrida: about Derrida himself; about his 'testament or his inheritance'. And about a specter, the shadow of Derrida, 'the *revenant* whose return so many raised voices today are attempting to conjure away' (Derrida, 2006: 120). Similarly, Sigmund Freud stresses thereon that 'uncanny in real experience' or 'actual occurrences of the uncanny' is the most 'horrible', the *un-heimlich*; it actually 'is what was once *heimisch*, homelike, familiar; the prefix "un" is the token of repression' (Freud 1919: 15–17).

Jacques Derrida experienced many times in his eventful life the legal language of uncanny. This is the language that interpellates the foreigner 'before the law of the country that welcomes or expels him; the foreigner is first of all foreign to the legal language in which the duty of hospitality is formulated, the right to asylum, its limits, norms, policing, etc. He has to ask for hospitality in a language which by definition is not his own, the one imposed on him by the master of the house, the host, the king, the lord, the authorities, the nation, the State. . . . This personage imposes on him translation into their own language, and that's the first act of violence' (Derrida and Dufourmantelle 2000: 15). According to Derrida, hospitality in the ordinary sense must be conceived as an act of state violence over the Levinasian face of the foreigner, where the 'encounter with a face is inevitably personal; with a seminal *pathos* whose sources lie beyond criteria of verification' (Bergo 2010: 2). The well-known 'Cambridge Affair' is just the tip of the iceberg (Glendinning 2011: 8; Smith 2005: 2). By the same token, Derrida is the most appropriate Levinasian face in order to speak about the peculiar slippage between *hostility* and *hospitality* — the so-called Derridean neologism of *hostipitality* (Derrida and Dufourmantelle 2000: 45), which 'raises in a radically new way the question of the subject of hospitality' (Derrida 2002: 356). 'Derrida's interest', John D. Caputo highlights repeatedly, 'is drawn to the fact that, by virtue of its etymology, the word "hospitality" carries its opposites within itself', which preserve 'the distance between one's own and the stranger. . . . So, there is always a little hostility in all hosting and hospitality, constituting a certain "hostil/pitality"' (Caputo 1999: 110). To put the matter different-ly, we could argue that Jacques Derrida is above this sui generis intellec-tual 'monster', which 'emerges from the lagoon of familiarity, shows it-self . . . but because we lack the *categories* to constitute it—and often because its very strangeness frightens us—we invest it with monstrosity' (Smith 2005: 2).

By making the uncanny familiar anew, Derrida brings to light the contradictory nature of Kantian state-centric conditional hospitality. In this specific regard, Kantian hospitality, as a paradox or a contradiction, constitutes, in accordance with Jacques Derrida, that great opportunity to deconstruct modern state sovereignty by prefixing deconstructive justice over state legality. 'The absolute or unconditional hospitality', he re-marks thereon, 'I would like to offer . . . presupposes a break with hospi-tality in the ordinary sense, with conditional hospitality, with the right to or pact of hospitality' (Derrida and Dufourmantelle 2000: 25). In other words, it presupposes the total recall of the uncanny as the familiar mon-strosity that inhabits within us. In Derridean terms, hospitality seems like a just 'impose' of justice on human affairs without the act of state vio-lence. Or to put it differently, it looks like the abolition of law via the justice.

> 'Absolute hospitality', he points out, 'requires that I open up my home and that I give not only to the foreigner (provided with a family name, with the social status of being a foreigner, etc.), but to the absolute, unknown, anonymous other, and that I *give place* to them, that I let them come, that I let them arrive, and take place in the place I offer them, without asking of them either reciprocity (entering into a pact) or even their names. The law of absolute hospitality commands a break with hospitality by right, with law or justice as rights. Just hospitality breaks with hospitality by right; not that it condemns or is opposed to it, and it can on the contrary set and maintain it in a perpetual progres-sive movement; but it is as strangely heterogeneous to it as justice is heterogeneous to the law to which it is yet so close, from which in truth it is indissociable' (Derrida and Dufourmantelle 2000: 25 and 27).

Derridean hospitality is the other face of monstrosity and vice versa, and from this perspective is the philosophical way in which Jacques Derrida tries to deconstruct overall the Western metaphysics of presence (Wort-ham 2010: 103). Hospitality begins 'with the unquestioning welcome, in a double effacement, the effacement of the question *and* the name' (Derrida and Dufourmantelle 2000: 29). Therefore, Derridean unconditional, im-possible, and absolute cosmopolitan hospitality is first and foremost the Nietzschean, or deconstructive, 'death' of state sovereignty as the deifica-tion of Hobbesian violence in political modernity.

We have to take seriously into consideration that monstrosity is a fundamental concept in Derridean ontological, political, and ethical philosophy. 'All experience open to the future', Jacques Derrida underlines, 'is prepared or prepares itself to welcome the monstrous *arrivant*' (Derrida 1995: 387). Nicholas Royle stresses thereon that 'the figure of the *arrivant* haunts everything he has ever said about the future and thus everything he has ever said about anything at all' (Royle 2003: 111). Hence, we could support in terms of Marx that the Derridean radical cosmopolitan project is a hauntology of hospitality as a familiar monstrosity. 'The question of the monstrous arrivant', Nicholas Royle points out emphatically, 'is a question of the border or threshold, of who or what comes to the shore or turns up at the door. . . . This "absolute *arrivant*" is "not an intruder", an invader, or a colonizer. . . . Rather the arrivant is "hospitality itself"'. In that Freudian and Levinasian sense, we support that Derridean corpus as a whole 'is a question of an "economy" of the uncanny . . . of rethinking the supposed opposition of the normal or familiar and the monstrous' (Royle 2003: 111–12). Adam Sharman highlights that 'because Derrida is interested in the ways in which impurity is denied and contamination suppressed, he pays constant attention to the places and figures (limits, frontiers, boundaries, demarcations; identities, essences, proper names) which attempt to separate out that which belongs from that which is alien, the proper from the improper, the official member of the group, nation or state from the outsider'. And, he concludes, 'all of Derrida's work takes place on and at the border. Be it the border that passes among things (territories, cultures or languages) or the border that passes between two apparently opposed concepts' (Simons 2004: 95).

In order to understand these new Derridean categories of thinking, acting, and judging, especially the markedly enigmatic and sometimes puzzling Derridean concept of hospitality, 'where that word', according to Emmanuel Levinas, 'already suggests being both a host and a guest' (Hand 2009: 111), we have to consider first and foremost this counter-ontology of hospitality, which the French postmodern philosopher introduces as a 'counter-monster' of deconstructive scepticism in the moralistic, juridical, and, in the final analysis, state-centric Kantian cosmopolitan reception of the 'foreigner' in the Western metaphysics of presence. In this spirit, the Derridean cosmopolitanism, or Jacques Derrida's cosmopolitan hospitality, requires one to speak about a definitely new political and ethical anti-ontology of hospitality beyond the modern hospitality, which to a large extent has been structured as a legal idea or discourse of state sovereignty, grounded on the violent exclusion of alterity. Someone looking for the mystical foundation of Derrida's thought must seek it mainly in the force of law (Derrida 2002: 228, 239): a very important open text in Derridean corpus, which founds the counter-ontology of a new ethics; a new world; a new cosmopolitan hospitality; beyond the constricting frontiers and thresholds of the modern state sovereignty; actually towards a New International, where people are subjects of hospitality and not objects of the violent Western metaphysics of the name and presence.

If we ought to paraphrase Jacques Derrida, we would claim that this new cosmopolitan hospitality is justice. Specifically, hospitality is deconstruction which is a kind of ontological justice (Derrida 2002: 243). '"Hospitality"', Derrida says in his famous seminars in Paris and in the United States on Hostipitality, 'the experience, the apprehension, the exercise of impossible hospitality, of hospitality as the possibility of impossibility (to receive another guest whom I am incapable of welcoming, to become capable of that which I am incapable of)—this is the exemplary experience of deconstruction itself. . . . Hospitality—this is a name or an example of deconstruction. . . . Hospitality is the deconstruction of the at-home; deconstruction is hospitality to the other, to the other than oneself, the other than "its other", to an other who is beyond any "its other"' (Derrida 2002: 364). More specifically, Derridean cosmopolitan hostipitality is the locus classicus of justice as event; as homelessness; as a decision between just and unjust; in final analysis, as a Platonic *pharmakon* where dominates the madness of undecidability (Lucy 2004: 90). In Jacques Derrida's terms, cosmopolitan hostipitality is that messianic Khôra where prevails the madness of the real Subject (Derrida 2002: 243, 244, 257, 258). 'The discourse on Khôra', Simon Morgan Wortham observes, 'gives rise to a certain *mise en abyme* which itself necessarily raises the question of the politics of the site, for instance that of the city or the state' (Wortham 2010: 126).

From this standpoint, we could support that Derridean theory of hospitality is a counter-theory of subjectivity in the late capitalism. As Emmanuel Levinas would have said, Derridean theory of hospitality is this new or counter-ethics which 'will present subjectivity as welcoming the Other, as hospitality' (Levinas 1991: 27). In other words, this Derridean new cosmopolitan ontological and political ethics should be seen not as 'an "ethics of hospitality" but as *ethics as hospitality*' (Hand 2009: 111). Derrida's biographer, Benoît Peeters, points out concerning the spinous question of hospitality: 'There were increasing bridges between his philosophical work and his political commitments. Hospitality . . . became a recurrent theme. . . . This was because the principle of hospitality concentrated within itself "the most concrete urgencies, those most proper to articulate the ethical on the political." . . . Hospitality is culture itself . . . *ethics is hospitality*' (Peeters 2013: 470). So, it should not be surprising that Jacques Derrida urges us, à la Marx, to highlight without hesitation the plagues of the New World Order (unemployment, ruthless economic war, inability to master the contradictions of the global market, aggravation of the foreign debt, arms industry and trade arms, spread of nuclear weapons, inter-ethnic wars, mafia and drug cartels on every continent, the present state of international law which favors the concept of state or national sovereignty), among which stands out without doubt 'the massive exclusion of homeless citizens' (Derrida 2006: 100).

In Derridean terms, cosmopolitan hospitality means actually thinking about the enclosures of casino capitalism in the era of neoliberal globalization. According to Massimo De Angelis, the new capitalistic enclosures are aimed to destroy those social, political, and ethical fields of life whose main feature is to ensure some degree of protection, especially to the homeless and deported people (De Angelis 2004). In this connection, Jacques Derrida points out with particular emphasis: 'Nowdays, a reflection on hospitality presupposes, among other things, the possibility of a rigorous delimitation of thresholds or frontiers: between the familial and the non-familial, between the foreign and the non-foreign, the citizen and the non-citizen, but first of all between the private and the public'. If we do not succeed to bring to light these new conceptual and practical aspects of contingent human relations in a totally globalized and multicultural world 'then every element of hospitality gets disrupted'. In that sense, if not I can offer freely 'my word, my friendship, my love, my help, to whomever I wish, and so invite whomever I wish to come into my home', Derrida concludes, then is probably clear that 'the intervention of the State becomes a violation of the inviolable in the place where inviolable immunity remains the condition of hospitality' (Derrida and Dufourmantelle 2000: 47, 49, 51).

As we shall see extensively below, Derridean cosmopolitan hospitality is by definition an unconditional hospitality, and in this perspective it is an impossible ideal (Deutscher 2005: 69, 68). Nevertheless, it must be clarified that Jacques Derrida is neither an idealist nor even more a nihilist. On the contrary, he is a realist, or it is even better to assert that he is a pragmatist in the era of capitalist cynicism. It is not necessary to say that possible impossibility in Derridean context has nothing to do with the Platonic utopian ideal. Especially, it has nothing to do with the 'un-realistic'. Impossibility in Jacques Derrida's oeuvre is only our egoistic weakness to transcend the narrow horizons of expectations. Impossibility means to go beyond the conditional or limited forms of thinking, acting, and judging. Impossibility means deconstruction as the experience of the impossible. A hospitality worthy of the name must remain open to the wholly unwelcomable 'foreigner'. In the final analysis, impossibility means to rethink and transform the conditional in the name of the unconditional, mainly in the fields of law, ethics, and politics (Wortham 2010: 75–76). So it is the impossibility of the other in a world of self-enclosed identities. It is a great opportunity to go one step beyond the parochial threshold (Deutscher 2005: 73–75). As Gury Gutting stresses emphatically, the Derridean 'view of ethics is to say that it is at root an openness to the other. . . . Such thought keeps us moving, as we must, toward another that will always lie beyond our current horizon' (Gutting 2001: 313).

In this specific regard, it could be indisputably supported that unconditional and impossible hospitality is a 'counter-metaphysics'; a metaphysics of exteriority, as Emmanuel Levinas usually says, which 'appears in the transcendence of the same (the self, consciousness, the I) by the other' (Stocker 2006: 121). From this point of view, Derridean new cosmopolitan hospitality is the crucial event of an ontological substitution, the unanticipatable event of an ontological hostageship with two faces: that between host and guest. It is the event *as if* the one is taking the place of another. 'So it is indeed the master', Derrida writes emphatically, 'the one who invites, the inviting host, who becomes the hostage—and who really always has been. And the guest, the invited hostage, becomes the one who invites, the master of the host. The guest becomes the host's host. The guest (hôte) becomes the host (hôte) of the host (hôte). These substitutions make everyone else's hostage. Such are the *laws of hospitality'* (Derrida and Dufourmantelle 2000: 123, 125). Summarizing thus far, we can claim that the concept of ethical and political cosmopolitanism in Jacques Derrida's later corpus presupposes this new counter-ontology of hospitality, which is centered around the poststructuralist and postmodern critique of Kantian state-centric cosmopolitanism, where hospitality, although characterized by rational universality, finally is by definition limited by the vital national interests of state sovereignty and legality. 'By taking this approach', Simon Morgan Wortham points out correctly, 'Derrida does not imagine for a moment that it would be practically possible . . . to sweep away sovereignty's borders and powers. Instead, his appeal to the "unconditional" confronts us with a continual responsibility to think of modifying or transforming them' (Wortham 2010: 191).

DECONSTRUCTING STATE-CENTRIC HOSPITALITY: ETHICAL, POLITICAL, AND INSTITUTIONAL INSPIRATIONS

Cities of refuge are the cities of Derridean radical cosmopolitan hospitality. The cities where hospitality is the outmost test of a critical ontological substitution: 'to be one at the place of the other, the hostage and the hôte of the other' (Derrida 2002: 387). By identifying the specific ontological content of impossible cosmopolitan hospitality, Jacques Derrida points out that in the final analysis, the guest becomes the host of the host. Ontologically, Derrida's ethical and political approach has been affected strongly by Louis Massignon's concept of sacred hospitality. Substitution is the metaphor of Holy Trinity. 'The hôte', he stresses, by referring to Louis Massignon, 'is the messenger of God . . . Abraham's hospitality is a sign announcing the final completion of the gathering of all nations, blessed in Abraham in this *Holy Land* (emphasis added) which must be monopolized by none. . . . This notion of sacred hospitality seems to me essential for a search after truth between men, in our itineraries and our work, here below, and toward the threshold of the hereafter. . . . With hospitality, we find the Sacred at the center of our destinies' mystery, like secret and divine alms. . . . This mystery touches the very bottom of the mystery of the Trinity, where God is at once Guest [*Hôte*], Host [*Hospitalier*], and Home [*Foyer*]' (Derrida 2002: 373). No doubt, cities of refuge are this Derridean Holy Land which belongs to none; an earthly substitution of Trinity, where 'God is at once Guest, Host, and Home' (Derrida 2002: 375). The cities are where the self-closed and self-alienated identities are deconstructed within the Derridean counter-ontological Khôra of justice. As asked above, is this specific city of refuge a new Platonic utopian city? In order to answer this critical question, it is required first to explore more the concept of cities of refuge in the context of the ethical philosophy of Emmanuel Levinas, and second to examine in depth the concept of this Derridean unconditional and impossible cosmopolitanism compared to a close reading with the Kantian conditional and state-centric cosmopolitanism.

In accordance with Emmanuel Levinas, city of refuge is a par excellence biblical institution. But what is most important to note is that he does not interpret this institution from a narrow and rigorous Zionist perspective. Not even from a Jewish religious viewpoint. To identify clearly the biblical institution of cities of refuge, he mainly uses the special term *humanitarian urbanism*. From this Levinasian point of view, perhaps the city of refuge can be understood better as a sui generis city of exile. 'Exile, of course', Emmanuel Levinas clarifies thereon, 'but no prison, no hard labour, and no concentration camp'. So city of refuge is the city of human fraternity—this Holy Land in which dominates two fundamental human values: indulgence and forgiveness. City of refuge in Levinasian terms is a 'question of the salvation of the world; of man's return to his true humanity' (Levinas 1994: 34, 37, 38, 42, 46, 47, 51). It is no accident that Derrida connects his problématique on hospitality with the concepts of forgiveness, friendship, and sovereignty. He writes: 'If one wanted systematically to pursue a search about forgiveness in Levinas, and from the point of view of hospitality, it is to the theme of cities of refuge . . . that one would have to return' (Derrida 2002: 356, 400). Regarding what links hospitality and forgiveness, he noted in a session which took place on 12 February 1997: 'Forgiving would be opening for and smiling to the other, whatever his fault or his indignity, whatever the offense or even the threat. *Whoever asks for hospitality, asks, in a way, for forgiveness and whoever offers hospitality, grants forgiveness* (emphasis added)—and forgiveness must be infinite or it is nothing' (Derrida 2002: 380). In his well-known seminal essay in 'On Forgiveness' (Derrida 2001: 27), Jacques Derrida refers to forgiveness as a kind of unconditional and impossible hospitality beyond state power and particularly state sovereignty. Therefore, it is worth remembering that he defines forgiveness as a 'forgiveness without power: unconditional but without sovereignty' (Derrida 2001: 59).

In this very particular ethical, political, and institutional regard, the Derridean cosmopolitan hospitality is first and foremost an unconditional, messianic, and almost surprising forgiving, which stands quite opposite to the modern metaphysical ontology of state power and state sovereignty. As we shall see below, sovereignty, especially the principle of nation-state sovereignty, is a key concept which crosses like a golden thread Jacques Derrida's radical criticism on Kantian cosmopolitanism. 'Hospitality', he observes, 'consists in welcoming the other that does not warn me of his coming. In regard of this messianic surprise, in regard of what must thus tear *any horizon of expectation* (emphasis added), I am always, if I can say so, always and structurally, lacking, at fault . . . , and therefore condemned to be forgiven . . . , or rather to have to ask for forgiveness for my lack of preparation, for an irreducible and constitutive unpreparedness. . . . Therefore', he concludes in a perfectly Levinasian way of thinking, 'I have to ask for forgiveness for abandonment . . . , forgiveness for not giving, forgiveness for not having known how to give' (Derrida 2002: 380, 381). State sovereignty is unprepared for this messianic hospitality and forgiveness because it is by definition conditional and framed from the force of law—this mystical foundation of state authority (Derrida 2002: 230). By separating the state positive laws from justice, Derrida argues that law is not justice. Justice, as Emmanuel Levinas always says, is a peculiar kind of humanism, whose basis is not the abstract Man, but rather the concrete Other. Justice is not the right of the state upon its spatial or national territory, but the other's right as an infinite right. *Justice is the right of homelessness—the rights of homeless people.* So, insofar as justice is not only a mere 'juridical or political concept', Jacques Derrida summarizes his radical poststructuralist and postmodern reflections on hospitality, forgiveness and state sovereignty, then unconditional hospitality opens up a new ontological place for the disclosure and appearance of the Other which means in Derridean terms that justice gives to the avenir the possibility for 'the transformation, the recasting or refounding of law and politics' ab initio (Derrida 2002: 239, 240, 244, 250, 256, 257, 258).

By the same token, Jacques Derrida introduces to his deconstructive discourse about state sovereignty the relevant concept of *rogue state*. His argument is quite simple. To the extent that state law is founded on state violence, the state is rogue by its nature. Hence the distinction between normal and abnormal states is based only on the right of the strongest. In other words, the right of the Hobbesian and Schmittian Sovereign (Derrida 2005: xi–xiii). In that sense, Jacques Derrida points out that sovereignty is a 'force that is stronger than all the other forces in the world. . . . There is no sovereignty without force, without the force of the strongest, whose reason—the reason of the strongest—is to win out over everything. . . . *Abuse of power* is constitutive of sovereignty itself. . . . Abuse is the law of use; it is the law itself, the "logic" of sovereignty that can reign only by not sharing . . . to reign without sharing. It can only tend toward *imperial hegemony*. . . . There are thus only *rogue states*, potentially or actually. The state is *voyou* (killer, murderer, slayer), a rogue, roguish . . . the most perverse, most destructive of rogue states would be, first and foremost' the so-called Great Powers or superpowers. 'Abuse of power', Derrida writes, 'is constitutive of sovereignty itself' (Derrida 2005: 100, 101, 102, 97). The rhetoric of a rogue state is the rhetoric of the United Nations Security Council. The United Nations, he concludes, is entrapped violently and arbitarily to the reason of the strongest, which 'not only determines the actual policy of that international institution but, well before that, already determined *the conceptual architecture of the charter itself, the law that governs, in its fundamental principles and in its practical rules* (emphasis added), the development of this institution' (Derrida 2005: 100).

From this perspective, it is quite difficult to comprehend sufficiently Derridean cosmopolitan unconditional hospitality, and especially Jacques Derrida's ambitious project of a New International beyond the state-centric logic of the United Nations, without adequately understanding this counter-ontological and most of all post-ethical and politically radical criticism on state sovereignty—mainly of the most powerful state players in the postwar and contemporary international system. 'The massive exclusion of homeless citizens', he points out emphatically in his seminal book on Marx's specters, 'from any participation in the democratic life of States, the expulsion or deportation of so many exiles, stateless persons, and immigrants from the so-called national territory already herald a new experience of frontiers and identity—whether national or civil. . . . A "new international" is being sought through these crises of international law; it already denounces the limits of a discourse on human rights that will remain inadequate, sometimes hypocritical, and in any case formalistic and inconsistent with itself. . . . The "New International"', Derrida summarizes, 'is not only that which is seeking a new international law through these crimes. It is a link of affinity, suffering, and hope. . . . It is "a link" without title, and without name . . . without contract, "out of joint", without coordination, without party, without country, without national community (International before, across, and beyond any national determination). . . . The name of New International is given here to what calls to the friendship of an alliance without institution among those who, even if they no longer believe or never believed in the socialist-Marxist International . . . , continue to be inspired by at least one of the spirits of Marx . . . in order to ally themselves, in a new, concrete, and real way, even if this alliance no longer takes the form of a party or of a worker's international, but rather of a kind of counter-conjuration, in the (theoretical and practical) critique of the state of international law, the concepts of State and nation . . . in order to renew this critique, and especially to radicalize it' (Derrida 1994: 101, 106, 107).

As mentioned above, this Derridean counter-conjuration is first and foremost a negative ontology or, in other words, a negative theology which approaches the pivotal Derridean principle of the Platonic *khôra* (Derrida 1998: 71). Khôra is 'what makes it possible to think the difference between "I" and "you"'. This '"not knowing" is the "being" of every "identity"' (Lucy 2004: 68–69). Khôra is the hard core of deconstruction. Khôra is the Holy Land of justice, the biblical city of refuge, the Levinasian city of exile. To put the matter differently, Derridean Khôra is undoubtedly this 'New International' beyond the modern state identity which, through the force of law, leads repeatedly to these massive exclusions of homeless and stateless citizens. Derridean Khôra is in a sense the Arendtian 'right to have rights' (Arendt 2004: 376). It is worth noting that Jacques Derrida explores extensively the concrete meaning of city of refuge in his monumental essay in 'On Cosmopolitanism', having inspired its basic elements, inter alia, from Hannah Arendt's work. By following the thought of Arendt, Derrida argues that 'whenever the State is neither the foremost author of, nor the foremost guarantor against the violence which forces refugees or exiles to flee, it is often powerless to ensure the protection and the liberty of its own citizens before a terrorist menace, whether or not it has a religious or nationalist alibi. This is a phenomenon', he underlines, 'with a long historical sequence, one which Hannah Arendt has called, in a text which we should closely scrutinise, "The Decline of the Nation-State and the End of the Rights of Man"' (Derrida 2001: 6). As a genuine republican thinker, Jacques Derrida comes close to the Arendtian notion of *polis* as a public space where citizens are free from discrimination due to sex, colour, nationality, or religion. This is, as he writes, a new horizon of possibility undreamt of by international state law. This city of refuge is a *ville franche* which could elevate itself above nation-states 'or at least free itself from them, in order to become, to coin a phrase in a new and novel way, a *free city*' (Derrida 2001: 9).

The Derridean cosmopolitan and republican city of hospitality is certainly the city for the other (Derrida 1999). This city of refuge is that which makes possible the event of impossible and unconditional hospitality and forgiveness, particularly, this city which realizes the Aristotelian political friendship 'beyond the principle of fraternity' (Derrida 2005a: viii). From this standpoint, city of refuge is a city of a new kind of friendship 'which may perhaps go beyond the fraternal tradition that establishes a certain restricted model of friendship as the basis of familial, social, and political relations generally' (Wortham 2010: 142). The city of hospitality is this unknown Khôra (perhaps T. S. Eliot's *The Waste Land*) that in the final analysis urges us to overcome as a messianic miracle or a possibility to come (the Derridean events) our selfish identities, and especially our enclosed discursive horizons. So this Derridean unknown

Khôra is not the metaphysical limit of a positive knowledge but a new ontological opportunity for the transcendence of the Same or a new way to see clearly that ethics and politics are most of all a calling into question of the Same (Derrida 2001a: 205). To put it another way, the Derridean city of refuge is an alternative way for the transcendence of the Same by the other (Stocker 2006: 122). 'It all seems', Derrida writes, 'to happen just *as if*—and the *as if* is important to us here—the fracture of this abyss were announced in a muted and subterranean way, preparing and propagating its simulacra and *mises en abyme: a series of mythic fictions embedded mutually in each other'* (Wolfreys 1998: 249). In that Derridean sense, cities of hospitality are places where citizens as mythic fictions are embedded mutually in each other.

Is city of refuge a fictional city? Absolutely not. Khôra is a counter-ontology of ethics and politics as we understand them conventionally in modernity. Jacques Derrida chooses the Kantian model of state-centric and conditional hospitality as the best exemplar (an original Kantian methodology) in order to show how this city of hospitality is possible in the late capitalism. It is worth noting that Derrida, as Benoît Peeters highlights in the excellent biography he wrote of the French thinker, used to say that Immanuel Kant is a great philosopher to the extent that you can 'find him at every crossroads' (Peeters 2013: 110). From this point of view, it is absolutely wrong to believe that Derrida unhesitatingly rejects the Kantian model of hospitality. On the contrary, he seeks to reformulate its state-centric logic within a postmodern frame. Towards this 'middle road' perspective, Garrett W. Brown argues that actually there is 'an alternative reading of Kant that can take into account Derrida's concern for asylum seekers' (Brown 2010: 324). Particularly, Brown claims that Immanuel Kant through the right of residence (*gastrecht*), which 'is not necessarily *xenophobic*' (emphasis added), tried 'to limit powerful European armies for claiming residence in the form of colonial expansion' (Brown 2010: 324). Indeed, anyone who reads carefully the 'Definite Article the Third' in Immanuel Kant's *Perpetual Peace* manifestly understands that the German philosopher on the one hand limits the right of visiting within the framework of a very particular beneficent contract or a special friendly agreement (Kant 1992: 106), and on the other hand criticizes sharply the inhospitable conduct of civilized commercial states, which make their visiting behavior synonymous with conquering (Kant 1993: 269–70).

Generally speaking, this alternative reading of Kant's *Perpetual Peace* is correct. But according to my argument in this chapter, Derrida seeks more to show an inherent contradiction in Kantian conditional cosmopolitanism which stems from his state-centric approach concerning the laws of hospitality. This is the whole point. Jacques Derrida rejects the Kantian cosmopolitanism as a universal right of humanity or as a cosmopolitan project that is 'continually advancing towards a perpetual peace' (Kant

1992: 108) because 'in defining hospitality in all its rigour as a law (which counts in this respect as progress), *Kant assigns to it conditions which make it dependent on state sovereignty* (emphasis added), especially when it is a question of the right of residence . . . hospitality . . . is dependent on and controlled by the law and the state police' (Derrida 2001: 22). Actually, Jacques Derrida accuses Immanuel Kant that his idea for a universal history with a cosmopolitan purpose is not as revolutionary as it has to be (Kant 1992: 41). The best way to comprehend the Derridean point of view on Kant's cosmopolitanism is Martin Wight's approach on Kantian international theory (Wight 2005: 63). The founding father of the English School of International Relations (Makris 2010) asking the question 'Was Kant a revolutionary?' (Wight 2005: 65) actually reveals the multiple faces of Kantian cosmopolitanism. According to Martin Wight, Kant's universality has two elemental sides. The first side is the evolutionary Kant who is the theoretician of a state-centric internationalism. This is a soft utopian Kant. The second side is the revolutionary Kant who is the theoretician of a world state cosmopolitanism. This is a hard utopian Kant (Wight 2005: 83). Nevertheless, in both cases, he remains entrapped within a state-centric perspective. The main participants in the international arena are either states (the case for a Kantian realism) or the world state (the case for a Kantian idealism). The decision-making processes are done by the states. They are at any rate the active actors.

Narrowly speaking, we could claim that Jacques Derrida is a hard utopian or a revolutionary Kantian idealist. This 'middle road' argument seems attractive but is ontologically and epistemologically wrong. Derrida's postmodern or otherwise critical cosmopolitanism is beyond soft internationalism, global governance concept, or world state theory (Griffiths and O'Callaghan 2006: 55, 124). Derrida's cosmopolitan approach is by definition non-state-centric. Especially, he rejects state sovereignty as the modern crystallization of pure violence in the force of law (*Gewalt*: violence but also legitimate power). From this point of view, he comes close to Hannah Arendt and Walter Benjamin (Wortham 2010: 56). As Garrett Wallace Brown and David Held write, 'Derrida offers a *critical examination* (emphasis added) of the idea of the cosmopolitan law and of Kant's conceptualization of a corresponding cosmopolitan right to hospitality' (Brown and Held 2012: 374). Actually, this critical examination presupposes consideration of all the above. From the very beginning, Derrida asks, 'How can we still dream of a *novel status* (emphasis added) for the city, and thus for the "cities of refuge", through a *renewal* of international law?' (Derrida 2001: 3). And he answers that cities of refuge 'must open themselves up to something more and other than merely banal articles in the literature on international law. They must, if they are to succeed in so doing, make an audacious call for a genuine innovation in the history of the right to asylum or the duty to hospitality (Derrida 2001: 4).

SOME CONCLUDING REMARKS

At the heart of Jacques Derrida's problématique on cosmopolitanism, the major question of state sovereignty is raised. According to the French philosopher, this rule of state sovereignty 'should no longer be the ultimate horizon for the cities of refuge. Is this possible?' (Derrida 2001: 4–5). Actually, he asks, 'How can the right of asylum be redefined and developed without repatriation and without naturalization? Could the City, equipped with new rights and greater sovereignty, open up new horizons of possibility previously undreamt of by international state law?' (Derrida 2001: 7–8). So could the city 'when dealing with the related questions of hospitality and refuge, elevate itself above nation-states or at least free itself from them, in order to become, to coin a phrase in a new and novel way, a *free city*?' (Derrida 2001: 9). This is a first conclusion in the form of some critical Derridean questions about the role of state power in the contemporary post–Cold War era. As a second conclusion, we ought to notice that city of refuge is a free city. Free city in Derridean terms means first and foremost a city in 'which one could retreat in order to escape from the threat of injustice' (Derrida 2001: 9). From this perspective, city of refuge or free city is by definition the city of justice. In a Derridean cosmopolitan context, these expressions are synonymous and in any case are metonyms of deconstruction itself. So it is obvious that city of refuge is the city of *différance*. The city 'appears as an impersonal agent performing many of the functions previously attributed to the conscious subject. Derrida inverts the subjectivist position and describes subjectivity precisely as "an effect of différance"' (Howells 1998: 133–34).

As a third conclusion, we can say that in accordance with Jacques Derrida, Kantian conditional and most of all state-centric cosmopolitanism (Caygill 1996: 137–38), as it formed mainly in his key texts — *Idea for a Universal History with a Cosmopolitan Purpose* (1784), *Perpetual Peace* (1795), and *Anthropology from a Pragmatic Point of View* (1798) (Kant 1993; Guyer 1995: 342; Hutchings 1996: 146; Fenves 1999) — is characterized by a strong inherent contradiction 'because the legal "conditions" he initiates within the laws of hospitality ultimately undermine the universality also suggested within Kant's cosmopolitan vision . . . this contradiction is due to the fact that Kantian cosmopolitanism requires an unconditional hospitality on one hand (a right to travel the world and engage in public reason) while simultaneously imposing a limitation on any right to residence on the other (settlement only by agreed contract with local inhabitants)'. From this Derridean perspective, 'cosmopolitanism becomes dependent on a legal apparatus, which . . . have been abused and "perverted" by the law and the enforcers of that law' (Brown and Held 2012: 374). For Derrida's view, there aren't easy answers to the problem of cosmopolitan hospitality. What is at stake is first and foremost practical: 'How can the hosts and guests of cities of refuge be helped to re-create, *through work and creative activity* (emphasis added) a living and durable network in new places and occasionally in a new language' (Derrida 2001: 12). Cities of refuge are not cities of charity. In that sense, Derrida clarifies that 'all these questions remain obscure and difficult'. So regarding the question of cities of refuge, 'it is a question of knowing how to transform and improve the law, and of knowing if this improvement is possible within an historical space which takes place *between* the Law of an unconditional hospitality, offered a priori to every other, to all newcomers, *whoever they may be*, and the conditional laws of a right to hospitality, without which *The* unconditional law of hospitality would be in danger of remaining a pious desire, without form and without potency, and of even being perverted at any moment' (Derrida 2001: 22–23).

Without doubt, Jacques Derrida is not a postmodern utopian thinker. Although in the last interview he gave to John Birnbaum, he did not hesitate to speak about a New International 'beyond "cosmopolitanism", beyond the notion of a "world citizen", beyond a new world nation-state, even beyond the logic'. In the final analysis, in his whole life he was looking ceaselessly for all the alter-globalist imperatives 'which appear more clearly today (though still insufficiently; in a chaotic and unthought way)' (Derrida 2007: 22–23; Derrida 2004: 96). Simon Critchley points out that 'Derrida would here seem to be trying to sketch the preconditions for a new socialist hegemonic articulation (emphasis added), a political decision taken in the name of justice and in the face of the world's afflictions' (Critchley 1999: 166). In the same spirit, 'the political center of gravity of debate . . . around his work', Geoffrey Bennington highlights, 'has undoubtedly been the Left. Derrida is, obviously and self-proclaimedly, on the Left' (Cohen 2001: 193). As Jacques Derrida writes on cosmopolitan unconditional and impossible hospitality and especially the cities of refuge as the free cities of the other to come, 'it's not a matter of speculation, of speculative movement within the academy. . . . It's a worldwide political question' (Derrida 2002a: 26–27). From this point of view, Jacques Derrida was and remains a par excellence political and social postmodern thinker (Sim 2013: 81).

BIBLIOGRAPHY

Arendt, H. (2004). *The Origins of Totalitarianism*. New York: Schocken Books.
Benhabib, S. (2004). *The Rights of Others. Aliens, Residents, and Citizens*. Cambridge: Cambridge University Press.
Bergo, B. (2010). 'The Face in Levinas: Toward a Phennomenology of Substitution'. *Journal of the Theoretical Humanities* 16, 1, 1–33.
Brown, G. W. (2010). 'The Laws of Hospitality, Asylum Seekers and Cosmopolitan Rights: A Kantian Response to Jacques Derrida'. *European Journal of Political Theory* 9, 3, 308–27.
——— and Held, D. (eds.) (2012). *The Cosmopolitan Reader*. Cambridge: Polity Press.

Caputo, J. D. (ed.) (1999). *Deconstruction in a Nutshell. A Conversation with Jacques Derrida*. New York: Fordham University Press.

Caygill, H. (1996). *A Kant Dictionary*. Oxford: Blackwell Publishers.

Cohen, T. (ed.) (2001). *Jacques Derrida and the Humanities: A Critical Reader*. Cambridge: Cambridge University Press.

Critchley, S. (1999). *Ethics-Politics-Subjectivity: Essays on Derrida, Levinas and Contemporary French Thought*. London and New York: Verso.

De Angelis, M. (2004). 'Separating the Doing and the Deed: Capital and the Continuous Character of Enclosures'. *Historical Materialism* 12, 57–87.

Derrida, J. (1994). *Specters of Marx: The State of Debt, the Work of Mourning and the New International*. London and New York: Routledge.

———. (1995). *Points . . . Interviews, 1974-1994*. Stanford, CA: Stanford University Press.

———. (1998) *Monolingualism of the Other; or, The Prosthesis of Origin*. Stanford, CA: Stanford University Press.

———. (1999). *Adieu to Emmanuel Levinas*. Stanford, CA: Stanford University Press.

———. (2001). *Cosmopolitanism and Forgiveness*. London and New York: Routledge.

———. (2001a). *The Work of Mourning*. Chicago and London: University of Chicago Press.

———. (2002). *Acts of Religion*. New York and London: Routledge.

———. (2002a). *Ethics, Institutions, and the Right to Philosophy*. New York: Rowman & Littlefield Publishers, Inc.

———. (2004). *The Last Interview*. New York: SV.

———. (2005). *Rogues: Two Essays on Reason*. Stanford, CA: Stanford University Press.

———. (2005a). *The Politics of Friendship*. London and New York: Verso.

———. (2006). *Specters of Marx: The State of the Debt, the Work of Mourning and the New International*. London and New York: Routledge.

———. (2007). *Learning to Live Finally: The Last Interview*. New York: Melville House Publishing.

——— and Dufourmantelle, A. (2000). *Of Hospitality*. Stanford, CA: Stanford University Press.

——— and Roudinesco, E. (2004). *For What Tomorrow . . . A Dialogue*. Stanford, CA: Stanford University Press.

Deutscher, P. (2005). *How to Read Derrida*. London: Granta Books.

Fenves, P. (ed.) (1999). *Raising the Tone of Philosophy: Late Essays by Immanuel Kant, Transformative Critique by Jacques Derrida*. Baltimore and London: The Johns Hopkins University Press.

Freud, S. (1919). *The Uncanny*, at web.mit.edu/allanmc/www/freud1.pdf .

Glendinning, S. (2011). *Derrida: A Very Short Introduction*. Oxford: Oxford University Press.

Griffiths, M. and O'Callaghan, T. (2006). *International Relations: The Key Concepts*. London and New York: Routledge.

Gutting, G. (2001). *French Philosophy in the Twentieth Century*. Cambridge: Cambridge University Press.

Guyer, P. (ed.) (1995). *The Cambridge Companion to Kant*. Cambridge: Cambridge University Press.

Hand, S. (2009). *Emmanuel Levinas*. London and New York: Routledge.

Howells, C. (1998). *Derrida: Deconstruction from Phenomenology to Ethics*. Cambridge: Polity Press.

Hutchings, K. (1996). *Kant, Critique and Politics*. London and New York: Routledge.

Kant, I. (1992). *Political Writings*. Cambridge: Cambridge University Press.

———. (1993). *Essays and Treatises Volume I*. Bristol: Thoemmes Press.

Levinas, E. (1991). *Totality and Infinity*. USA and Canada: Kluwer Academic Publishers.

———. (1994). *Beyond the Verse: Talmudic Readings and Lectures*. London: The Athlone Press.

Lucy, N. (2004). *A Derrida Dictionary*. Oxford: Blackwell Publishing.

Makris, S. (2010). *Hegemonism, American Foreign Policy and International Society: Alternative Perspectives*. Bruxelles: Établissements Émile Bruylant, S. A.

Peeters, B. (2013). *Derrida: A Biography*. Cambridge: Polity Press.

Royle, N. (2003). *Jacques Derrida*. London and New York: Routledge.

Sim, S. (2013). *Fifty Key Postmodern Thinkers*. London and New York: Routledge.

Simons, J. (ed.) (2004). *Contemporary Critical Theorists: From Lacan to Said*. Edinburgh: Edinburgh University Press.

Smith, J. K. A. (2005). *Jacques Derrida: Live Theory*. New York and London: Continuum.

Stocker, B. (2006). *Derrida on Deconstruction*. London and New York: Routledge.

Wight, M. (2005). *Four Seminal Thinkers in International Theory: Machiavelli, Grotius, Kant and Mazzini*. Oxford: Oxford University Press.

Wolfreys, J. (ed.) (1998). *The Derrida Reader: Writing Performances*. Edinburgh: Edinburgh University Press.

Wortham, S. M. (2010). *The Derrida Dictionary*. London and New York: Continuum.

Index

About the Authors

Sybille De La Rosa is assistant chair in the Department of Political Science at the University of Heidelberg, Germany. She is author of *Aneignung und interkulturelle Repräsentation* (2012) and coeditor of *Steuerung durch diskursive Praktiken, Argumente und Symbole. Studien zu einem Konzept weicher Steuerung* (2009, with Gerhard Göhler and Ulrike Höppner) and *Transdisziplinäre Governanceforschung. Gemeinsame Blicke hinter den Staat* (2000, with Matthias Kötter and Ulrike Höppner). She has written articles for major German jounals such as *Politische Vierteljahresschrift* and *Leviathan Berliner Zeitschrift für Sozialwissenschaft*.

Sneja Gunew is professor of English and Women's and Gender Studies at the University of British Columbia, Canada. She has taught in England, Australia, and Canada and has published widely on multicultural, postcolonial, and feminist critical theory. Her forthcoming book is provisionally entitled *Back to the Future: Post-multiculturalism; Immanent Cosmopolitanism*. faculty.arts.ubc.ca/sgunew/

Martin Hewson is associate professor in Politics and International Studies at the University of Regina, Canada. His research interests lie in the areas of global governance and global conflict and international relations theory.

Sae-Hee Lee is a researcher in the political section at the embassy of the Republic of Korea in India. The views expressed in this article are those of the author and do not necessarily represent the views of, and should not be attributed to, the Korean Embassy in India or the South Korean government.

Spiros Makris is a lecturer in the Department of International and European Studies of the School of Social Sciences, Humanities and Arts at the University of Macedonia in Thessaloniki, Greece, and a research fellow at the Academy of Athens. His recent publications in English include *Hegemonism. American Foreign Policy and International Society: Alternative Perspectives*.

Amos Nascimento is associate professor of Philosophy at the University of Washington. His current research focuses on cosmopolitanism, human rights, and environmental ethics. His latest publications are *Building Cosmopolitan Communities* (2013) and *Human Rights, Human Dignity, and Cosmopolitan Ideals* (2014, editor with Matthias Lutz-Bachmann).

Darren O'Byrne is Reader of Sociology and Human Rights at Roehampton University, UK. He has published widely in the areas of globalization studies, human rights, and sociological theory. He is the author of *Human Rights: An Introduction* (2003), *The Dimensions of Global Citizenship* (2003), *Theorizing Global Studies* (2011, with Alexander Hensby), *Introducing Sociological Theory* (2011), and *Human Rights in a Globalizing World* (2015), and he is coeditor of *Global Ethics and Civil Society* (2005, with John Eade). He has written articles for such major journals as *Sociology, International Journal of Human Rights* and *Cross-Cultural Management: An International Journal*. He was the founding chair of the Global Studies Association and organized the 2013 conference from which this volume emerges.

Angie Pepper is a teaching fellow in Political Philosophy in the Department of Politics at the University of York. Angie works on a number of topics in moral and political philosophy including social justice, global justice, feminism, and animal ethics.

Geneviève Souillac is currently researching peace ethics at the University of KU Leuven. Previously, she was Senior Researcher at the Tampere Peace Research Insitute at the University of Tampere, Finland, and Senior Associate Professor at the International Christian University in Tokyo, Japan. Her most recent publications include *A Study in Transborder Ethics: Justice, Citizenship, Civility* (2012) and *The Burden of Democracy: The Claims of Cultures, Public Culture and Democratic Memory* (2011).

Anne Surma lectures in the English and Creative Arts program at Murdoch University in western Australia. Her book, *Imagining the Cosmopolitan in Public and Professional Writing* (2013), explores the ways in which writing in the public domain might support or inhibit the cosmopolitan project.